FAMILY FAVORITES
FROM COUNTRY KITCHENS

Other cookbooks by *FARM JOURNAL*

FAMILY FAVORITES
FROM COUNTRY KITCHENS

A collection of outstanding recipes

from the best cooks in the country . . .

selected and tested by the Food Editors of

FARM JOURNAL

Edited by ELISE W. MANNING

FARM JOURNAL Food Editor

Photography Supervised by AL J. REAGAN

FARM JOURNAL Art Staff

Doubleday & Company, Inc., Garden City, New York

1973

ISBN: 0-385-05095-X
Library of Congress Catalog Card Number 73–83599
Copyright © 1973 by Farm Journal, Inc.

CONTENTS

COLOR ILLUSTRATIONS

Color photographs by: William Hazzard/Hazzard Studio and Ted Hoffman, Chas. P. Mills & Son

FAMILY FAVORITES
FROM COUNTRY KITCHENS

Introduction

FAMILY FAVORITES...
GOOD EATING EVERY DAY

A good cook is judged not only by the meals she prepares for guests or for special occasions, but especially by what she puts on her family table day after day. Farm women take everyday cooking seriously and confess particular pride in compliments from the family, as well as from guests. A tried-and-true family favorite usually is a sure winner with guests too.

Good eating always has been such a part of family and community life in the country that recipes acquire values far beyond their tangible ingredients. They are often handed down from one generation to the next—but also updated by adapting them to changes in ingredients or habits. Country women are always curious about what other women fix for their families. And in a neighborly fashion they exchange such recipes as "Aunt Sarah's Chocolate Fudge Brownies" or "Mabel's Best Butterscotch Bars."

When we printed a brief paragraph in FARM JOURNAL magazine asking women to send the recipe for their family's favorite, the response was unusually high. Recipes were accompanied by warm, friendly letters telling why this recipe was a favorite, where it originated, when they prepare and serve it. From 10,000 recipes, we selected over 450 family favorites. Then, we tested, tasted and perfected them in our Countryside Test Kitchens for this book.

Within each of the twelve chapters, we have grouped recipes into "situation" categories. In the cookie chapter, for instance, we present four or five excellent cookies that farm women pack into lunch boxes. Another group of cookie recipes are those made as gifts for Christmas.

In the casserole chapter we give recipes for those dishes that home-makers say go over well at church suppers and bazaars. There's also a supper-in-a-jiffy category . . . and others. We share recipes for pies which farm women say men especially like; pies that take honors on holiday tables; pies that won prizes at fairs.

Farm women enjoy preparing food their husbands and children eat with pleasure, but they are also aware of the importance of good nutrition. They know that just "filling up" a family is not enough and that every meal must supply essentials for body growth, repair and function. So the Basic Four—the Milk Group, Vegetable/Fruit Group, Meat Group and Bread/Cereal Group—enter into daily meal planning by good farm cooks.

Notice the imaginative ways in which milk, cheese and ice cream are incorporated in recipes in this cookbook. The Vegetable/Fruit Group is a basic part of at least two meals a day, with emphasis on citrus fruits, dark green and yellow vegetables in a variety of scrumptious dishes. The Meat Group and dry lentils, nuts, peanuts and peanut butter are standard protein contributors. The Bread/Cereal Group contributes whole grain enriched breads and ready-to-eat cereal recipes.

In these family-favorite recipes, vegetables are made interesting by serving them in variety and in combinations. A light puffy carrot or spinach soufflé will entice the family to eat vegetables otherwise not high on their preference list. Many a favorite casserole is loaded with good nutrition as well—a combination of cheeses, meat and tomatoes, for example.

After a well-balanced meal, a prized family dessert is often served at the farm table. Everyone likes a sweet treat and farm women can and do turn out the highest cakes, the most velvety custard pies and the creamiest cheese cakes. Notice how many of the dessert recipes contain generous amounts of nourishing eggs, milk and cheese.

We think you will enjoy browsing through this book and reading women's comments on why their families like a certain dish. You'll find lots of ideas for dishes to show off at the community supper, family reunion or barbecue, and to delight guests in your home. Being family favorites, most of the recipes appeal to both men and children.

We hope that you will have as much pleasure and satisfaction from tasting these tried-and-true family favorites as we did when we tested —and tasted—them in our FARM JOURNAL Countryside Test Kitchens. It was a year of fine eating!

Chapter 1

MEATS THAT RATE WITH THE WHOLE FAMILY

"My husband is a meat and potato man"—this is a remark we hear over and over when we chat with farm women. And they know how to please the men in their family when it comes to meat dishes. They are experts in adding a zippy sauce or a pinch of herbs to make a stew taste "just right."

The meat recipes in this chapter are favorites from farm homes all over the country. We have an assortment of succulent ground beef dishes that are everyday but out-of-the-ordinary, such as Potato/Beef Roll. An Ohio woman says "My husband likes this because it's a combination of his favorite foods. It's easy for me to fix and freeze ahead too."

We give you a family reunion must, Meatballs in Tomato Sauce—the sauce simmers thick and is laced just right with spices and herbs. Children will love the Pizza Meat Loaf for picnics. Adults will request seconds when you serve Savory Meat Squares—a moist meat loaf baked in a square pan. The first time a Pennsylvania homemaker took her Country Fair Ham Loaf to the family picnic it became an instant hit.

There's an interesting medley of pork recipes for family and company meals. Pork Steaks with Mushroom Gravy are delicious served with snowy mounds of mashed potatoes. Guests will rave when you pass the Baked Pork Chops with Dressing—the dressing puffs to a golden mound and is seasoned to perfection. At the next barbecue, make a batch of Pork Kabobs for a tasty treat—they look pretty, too, with chunks of green pepper, mushrooms, quartered tomatoes and pork.

We have several buffet beauties that you'll be proud to present. Calabrian Rolled Beef is bread-stuffed beef simmered in basil-scented tomato sauce. From Oregon we feature Succulent Sirloin Steak—men especially like the zippy sauce of ginger, soy sauce and garlic. For a company meal Chilled Apricot Glazed Ham is spectacular, and it's so easy to fix. When your family is in the mood for ham, treat them to Apple Upside-Down Ham Loaf.

"Even liver haters like my Slivered Liver," an Indiana woman wrote us. It's the hint of chili powder that makes the difference.

Surprise your children and pack Miniature Cheese Loaves in their lunch boxes or slice the Grated Vegetable Meat Loaf and stuff it into hot dog buns for a treat.

Two pot roasts you will want to try are Pot Roast with Vegetable Gravy and the Company Pot Roast. Both produce delightfully flavored juices to thicken into a rich gravy.

We think your family will approve every one of these meat dishes.

MEAT AND POTATO DISHES MEN LIKE

"Hearty food, nothing fancy is what my husband prefers . . . he means meat and potatoes." These recipes cater to just that. Sturdy meats, seasoned perfectly—in some, the potatoes and vegetables cook along with the meat.

DELICIOUS BEEF STEW

"I usually serve this with a molded salad, muffins and fresh fruit"

½ lb. bacon	1 c. chopped onion
1½ lbs. round steak, cut in 1½″ cubes	1 clove garlic, minced
1 tsp. salt	6 medium potatoes, pared and quartered
⅛ tsp. pepper	2 c. tomato juice
2½ c. sliced carrots	1 tsp. orégano leaves
1 (8 oz.) can sliced mushrooms	¼ tsp. basil leaves

Fry bacon in large skillet until partially cooked, but not crisp. Add meat, salt and pepper. Sauté until meat cubes are well browned.

Add carrots, undrained mushrooms, onion, garlic, potatoes, tomato juice, orégano and basil. Bring to a boil; reduce heat. Cover. Simmer for 1 hour or until vegetables and meat are tender. Makes 6 servings.

POT ROAST WITH VEGETABLE GRAVY

"One of the best pot roasts we've ever tasted . . . wonderful gravy"

3 lbs. boned beef rump roast	1 clove garlic, minced
½ tsp. salt	1 beef bouillon cube
⅛ tsp. pepper	1 c. water
1 tblsp. cooking oil	1 (8 oz.) can tomato sauce
1 c. chopped celery	½ tsp. orégano leaves
½ c. chopped onion	2 tblsp. cornstarch
½ c. diced carrots	½ c. water

Season meat with salt and pepper. Brown well in hot oil in Dutch oven. Remove meat. Add celery, onion, carrots and garlic to hot oil; sauté until tender (do not brown). Add bouillon cube, 1 c. water, tomato sauce and orégano. Bring to a boil. Return meat to Dutch oven. Cover. Bake in slow oven (325°) 2 hours 30 minutes or until tender.

Remove meat and keep warm. Skim off excess fat. Slowly stir combined cornstarch and ½ c. water into pan juices. Bring to a boil; boil for 1 minute. Makes 6 to 8 servings.

SUCCULENT SIRLOIN STEAK

"My husband likes this with home-fried potatoes and sliced tomatoes"

3 lbs. sirloin steak, 2″ thick	2 tblsp. butter or regular margarine
Meat tenderizer	
3 tblsp. melted butter or regular margarine	1½ tblsp. lemon juice
	1 tsp. sugar
2 tblsp. cooking oil	½ tsp. ground ginger
¼ c. soy sauce	1 clove garlic, minced

Sprinkle meat with meat tenderizer following package directions. Slice in ¼″ slices. Sauté meat in 3 tblsp. melted butter and oil in skillet, for about 30 seconds on each side. Place browned meat in 11 × 7 × 1½″ baking dish.

Combine soy sauce, 2 tblsp. butter, lemon juice, sugar, ginger and garlic in small saucepan. Simmer, uncovered, for 5 minutes. Pour over meat slices.

Bake in moderate oven (350°) 7 minutes. Makes 6 servings.

BARBECUED SHORT RIBS

"My family thinks nobody makes short ribs as good as mine"

8 large beef short ribs	3 tblsp. Worcestershire sauce
1 tblsp. cooking oil	2 tsp. salt
1 c. chopped onion	1 tsp. prepared mustard
1 c. ketchup	½ c. chopped celery
¼ c. vinegar	¼ c. water
2 tblsp. brown sugar	

Brown meat in hot oil in Dutch oven. Remove.

Add onion; sauté until tender (do not brown). Add ketchup, vinegar, brown sugar, Worcestershire sauce, salt, mustard, celery, water and meat. Bring to a boil; reduce heat. Cover. Simmer for 1 hour 30 minutes or until meat is tender. Makes 4 servings.

OVEN-BARBECUED LAMB CHOPS

Buttered noodles tossed with chopped parsley go well with this

6 shoulder lamb chops (about 2½ lbs.)	1½ tblsp. vinegar
1 tsp. salt	1 tblsp. Worcestershire sauce
¼ tsp. pepper	1½ tsp. ground ginger
¼ c. cooking oil	1½ tsp. dry mustard
½ c. chopped onion	¼ tsp. garlic salt
3 tblsp. chili sauce	¼ c. water

Season chops with salt and pepper. Brown in hot oil in large skillet. Remove from skillet. Place in 13 × 9 × 2″ baking pan.

Sauté onion in hot oil until tender (do not brown). Stir in chili sauce, vinegar, Worcestershire sauce, ginger, mustard, garlic salt and water. Bring mixture to a boil. Pour over chops.

Bake in moderate oven (350°) 40 minutes or until meat is tender, basting occasionally. Makes 6 to 8 servings.

CHILI DUMPLING STEW

Crowned with puffy light dumplings, this is fine enough for company

2 lbs. ground beef	1 tsp. savory leaves
2 tblsp. cooking oil	½ tsp. orégano leaves
1 c. chopped onion	½ tsp. pepper
½ c. chopped green pepper	2 c. sifted flour
2 (8 oz.) cans tomato sauce	4 tsp. baking powder
2 c. water	¼ tsp. salt
2 (1 lb.) cans red kidney beans, drained	1 tblsp. cooking oil
	1 egg, beaten
4 tsp. chili powder	¾ c. milk
1½ tsp. salt	

Sauté ground beef in 2 tblsp. hot oil in 4-qt. Dutch oven. Add onion and green pepper; cook until meat is browned. Add tomato sauce, water, kidney beans, chili powder, 1½ tsp. salt, savory, orégano and pepper. Bring to a boil; reduce heat. Simmer, uncovered, for 30 minutes.

Sift together flour, baking powder and ¼ tsp. salt. Add 1 tblsp. oil, egg and milk; stir until just blended. Drop by spoonfuls into stew. Cover. Simmer for 15 minutes. Makes 8 servings.

MEATBALL STEW

An easy-to-prepare stew that is perfect for potluck suppers

1½ lbs. ground beef	1 (10½ oz.) can condensed tomato soup
1 c. soft bread crumbs	
¼ c. finely chopped onion	1 (10½ oz.) can condensed beef broth
1 egg, beaten	
1 tsp. salt	4 medium potatoes, pared and quartered
½ tsp. marjoram leaves	
¼ tsp. thyme leaves	4 carrots, cut in 1" chunks
⅛ tsp. pepper	8 small white onions
2 tblsp. cooking oil	2 tblsp. chopped fresh parsley

Combine ground beef, bread crumbs, ¼ c. onion, egg, salt, marjoram, thyme and pepper. Mix lightly, but well. Shape into 24 meatballs.

Brown meatballs in hot oil in 4-qt. Dutch oven. Remove as they brown. Combine soup and broth in Dutch oven. Add meatballs, potatoes, carrots and small onions. Bring to a boil; reduce heat. Cover. Simmer for 30 minutes or until vegetables are tender. Garnish with parsley. Makes 6 to 8 servings.

BAKED PORK CHOPS WITH DRESSING

Serve with a marinated green bean salad and lemon pie for dessert

6 pork chops, ¾" thick
¼ tsp. salt
⅛ tsp. pepper
1 tblsp. cooking oil
½ c. chopped onion
¼ c. butter or regular margarine
4½ c. bread cubes (½")
½ tsp. poultry seasoning

¼ tsp. celery salt
¼ c. water
3 medium potatoes, pared and quartered
Cooking oil
1 (10½ oz.) can condensed cream of mushroom soup
½ c. water

Season pork chops with salt and pepper. Brown chops in 1 tblsp. hot oil in skillet. Remove from skillet. Place in 13 × 9 × 2" baking dish.

Sauté onion in melted butter in small skillet until tender (do not brown). Combine onion with bread cubes, poultry seasoning, celery salt and ¼ c. water. Mix lightly. Shape dressing in mounds on top of chops.

Coat potatoes with oil; place around chops.

Combine soup and ½ c. water. Pour over chops and potatoes.

Bake in moderate oven (350°) 1 hour or until meat is tender. Makes 6 servings.

PORK STEAKS WITH MUSHROOM CREAM GRAVY

There's lots of smooth brown gravy to ladle over mashed potatoes

6 lean pork steaks or chops, about ¾" thick (2½ lbs.)
½ tsp. salt
¼ tsp. pepper
2 tblsp. cooking oil
½ c. chopped onion

1 (8 oz.) can mushrooms
1 (10½ oz.) can condensed beef broth
1 tsp. Worcestershire sauce
1 c. evaporated milk
1 tblsp. flour

Season pork steaks with salt and pepper. Brown well in hot oil in large skillet. Remove. Add onion; sauté until tender (do not brown).

Drain mushrooms, reserving liquid. Add reserved mushroom liquid, beef broth, Worcestershire sauce and meat to skillet. Cover. Simmer for 1 hour or until meat is tender.

Remove meat and keep warm. Add mushrooms to pan juices in skillet. Bring mixture to a boil. Combine evaporated milk and flour. Slowly stir into hot liquid. Cook over medium heat, stirring constantly, until thickened. (Do not boil.) Makes 6 servings.

QUICKIES THAT SIMMER IN A SKILLET

On days when there doesn't seem to be a minute to spare—and the clock tells you dinner hour is fast approaching—turn to these recipes that can be put together in minutes. They simmer on top of the range while you put the finishing touches on the rest of the meal.

BACON NOODLE SKILLET

"A fast, simple well-balanced main dish that my family enjoys"

1 lb. bacon	⅛ tsp. pepper
½ c. chopped green pepper	2 (1 lb.) cans stewed tomatoes
½ c. chopped onion	2 c. water
1 tsp. salt	1 (8 oz.) pkg. wide noodles
½ tsp. marjoram leaves	1½ c. shredded Cheddar cheese
½ tsp. thyme leaves	

Cook bacon until crisp in 10″ skillet. Drain on paper towels. Pour off bacon drippings, reserving 2 tblsp. Sauté green pepper and onion in bacon drippings until tender (do not brown). Stir in salt, marjoram, thyme, pepper, tomatoes and water. Bring mixture to a boil. Add noodles. Cover. Simmer for 20 minutes.

Crumble half of bacon and stir into mixture. Top with cheese and remaining bacon strips. Simmer, covered, for 5 minutes or until cheese melts. Makes 6 servings.

ZUCCHINI ITALIANO

"A favorite busy-day dinner . . . it's ready to serve in 30 minutes"

1 lb. bulk pork sausage
1 c. chopped onion
1 green pepper, cut in strips
1 clove garlic, minced
1 (1 lb.) can tomatoes
1 (8 oz.) can tomato sauce
1¼ tsp. salt

1 tsp. orégano leaves
¼ tsp. cayenne pepper
1¼ lb. zucchini, cut in ¼" thick slices
1 c. wide noodles
1 c. water
1 c. shredded Cheddar cheese

Brown sausage in 12" skillet or Dutch oven. When meat begins to change color, add onion, green pepper and garlic. Sauté until meat is well browned.

Stir in tomatoes, tomato sauce, salt, orégano, cayenne pepper, zucchini, uncooked noodles and water. Bring to a boil; reduce heat. Cover. Simmer for 15 minutes.

Top with cheese. Cook until cheese melts. Makes 6 servings.

GERMAN SKILLET DINNER

"An old German dish that has become popular in my family"

1 lb. ground beef
2 tblsp. butter or regular margarine
1 c. chopped onion
1¼ tsp. salt
½ tsp. pepper

1 c. regular rice
2 (8 oz.) cans tomato sauce
1 (1 lb.) can sauerkraut
½ tsp. caraway seeds
1 c. water

Brown ground beef in butter in 10" skillet. When meat begins to turn color, add onion, salt and pepper. Sauté until meat is well browned.

Stir in rice, tomato sauce, sauerkraut, caraway seeds and water. Bring to a boil; reduce heat. Cover. Simmer for 25 minutes or until rice is tender. Makes 6 servings.

EASY GROUND BEEF SKILLET

A good hearty cold-weather dish that is easy to fix and flavorful

2 lbs. ground beef	1 tblsp. bottled steak sauce
1 c. thinly sliced onion	1 tsp. salt
1 c. chopped green pepper	1 tsp. marjoram leaves
1 (1 lb.) can whole kernel corn	¼ tsp. pepper
1 (1 lb.) can red kidney beans	1 bay leaf
2 (8 oz.) cans tomato sauce	

Brown ground beef in 10" skillet. When meat begins to turn color, add onion and green pepper. Sauté until meat is well browned.

Add undrained corn, undrained kidney beans, tomato sauce, steak sauce, salt, marjoram, pepper and bay leaf. Bring to a boil; reduce heat. Cover. Simmer for 15 minutes, adding water, if necessary. Makes 4 to 6 servings.

VEGETABLE SKILLET SUPPER

An attractive dish with a good combination of colorful vegetables

3 strips bacon	1 tblsp. Worcestershire sauce
1 lb. ground beef	2 medium potatoes, pared and diced
1 c. sliced onion	
1 (1 lb.) can tomatoes	1 c. green pepper strips
½ c. water	2 c. coarsely chopped cabbage
1 tsp. salt	1 c. chopped celery
¼ tsp. pepper	

Fry bacon in skillet until crisp. Remove and drain on paper towels. Crumble.

Sauté ground beef and onion in 2 tblsp. of bacon fat until meat is well browned.

Add tomatoes, water, salt, pepper, Worcestershire sauce, potatoes, green pepper, cabbage, celery and bacon. Bring to a boil; reduce heat. Cover. Simmer for 20 minutes or until vegetables are tender. Makes 4 to 5 servings.

PORK CHOP SKILLET DINNER

All the favorite winter vegetables cook along with the pork chops

6 lean pork chops
½ tsp. salt
¼ tsp. pepper
1 tblsp. cooking oil
½ tsp. savory leaves
½ bay leaf
2 c. tomato juice

½ c. water
1 small cabbage, cut in 6 wedges
6 carrots, cut in 1" pieces (2 c.)
1½ c. coarsely chopped onion
3 medium potatoes, pared and quartered
¼ tsp. salt

Season pork chops with ½ tsp. salt and pepper. Brown chops in hot oil in large skillet. Add savory, bay leaf, tomato juice and water. Cover. Simmer for 30 minutes.

Add cabbage, carrots, onion, potatoes and ¼ tsp. salt. Cover. Simmer for 35 minutes or until vegetables are tender. Makes 6 servings.

HAM JAMBALAYA STYLE

Crusty golden brown corn muffins and a salad complete the meal

2 c. chopped green pepper
2 c. chopped celery
1 c. chopped onion
1 clove garlic, minced
⅓ c. cooking oil
2 (15 oz.) cans tomato sauce

½ tsp. chili powder
1½ lbs. cooked ham, cut in julienne strips
½ c. tomato juice
Few drops Tabasco sauce
Hot, cooked rice

Sauté green pepper, celery, onion and garlic in hot oil in 10" skillet until tender (do not brown).

Add tomato sauce and chili powder. Simmer, uncovered, for 20 minutes.

Stir in ham, tomato juice and Tabasco sauce. Cook over low heat for 5 minutes. Serve over rice. Makes 6 to 8 servings.

BEEF AND NOODLE MEDLEY

A fast-fix skillet dinner that's served often on a Montana ranch

1 lb. ground beef	1 (1 lb.) can red kidney beans
2 tblsp. cooking oil	1 (2 lb. 3 oz.) can tomatoes
1½ c. chopped celery	1 (4 oz.) can mushrooms
½ c. chopped onion	2½ tsp. salt
½ c. chopped green pepper	¾ tsp. chili powder
2 c. wide noodles	¼ tsp. pepper

Sauté ground beef in hot oil in skillet. When meat begins to turn color, add celery, onion and green pepper. Cook until well browned.

Add uncooked noodles, undrained kidney beans, tomatoes, undrained mushrooms, salt, chili powder and pepper. Bring mixture to a boil; reduce heat. Cover. Simmer for 20 minutes or until noodles are tender. Makes 6 to 8 servings.

SPANISH-STYLE SQUASH

Well-seasoned skillet meal that is ready to serve in just minutes

1 lb. ground beef	¼ tsp. garlic salt
⅓ c. chopped onion	¼ tsp. ground cumin
1½ lbs. zucchini squash, sliced	1/16 tsp. pepper
(about 5 c.)	1 (8 oz.) can tomato sauce
½ tsp. salt	1 (12 oz.) can mexicorn

Sauté ground beef and onion in medium skillet until meat is well browned.

Add squash, salt, garlic salt, cumin and pepper. Cook over medium heat for 3 to 5 minutes.

Add tomato sauce and corn. Bring to a boil; reduce heat. Cover. Simmer for 10 minutes or until squash is tender. If mixture is too thick, add a little water. Makes 6 servings.

COMPANY'S COMING

Imaginative and irresistible are the words for these savory meat dishes that are baked, simmered or broiled to perfection. Some are easy to fix, while others take a bit more time, but they all look spectacular when you take them to the company table.

PORK KABOBS

Arrange on a bed of rice and border with bright green parsley

1 c. finely chopped onion	¼ tsp. pepper
¼ c. cooking oil	1½ lbs. pork, cut in 1½″ cubes
1 c. ketchup	3 green peppers, cut in large
¼ c. brown sugar, firmly packed	pieces
¼ c. lemon juice	½ lb. fresh mushrooms, sliced
1 tsp. salt	3 medium tomatoes, quartered

Sauté onion in hot oil in saucepan until tender (do not brown). Stir in ketchup, brown sugar, lemon juice, salt and pepper. Simmer, uncovered, for 5 minutes. Cool slightly.

Pour sauce over pork cubes in a bowl. Cover. Refrigerate for 1 hour.

Place marinated pork cubes on broiler pan. Broil 7″ from source of heat for 6 minutes. Turn and brush with sauce. Broil for 6 more minutes.

Meanwhile, simmer green pepper with water in small saucepan until tender.

Thread meat, green pepper, mushrooms and tomatoes on skewers. Brush with sauce. Broil for 5 to 6 minutes. Brush with sauce and broil for 5 more minutes or until meat is well browned. Makes 6 servings.

FRUITED PORK CHOPS

Serve with hot fluffy rice, buttered green beans and hot rolls

6 pork chops, about ¾″ thick (about 2½ lbs.)	1¼ c. reconstituted orange juice
1 tsp. salt	¼ tsp. ground nutmeg
⅛ tsp. pepper	2 whole cloves
2 tblsp. cooking oil	1 (13½ oz.) can pineapple chunks, drained
¼ c. chopped onion	12 prunes

Season pork chops with salt and pepper. Brown chops in hot oil in skillet. Remove and place in 13 × 9 × 2″ baking dish.

Remove all but 2 tblsp. fat. Add onion; sauté until tender (do not brown). Add orange juice, nutmeg and cloves. Bring to a boil, stirring constantly.

Arrange pineapple chunks and prunes around pork chops. Pour orange juice mixture over all. Cover with aluminum foil.

Bake in moderate oven (350°) 1 hour or until meat is tender. Makes 6 servings.

CHILLED APRICOT-GLAZED HAM

Make this the focal point of a hot summer night supper on the porch

¼ c. dark corn syrup	1 c. apricot nectar
1 tblsp. cornstarch	2 tblsp. lemon juice
¼ tsp. ground cloves	8 lb. canned precooked ham

Combine corn syrup, cornstarch and cloves in small saucepan. Stir in apricot nectar and lemon juice. Cook over medium heat, stirring constantly, until mixture comes to a boil. Boil for 1 minute. Cool slightly.

Spread over ham in 13 × 9 × 2″ baking dish. Cover with plastic wrap. Chill several hours or overnight.

Slice thinly and serve cold. Makes 24 servings.

CRANBERRY / ORANGE GLAZED HAM

Certain to be the center of attention at your Christmas dinner

1 (10 to 12 lb.) fully cooked bone-in ham	2 tblsp. prepared mustard
2 large oranges, sliced	1 c. cranberry cocktail
3 maraschino cherries, halved	¼ c. cider vinegar
Whole cloves	¼ c. honey
1 tblsp. flour	2 tblsp. butter or regular
⅓ c. brown sugar, firmly packed	margarine

Trim and score ham. Place fat side up on rack in shallow pan. Insert meat thermometer into center; do not let it touch bone. Bake in moderate oven (350°) 1 to 1 hour 30 minutes. Remove from oven. Cover top and sides with orange slices. Place a cherry half in center of each orange slice. Insert cloves around edge of each cherry.

In 1½-qt. saucepan, combine flour, brown sugar and mustard; stir in cranberry cocktail, vinegar, honey and butter. Bring to a full boil; cook for 1 minute. Pour over hot ham. Return to oven. Continue baking 30 minutes or until thermometer registers 160°, basting often with the glaze. Makes about 20 servings.

BAKED VEAL CUTLET WITH EGGPLANT

Serve with spaghetti, crisp spinach salad and hot crusty rolls

1½ lbs. veal cutlets
1 tsp. salt
¼ c. cooking oil
½ c. chopped onion
½ c. chopped green pepper
1 clove garlic, minced
1 (1 lb.) can tomatoes
½ tsp. salt
½ tsp. orégano leaves
¼ tsp. pepper
1 medium eggplant, peeled and sliced
½ c. grated Parmesan cheese
½ lb. mozzarella cheese, sliced

Season veal cutlets with 1 tsp. salt. Brown in hot oil in skillet. Remove from skillet. Add onion, green pepper and garlic; sauté until tender (do not brown). Add tomatoes, ½ tsp. salt, orégano and pepper. Bring mixture to a boil.

Place a layer of eggplant in 11 × 7 × 1½" baking dish. Top with sauce and then meat. Repeat layers. Sprinkle with Parmesan cheese. Cover with aluminum foil.

Bake in moderate oven (350°) 50 minutes. Uncover. Top with mozzarella cheese. Bake for 10 more minutes. Makes 6 servings.

STUFFED STEAK ROLLS

Hot parslied noodles and buttered whole beets go well with this

2 lbs. round steak, ¼" thick
3 strips bacon
⅓ c. finely chopped onion
¼ c. finely chopped celery
2 c. soft bread crumbs
2 tblsp. chopped fresh parsley
1 tsp. poultry seasoning
1 egg, beaten
½ c. flour
¾ tsp. salt
¼ tsp. pepper
¼ tsp. rubbed sage
¼ c. cooking oil
1 (10½ oz.) can condensed beef broth
1 bay leaf

Pound meat with meat mallet or edge of heavy plate. Cut into 4 × 3" pieces.

Fry bacon in small skillet until crisp. Remove and drain on paper towels. Crumble bacon.

Sauté onion and celery in bacon fat until tender (do not brown).

Combine bread crumbs, parsley, poultry seasoning, egg, bacon and sautéed onion mixture. Mix lightly, but well.

Place a small amount of stuffing on each piece of meat. Roll up, starting at narrow end. Secure with toothpick or lace with thread, if necessary. Dredge with combined flour, salt, pepper and sage.

Brown rolls in hot oil. Remove and place in 2-qt. casserole. Bring beef broth and bay leaf to a boil; pour over beef rolls. Cover.

Bake in moderate oven (375°) 1 hour 10 minutes or until meat is tender. Skim off excess fat. Remove bay leaf. If you wish, thicken pan juices. Makes 6 to 8 servings.

CALABRIAN BEEF ROLLS

Flank steak with an unusual and most delicious Italian stuffing

2 lbs. flank steak, 1½" thick
1 c. soft bread crumbs
2 hard-cooked eggs, chopped
½ c. chopped walnuts
½ c. grated Parmesan cheese
¼ c. golden raisins
1 tblsp. melted butter or regular margarine
2 tblsp. chopped fresh parsley
½ tsp. salt

⅛ tsp. pepper
½ c. cooking oil
1 (2 lb. 3 oz.) can plum tomatoes
1 clove garlic, minced
½ tsp. basil leaves
½ tsp. salt
½ bay leaf
¼ c. golden raisins

Cut meat in half lengthwise, making two ¾" thick slices. Cut each into four pieces.

Combine bread crumbs, eggs, walnuts, Parmesan cheese, ¼ c. raisins, butter, parsley, ½ tsp. salt and pepper. Mix lightly, but well. Place about ⅓ c. stuffing on each piece of meat. Roll up, starting at narrow end. Secure with toothpick or lace with thread, if necessary.

Brown meat rolls in hot oil. Stir in tomatoes, garlic, basil, ½ tsp. salt, bay leaf and ¼ c. raisins. Bring to a boil; reduce heat. Cover. Simmer for 1 hour or until meat is tender. Stir occasionally. Makes 4 to 6 servings.

KOREAN-STYLE STEAK

Let your guests try to guess all the ingredients in the marinade

1½ lbs. round steak, ½" thick
¼ c. soy sauce
3 tblsp. cooking oil
⅓ c. finely chopped onion
2 tblsp. toasted sesame seeds

1 clove garlic, minced
2 tsp. sugar
½ tsp. ground ginger
¼ tsp. pepper

Pound meat with meat mallet or edge of heavy plate. Score meat by crisscrossing shallow diamond-shaped cuts on both sides of meat. Cut into 4 × 3" pieces.

Combine soy sauce, oil, onion, sesame seeds, garlic, sugar, ginger and pepper; mix well. Add meat and marinate at room temperature for 1 hour.

Arrange meat on broiler rack. Broil 3" from the source of heat. Broil for 6 minutes, turning once; baste with marinade as necessary. Makes 6 servings.

CHINESE PEPPER STEAK

Pleasant touch of oriental subtlety with bright fresh color

1 lb. beef chuck, cut in 3 × 1"
  strips
1 tsp. salt
¼ c. cooking oil
2 tblsp. soy sauce
1 clove garlic, minced
½ c. water

1 c. green pepper strips
1 c. sliced onion
½ c. sliced celery
2 tomatoes, cut in 8 wedges
1 tblsp. cornstarch
1 c. water
Hot, cooked rice

Season meat with salt. Brown meat in hot oil in large skillet. Add soy sauce, garlic and ½ c. water. Bring to a boil; reduce heat. Cover. Simmer for 45 minutes or until meat is tender.

Add green pepper, onion and celery. Cover. Simmer for 10 minutes. Add tomatoes.

Combine cornstarch and 1 c. water. Slowly stir into mixture. Bring to a boil; boil for 1 minute. Serve on rice. Makes 6 servings.

FRUITED SWISS STEAK

A tart cranberry-studded gravy makes this Swiss steak different

2 lbs. round steak (½″ thick)	½ c. water
3 tblsp. flour	1 (1 lb.) can whole cranberry
1 tsp. salt	sauce
⅛ tsp. pepper	½ c. chopped celery
2 tblsp. cooking oil	1 clove garlic, minced
¼ c. lemon juice	1 tblsp. sugar
½ tsp. Worcestershire sauce	1 tsp. grated lemon rind

Dredge meat with combined flour, salt and pepper. Brown in hot oil in large skillet.

Combine lemon juice, Worcestershire sauce and water; mix well. Pour over steak. Bring to a boil; reduce heat. Cover. Simmer for 45 minutes.

Mix together cranberry sauce, celery, garlic, sugar and lemon rind. Pour over meat. Cover. Simmer for 1 more hour or until meat is tender. Makes 6 servings.

OLD WORLD SAUERBRATEN

For an even spicier flavor, try marinating the roast 3 or 4 days

3 to 4 lbs. boned beef rump roast	1 c. chopped onion
1 c. cider vinegar	1 c. sliced carrots
1 c. water	1 c. sliced celery
¼ c. brown sugar, firmly packed	2 tblsp. flour
2 tsp. salt	3 tblsp. cooking oil
¼ tsp. pepper	¼ c. gingersnap crumbs
¼ tsp. ground cloves	½ c. dairy sour cream
1 bay leaf	

Place meat in large bowl. Combine vinegar, water, brown sugar, salt, pepper and cloves. Pour over meat, turning meat to coat all sides. Add bay leaf, onion, carrots and celery. Cover. Refrigerate meat for 2 days, turning meat several times.

Remove meat from marinade. Pat dry with paper towels. Roll meat in flour. Brown well in hot oil in Dutch oven. Add marinade and vegetables; bring to a boil. Reduce heat. Cover. Simmer for 3 hours or until meat is tender.

Remove meat and keep warm. Skim off fat. Strain liquid. Press vegetables through a sieve and return to liquid. Stir in gingersnaps. Cook over medium heat, stirring constantly, until gravy thickens slightly. Blend in sour cream. (Do not boil.) Makes 6 to 8 servings.

COMPANY POT ROAST

Whisper of ginger and cloves adds the extra special flavor

3 to 4 lbs. beef rump roast	½ tsp. ground ginger
½ tsp. salt	1 (10½ oz.) can condensed
⅛ tsp. pepper	beef broth
¼ c. cooking oil	1 c. water
4 strips bacon, diced	3 tblsp. cornstarch
1 c. chopped onion	½ c. water
2 cloves garlic, minced	1 tsp. prepared mustard
2 bay leaves	¼ tsp. bottled sauce for gravy
4 whole cloves	

Rub surface of meat with salt and pepper. Brown well in hot oil in Dutch oven. Remove meat.

Add bacon, onion and garlic; sauté until onion is tender (do not brown). Add bay leaves, cloves, ginger, beef broth and 1 c. water. Return meat to Dutch oven. Bring to a boil; reduce heat. Cover. Simmer for 2½ to 3 hours or until meat is tender.

Remove meat and keep warm. Remove excess fat. Strain pan juices into a large measuring cup. Add water, if necessary, to make 3½ c. liquid. Return to Dutch oven. Bring to a boil. Slowly stir in combined cornstarch, ½ c. water, mustard and bottled sauce for gravy. Bring to a boil; boil for 1 minute. Makes 6 to 8 servings.

MEDLEY OF MEAT LOAVES

Farm women have wonderful ways with meat loaves. We have a prized collection of some of the best; each one is distinctive and tasty as can be. Some are "frosted," some have a zingy bake-on glaze and some are plain but perfectly flavored.

STUFFED MEAT LOAF

Surround the loaf with buttered carrot chunks sprinkled with parsley

1 lb. lean ground beef	1 (4 oz.) can mushrooms,
1 lb. ground pork	drained and chopped
1 c. dry bread crumbs	1 tblsp. finely chopped onion
½ c. grated carrots	2 tblsp. butter or regular marga-
¼ c. finely chopped onion	rine
2 eggs, beaten	2 c. soft bread crumbs
½ c. milk	1 tblsp. chopped fresh parsley
2 tsp. salt	½ tsp. poultry seasoning
1 tsp. Worcestershire sauce	¼ tsp. salt
⅛ tsp. pepper	

Mix together ground beef, ground pork, dry bread crumbs, carrots, ¼ c. onion and eggs. Add milk, 2 tsp. salt, Worcestershire sauce and pepper. Mix lightly, but well.

Place on a double-thick square of greased aluminum foil. Shape into a 14 × 8″ rectangle.

Sauté mushrooms and 1 tblsp. onion in melted butter in small skillet over medium heat. Combine with soft bread crumbs, parsley, poultry seasoning and ¼ tsp. salt.

Spread stuffing over meat mixture; roll up, starting with long side. Press overlapping edge into roll to seal. Bring foil edges together in a tight double fold on the top. Fold ends up, using tight double folds. Place wrapped meat loaf on rack in shallow pan.

Bake in moderate oven (375°) 1 hour. Open foil; continue baking for 15 minutes or until loaf browns. Makes 4 to 6 servings.

Note: If you freeze meat loaf, bake it wrapped in very hot oven (450°) 1 hour 30 minutes, then brown as directed.

SAVORY MEAT SQUARES

An Oregon family is especially fond of this . . . stays moist and juicy

2 lbs. ground beef	1¾ tsp. salt
1 c. soft bread crumbs	½ tsp. basil leaves
1½ c. chopped, pared apples	½ tsp. orégano leaves
¾ c. chopped onion	⅛ tsp. pepper
2 tblsp. chopped fresh parsley	2 eggs, beaten

Combine all ingredients. Mix lightly, but well. Press mixture into greased 8″ square baking pan.

Bake in moderate oven (375°) 1 hour or until done. Cut into squares. Makes 6 servings.

PIZZA MEAT LOAF

Bake a big casserole of scalloped potatoes to serve with this loaf

½ c. chopped onion	1 tsp. orégano leaves
1 (6 oz.) can tomato paste	¼ tsp. basil leaves
¼ tsp. salt	¼ tsp. pepper
1 c. water	½ clove garlic, minced
1½ lbs. ground beef	1 egg, beaten
1 c. soft bread crumbs	1 tblsp. grated Parmesan cheese
1½ tsp. salt	1 c. shredded mozzarella cheese

Combine onion, tomato paste, ¼ tsp. salt and water in small saucepan. Bring to a boil; reduce heat. Simmer, uncovered, for 20 minutes.

Combine ground beef, bread crumbs, 1½ tsp. salt, orégano, basil, pepper, garlic, egg and ½ c. cooked sauce. Mix lightly, but well. Shape into a loaf on greased 11 × 7 × 1½″ baking dish.

Bake in moderate oven (375°) 1 hour. Pour remaining sauce over meat loaf. Sprinkle with Parmesan cheese and mozzarella cheese. Bake for 10 more minutes. Makes 6 servings.

HAM AND VEAL LOAF

Fill the center of the ring with sliced buttered carrots and peas

1 lb. ground cooked ham	¼ c. ketchup
1 lb. ground veal	½ tsp. celery seeds
1 c. saltine cracker crumbs	½ tsp. salt
¼ c. finely chopped onion	2 eggs, beaten
2 tblsp. chopped green pepper	½ c. milk
2 tblsp. quick-cooking rolled oats	4 c. water

Combine all ingredients, except water. Mix lightly, but well. Press mixture into well-greased 5-cup ring mold.

Bring water to a boil in Dutch oven. Place mold in water. Cover. Steam for 1 hour 30 minutes or until done. Makes 6 servings.

POTATO / BEEF ROLL

"My husband likes this because it contains all his favorite foods"

¾ c. chopped onion
1 clove garlic, minced
1 tblsp. cooking oil
2 lbs. lean ground beef
1½ tsp. salt
½ tsp. rubbed sage
¼ tsp. pepper
4 slices bread, cut in 1" cubes

2 eggs, beaten
½ c. milk
½ c. dry bread crumbs
2 c. stiff, seasoned mashed
   potatoes
2 tsp. minced fresh parsley
4 strips bacon

Sauté onion and garlic in hot oil in skillet until tender (do not brown).

Combine ground beef, salt, sage, pepper, cubed bread, eggs, milk and sautéed onion mixture. Mix lightly, but well.

Sprinkle bread crumbs on a piece of waxed paper, making a 12 × 8" rectangle. Pat meat mixture in an even layer on bread crumbs. Spread with mashed potatoes and sprinkle with parsley. Roll up like a jelly roll, starting at wide end, using waxed paper in rolling. Place in greased shallow roasting pan. Top with bacon strips.

Bake in moderate oven (350°) 1 hour or until done. Makes 6 to 8 servings.

MINIATURE CHEESE LOAVES

Light golden Swiss cheese melts all through these little loaves

2 lbs. ground beef
2¾ c. soft bread crumbs
¾ c. chopped onion
½ c. chopped green pepper
2 tblsp. chopped fresh parsley
1 tsp. salt
¼ tsp. basil leaves
¼ tsp. pepper

1 (10½ oz.) can condensed vegetable or vegetarian vegetable
   soup
¼ c. milk
½ c. cubed Swiss cheese
1 (1 lb.) jar meatless spaghetti
   sauce

Combine ground beef, bread crumbs, onion, green pepper, parsley, salt, basil, pepper, soup and milk. Mix lightly, but well. Shape in 8 small meat loaves. Place on 15½ × 10½ × 1" jelly roll pan. Press cheese cubes into each loaf, covering with meat mixture. Bake in hot oven (400°) 35 minutes or until brown.

Cool and refrigerate. To serve, heat in spaghetti sauce. Makes 8 servings.

GRATED VEGETABLE MEAT LOAF

The vegetables add wonderful flavor . . . makes good sandwiches

2 lbs. ground beef	2 tsp. salt
1 c. grated potato	1 tsp. savory leaves
½ c. grated carrots	½ tsp. ground nutmeg
½ c. chopped onion	¼ tsp. pepper
¼ c. chopped green pepper	2 eggs, slightly beaten
2 tblsp. diced pimientos	¼ c. water

Combine all ingredients. Mix lightly, but well. Press mixture into greased 9 × 5 × 3″ loaf pan.

Bake in moderate oven (350°) 1 hour or until done. Makes 6 to 8 servings.

CLARA'S MEAT LOAF

Bake and chill overnight and take to the picnic the next day

2 lbs. ground beef	¼ tsp. pepper
1 c. saltine cracker crumbs	1¼ c. milk
3 eggs, slightly beaten	½ c. ketchup
½ c. finely chopped onion	2 tsp. dry mustard
¼ c. chopped green pepper	1 tsp. brown sugar
1½ tsp. salt	½ tsp. ground nutmeg
½ tsp. rubbed sage	

Combine ground beef, cracker crumbs, eggs, onion, green pepper, salt, sage, pepper and milk. Mix lightly, but well. Shape into a 12″ loaf on greased 15½ × 10½ × 1″ jelly roll pan or shallow roasting pan.

Bake in moderate oven (350°) 30 minutes.

Combine ketchup, mustard, brown sugar and nutmeg. Spread on loaf. Continue baking for 30 more minutes. Makes 8 servings.

APPLE UPSIDE-DOWN HAM LOAF

Glazed apple slices make a handsome topping for this moist loaf

1 lb. ground cooked ham	1 tblsp. butter or regular marga-
½ lb. ground beef	rine
½ c. dry bread crumbs	½ c. brown sugar, firmly packed
¼ c. chopped celery	⅛ tsp. ground cloves
¼ c. chopped onion	⅛ tsp. ground cinnamon
½ tsp. dry mustard	2 apples, pared and sliced
2 eggs, beaten	3 maraschino cherries, halved
¾ c. milk	1 tblsp. raisins

Combine ham, ground beef, bread crumbs, celery, onion, mustard, eggs and milk. Mix lightly, but well.

Melt butter in bottom of 9 × 5 × 3″ loaf pan. Combine brown sugar, cloves and cinnamon. Sprinkle mixture in loaf pan. Arrange apple slices, maraschino cherries and raisins on sugar mixture. Press meat mixture into loaf pan.

Bake in moderate oven (350°) 1 hour 15 minutes or until done. Remove from oven. Let stand for 5 minutes. Pour off excess liquid. Invert pan on serving platter; wait a few seconds and remove pan. Makes 6 servings.

COUNTY FAIR HAM LOAF

Three types of meat and lots of seasonings makes this extra special

2 lbs. ground cooked ham	3 eggs, beaten
1 lb. ground pork	1½ c. milk
1 lb. ground veal	1 (10½ oz.) can condensed to-
2 c. graham cracker crumbs	mato soup
½ c. chopped onion	1 c. brown sugar, firmly packed
1 tblsp. prepared mustard	1 tblsp. dry mustard
¼ tsp. ground cloves	½ c. vinegar
¼ tsp. pepper	½ c. water

Combine ground meats, graham cracker crumbs, onion, prepared mustard, cloves, pepper, eggs and milk. Mix lightly, but well. Shape into a loaf on greased 15½ × 10½ × 1″ jelly roll pan or shallow roasting pan.

Combine tomato soup, brown sugar, dry mustard, vinegar and water; mix well. Pour over loaf.

Bake in moderate oven (375°) 1 hour 45 minutes, basting frequently. Makes 10 to 12 servings.

FAMILY STAND-BYS

We have a combination of everyday meat dishes that will suit every member of the family . . . children's specials, teen-agers' favorites and some for the man of the family. Others have been popular with the field crew during planting and harvesting time. When we tested and tasted these dishes in the FARM JOURNAL Countryside Test Kitchens, the verdict was enthusiastic: "Good eating for everyday!"

CORNMEAL / BEAN SQUARES

A bit different and so good . . . make several and freeze ahead

5½ c. water	⅓ c. chopped onion
2 c. yellow cornmeal	1 clove garlic, minced
2 c. cold water	1 bay leaf
2 tsp. salt	1½ tsp. orégano leaves
2 tsp. sugar	½ tsp. salt
⅓ c. chopped onion	¼ tsp. pepper
2 tblsp. butter	⅟₁₆ tsp. cayenne pepper
1 c. shredded Cheddar cheese	2 (1 lb.) cans tomatoes
½ lb. red kidney beans, cooked and drained (about 3 c.)	1 (15 oz.) can tomato sauce
	½ tsp. sugar
¾ lb. ground beef	2 tblsp. chopped green pepper
⅓ c. cooking oil	1 c. shredded Cheddar cheese

Bring 5½ c. water to a boil in 4-qt. saucepan.

Combine cornmeal, 2 c. water, 2 tsp. salt and 2 tsp. sugar. Gradually stir into boiling water. Cook, over medium heat, stirring constantly, until mixture is thick. Reduce heat. Cover. Cook over low heat, stirring occasionally, for 25 minutes.

Sauté ⅓ c. onion in melted butter in skillet until tender (do not brown). Stir onion and 1 c. cheese into cornmeal mixture. Stir in kidney beans. Pour mixture into 13 × 9 × 2″ baking pan. Refrigerate until mixture sets.

Meanwhile, sauté ground beef in hot oil. When meat begins to turn color, add ⅓ c. onion, garlic, bay leaf, orégano, ½ tsp. salt, pepper and cayenne pepper. Cook until well browned.

Blend tomatoes in blender until smooth. Add tomatoes, tomato sauce, ½ tsp. sugar and green pepper to meat mixture. Bring to a boil; reduce heat. Simmer, uncovered, for 50 minutes.

Cut cornmeal mixture into 24 pieces. Arrange in two 13 × 9 × 2″ baking dishes. Pour half of meat sauce over each. Sprinkle remaining 1 c. cheese on top.

Bake in moderate oven (350°) 30 minutes or until well heated. Makes 12 servings.

BARBECUED RIBS

Subtle undertone of lime juice adds zest to this outdoor favorite

6 lbs. spareribs	¼ c. lime juice
1 tsp. salt	2 tblsp. brown sugar
½ c. chopped onion	1½ tsp. soy sauce
2 tblsp. butter	1 tsp. salt
¾ c. ketchup	1 tsp. dry mustard
¾ c. pineapple juice	

Cut ribs into serving pieces. Place in large saucepan and cover with water. Add 1 tsp. salt. Simmer for 45 minutes or until tender. Drain well.

Sauté onion in melted butter in saucepan until tender (do not brown). Stir in ketchup, pineapple juice, lime juice, brown sugar, soy sauce, 1 tsp. salt and dry mustard. Bring mixture to a boil. Remove from heat.

Grill ribs over hot coals, basting frequently with sauce, until tender and crisp. Makes 6 to 8 servings.

BARBECUED BEEF PATTIES

Accompany with chunks of crusty French bread to mop up the gravy

1 lb. ground beef	½ c. ketchup
1 c. soft bread crumbs	½ c. water
1 tblsp. chopped onion	½ c. chopped green pepper
1 tsp. salt	½ c. chopped onion
½ tsp. marjoram leaves	3 tblsp. vinegar
⅛ tsp. pepper	1½ tblsp. Worcestershire sauce
½ c. milk	1 tblsp. sugar

Combine ground beef, bread crumbs, 1 tblsp. onion, salt, marjoram, pepper and milk. Mix lightly, but well. Shape into four patties. Place in greased 9″ square baking pan.

Combine ketchup, water, green pepper, ½ c. onion, vinegar, Worcestershire sauce and sugar; mix well. Pour over beef patties.

Bake in moderate oven (375°) 1 hour or until done. Makes 4 servings.

MEATBALLS IN TOMATO SAUCE

Meatballs bake in spicy sauce . . . taste even better when reheated

1 lb. ground beef
½ c. soft bread crumbs
¼ c. finely chopped onion
2 tblsp. minced fresh parsley
1 tsp. salt
½ tsp. marjoram leaves
¹⁄₁₆ tsp. pepper
1 egg, beaten
¼ c. milk

¼ c. cooking oil
1 (10½ oz.) can condensed tomato soup
½ c. bottled barbecue sauce
½ c. water
1 tblsp. Worcestershire sauce
2 tblsp. finely chopped onion
½ clove garlic, minced

Combine ground beef, bread crumbs, ¼ c. onion, parsley, salt, marjoram, pepper, egg and milk. Mix lightly, but well. Shape into meatballs. Brown, a few at a time, in hot oil in small skillet. Remove from skillet and place in 11 × 7 × 1½″ baking dish.

Combine tomato soup, barbecue sauce, water, Worcestershire sauce, 2 tblsp. onion and garlic; mix well. Pour over meatballs.

Bake in slow oven (325°) 1 hour or until done. Makes 4 servings.

SPAGHETTI WITH MEAT SAUCE

Toss a salad with oil and vinegar dressing and pass hot garlic bread

1 lb. ground beef
1 lb. bulk pork sausage
1 c. chopped onion
2 cloves garlic, minced
2 (1 lb. 12 oz.) cans tomatoes
1 (8 oz.) can tomato sauce
1 (6 oz.) can tomato paste
1 c. water

2 (1½ oz.) pkgs. spaghetti sauce mix with mushrooms
2 tsp. salt
1 tsp. orégano leaves
1 tsp. sugar
⅛ tsp. pepper
1 bay leaf
Hot, cooked spaghetti

Sauté ground beef and sausage in 4-qt. Dutch oven. When meat begins to turn color, add onion, sauté until meat is well browned. Add garlic; cook for 1 minute.

Blend tomatoes in a blender for a few seconds to make them smooth. Add tomatoes, tomato sauce, tomato paste, water, spaghetti sauce mix, salt, orégano, sugar, pepper and bay leaf to meat mixture. Bring to a boil; reduce heat. Cover. Simmer for 1 hour 30 minutes. Stir occasionally. If you wish a thinner sauce, add a little water. Serve on spaghetti. Makes 2½ quarts.

SLIVERED BEEF LIVER

"My children will eat every bit of liver when I fix it like this"

1 lb. beef liver	½ tsp. salt
¼ c. butter or regular margarine	½ tsp. chili powder
1 large onion, sliced	⅛ tsp. pepper

Cut liver into ¼" slivers.

Melt butter in 10" skillet. Sauté onion rings in butter until tender (do not brown).

Add liver. Season with salt, chili powder and pepper. Cook over medium heat, stirring occasionally, for 5 minutes. Makes 4 servings.

SPANISH-STYLE PORK CHOPS

"There's never a bite left over when I make this for the family"

6 pork chops, ¾" thick	½ c. chopped green pepper
1 tsp. salt	½ c. chopped celery
⅛ tsp. pepper	¼ c. regular rice
1 tblsp. cooking oil	2 tsp. parsley flakes
1 (1 lb.) can tomatoes	½ bay leaf
½ c. chopped onion	½ c. water

Season pork chops with salt and pepper. Brown chops in hot oil in large skillet. Add tomatoes, onion, green pepper, celery, rice, parsley flakes, bay leaf and water. Bring to a boil; reduce heat. Cover. Simmer for 45 minutes or until meat is tender. Makes 6 servings.

HAMBURGER PIE

Complete the meal with a salad, biscuits and a chilled fruit compote

1½ lbs. ground beef	1 tblsp. Worcestershire sauce
1 tblsp. cooking oil	1 tsp. chili powder
½ c. chopped celery	Dash of Tabasco sauce
¼ c. chopped green pepper	Pastry for 2-crust 9″ pie
1 clove garlic, minced	Sesame seeds
1 (8 oz.) can tomato sauce	Vegetable Sauce (recipe follows)

Brown ground beef in hot oil in 10″ skillet. When meat begins to change color, add celery, green pepper and garlic. Sauté until meat is well browned.

Add tomato sauce, Worcestershire sauce, chili powder and Tabasco sauce. Simmer, uncovered, for 15 minutes. Cool well.

Meanwhile, line pie plate with pastry. Pour in cooled meat mixture. Roll out remaining pastry. Cut into ½″ strips. Lay half of strips over filling about 1″ apart. Repeat with remaining strips, placing them in opposite direction in diamond or square pattern. Trim strips even with pie edge. Turn bottom crust up over rim and ends of strips. Press firmly to seal edge. Sprinkle pastry strips with sesame seeds.

Bake in hot oven (400°) 25 minutes or until golden brown. Serve hot with Vegetable Sauce. Makes 6 servings.

Vegetable Sauce: Melt 3 tblsp. butter in medium saucepan. Stir in ¼ c. flour. Gradually stir in 2 c. beef bouillon. Cook over medium heat, stirring constantly, until thickened. Add 1 c. cooked peas, 1 c. diced, cooked carrots and 1 tblsp. chopped fresh parsley. Heat mixture well.

Chapter 2

WE COULD EAT CHICKEN
EVERY DAY

Whether it is everyday or dressed up, chicken is a top favorite with farm families. Whenever birthdays come up in one Kansas family, and the celebrant is given a choice for dinner, it's Sweet and Sour Chicken. For a spur of the moment barbecue, an Arizona family serves prized Golden Broiled Chicken. And in Texas, a big pot of Chili Chicken Stew is a popular dinner on busy days.

Chicken is economical as well as a valuable source of protein, and it's a low calorie choice if served broiled or boiled.

Keep several chickens in your freezer and when unexpected family or guests arrive, try the recipes in this chapter. There's one to suit every taste and occasion. Rich tomato-sauced Chicken Cacciatore, Chicken in Spicy Sauce, Crispy Baked Chicken—any one of these dishes is perfect for the busy hostess.

Even those who don't care for chicken livers just love Spaghetti Caruso, an Illinois farm woman says. For the holidays, serve Roast Chickens with Sausage Stuffing; use the leftover chicken for a batch of golden-brown Chicken-Rice Pyramids.

A popular meal with an Iowa family is Bulgarian Chicken. It's an interesting medley of cabbage, sauerkraut, onion, rice and tomatoes topped with chicken pieces and baked. Sometimes duck or turkey is substituted for the chicken.

Everyone will rave when you serve Crisp Oven-Fried Chicken. Coated with spices and dipped in milk and crumbs before it bakes, this dish is a great favorite for a buffet party meal.

CHICKEN COMPANY SPECIALS

These chicken dishes will "do you proud" when you present them to your guests. And best of all, they are economical as well as elegant. Some are broiled, some baked, some cook on top of your range. There's roast chicken with a choice of several savory stuffings, pineapple sauced chicken, curry scented baked chicken and a marinated broiled chicken dish that is just supreme.

CRISPY BAKED CHICKEN

Surprise unexpected supper guests with this quick and easy main dish

2 c. dry bread crumbs
2 tsp. onion salt
1¼ tsp. garlic salt
1 tsp. pepper
1 tsp. savory leaves

1 tsp. curry powder
2 (2½ lb.) broiler-fryers, cut in serving pieces
¾ c. mayonnaise

Combine bread crumbs, onion salt, garlic salt, pepper, savory and curry powder. Coat chicken pieces with crumb mixture. Place in 15½ × 10½ × 1″ jelly roll pan, skin side up.

Bake in hot oven (400°) 15 minutes. Remove from oven. Brush chicken pieces with mayonnaise. Reduce oven temperature to slow oven (300°) and bake 1 hour or until chicken is tender and golden. Makes 8 servings.

PINEAPPLE CHICKEN

Delicious served with fluffy hot rice and a crisp tossed green salad

2 (2½ to 3 lb.) broiler-fryers, cut up
2 tsp. salt
1 tsp. rosemary leaves
½ tsp. pepper
10 small white onions, parboiled for 15 minutes

2 c. unsweetened pineapple juice
1 tsp. ground ginger
1 tblsp. cornstarch
1 tblsp. water
Fresh parsley

Rub chicken with a mixture of salt, rosemary and pepper. Place skin side up in $13 \times 9 \times 2''$ baking dish. Arrange onions around chicken. Combine pineapple juice and ginger; pour over chicken.

Bake in moderate oven (350°), uncovered, 1 hour or until chicken is tender. Remove chicken and onions from pan and arrange on platter. Combine cornstarch and water. Slowly stir into pan juices. Bring to a boil; boil for 1 minute. Pour ⅓ c. sauce over chicken; pour remaining sauce into serving bowl. Garnish with parsley. Makes 6 to 8 servings.

ROAST CHICKENS WITH SAUSAGE STUFFING

Company fare when served with buttered peas and mushrooms

2 (3 lb.) whole broiler-fryers	6 c. fresh bread cubes (½")
Salt	1 tsp. rubbed sage
Pepper	½ tsp. salt
1 lb. bulk pork sausage	½ tsp. thyme leaves
1 (4 oz.) can mushroom pieces, drained	¼ tsp. savory leaves
1 c. chopped onion	¼ tsp. pepper
½ c. chopped celery	½ c. milk
2 tblsp. chopped celery leaves	Melted butter or regular margarine

Rub neck and body cavities with salt and pepper. Prepare stuffing.

Sauté sausage in skillet until it begins to turn color. Stir in mushrooms, onion, celery and celery leaves. Cook until meat is browned. Cool slightly.

Combine cooled sausage mixture with bread cubes, sage, salt, thyme, savory, pepper and milk; toss lightly.

Stuff neck cavity lightly. Pull neck skin back; secure with skewer. Pull each wing out and force tip back until it rests against neck skin. Stuff body cavity loosely. Tie drumsticks to tail. Repeat with other chicken.

Place chickens, breast side up on wire rack in shallow roasting pan. Brush chickens with melted butter. Roast in moderate oven (375°) 1 hour 45 minutes or until tender. Chicken is done if drumstick twists easily out of thigh joint. Remove skewers and string; place on heated platter. Makes 8 servings.

POTATO FILLING

A filling that is sure to become a holiday tradition in your family

10 c. seasoned mashed potatoes	2 tsp. rubbed sage
2 eggs	½ tsp. salt
3 c. chopped onion	¼ tsp. pepper
3 c. chopped celery	2 tblsp. butter or regular
⅔ c. butter or regular	margarine
margarine	2 tblsp. milk
6 c. soft bread cubes (½″)	Paprika
½ c. minced fresh parsley	

Mix eggs with mashed potatoes; set aside.

Sauté onion and celery in ⅔ c. melted butter in skillet until tender (do not brown). Add bread cubes, parsley, sage, salt and pepper; toss until golden.

Combine with mashed potato mixture. Turn into buttered 3-qt. casserole. Dot with 2 tblsp. butter and sprinkle with milk and paprika. Bake in moderate oven (375°) 40 minutes or until golden brown. Makes 10 servings.

MUSHROOM BREAD STUFFING

Valuable addition to your recipe files . . . perfect for company dinner

1 c. chopped onion	¼ tsp. pepper
1 (4 oz.) can sliced mushrooms, drained	¼ c. melted butter or regular margarine
¼ c. butter or regular margarine	1 (10½ oz.) can condensed cream of mushroom soup
12 c. soft bread cubes (¾″)	1 tblsp. milk
¼ c. minced fresh parsley	
1 tsp. rubbed sage	

Sauté onion and mushrooms in ¼ c. melted butter in skillet until tender (do not brown). Toss together bread cubes, parsley, sage, pepper, ¼ c. melted butter and sautéed vegetables. Stir soup and add to mixture.

Place in greased 2-qt. casserole and sprinkle with milk. Bake in moderate oven (350°) 35 minutes or until brown. Makes 6 to 8 servings.

GOLDEN BROILED CHICKEN

Cook this tasty chicken on the outdoor grill with baked potatoes

1 c. cider vinegar	1 egg, beaten
¾ c. cooking oil	½ c. sliced onion
4½ tsp. salt	2 (3 lb.) broiler-fryers,
1 tblsp. poultry seasoning	quartered
½ tsp. white pepper	

Combine vinegar, oil, salt, poultry seasoning, pepper, egg and onion in 2-qt. saucepan. Stirring constantly, bring mixture to a boil. Pour over chicken and let stand at room temperature for 1 hour.

Place chicken, skin side down on broiler pan. Place pan in broiler, 7 to 9" from heat. Broil for 30 minutes, basting frequently with marinade. Turn chicken over and baste. Broil another 15 minutes or until chicken is tender and golden. Makes 8 servings.

SWEET AND SOUR CHICKEN

Succulent chunks of golden fried chicken make this dish special

2 whole chicken breasts, skinned, boned and cut in 1" chunks	1 tblsp. paprika
½ tsp. salt	1 (1 lb. 4 oz.) can pineapple chunks
1 egg, beaten	¼ c. soy sauce
¾ c. biscuit mix	¼ c. cider vinegar
1 c. cooking oil	1 c. green pepper strips
⅔ c. sugar	½ c. sliced onion
2 tblsp. cornstarch	2 medium tomatoes, cut up
	Hot, cooked rice

Sprinkle chicken with salt. Coat with egg and then biscuit mix. Fry chicken in hot oil (400°) in small skillet until golden brown. Remove; drain on paper towels. Place in very slow oven (250°) to keep warm.

Combine sugar, cornstarch and paprika in 10" skillet. Drain pineapple; add enough water to make 2 c. Add pineapple juice, soy sauce and vinegar to cornstarch mixture. Cook, stirring constantly, until mixture boils. Boil for 1 minute. Add green pepper and onion. Cover;

cook vegetables until tender crisp (about 5 minutes). Add pineapple chunks and tomatoes; heat well. Add chicken chunks.

Serve with rice. Makes 6 to 8 servings.

DELUXE CHICKEN SUPPER

"First prize by a landslide in my home demonstration club contest"

3 strips bacon
¾ c. chopped onion
½ c. chopped celery
¼ c. chopped green pepper
1 (4 oz.) can sliced mushrooms, drained
1 (10½ oz.) can condensed cream of celery soup
1 c. dairy sour cream
3 c. cubed, cooked chicken
¼ tsp. salt
2 tsp. Worcestershire sauce
⅛ tsp. pepper
1 tblsp. milk
2 c. biscuit mix
2 eggs, slightly beaten
½ c. milk
1 tblsp. chopped pimientos
1 c. shredded Cheddar cheese

Fry bacon in skillet until crisp. Remove and drain on paper towels. Crumble.

Sauté onion, celery, green pepper and mushrooms in bacon drippings until tender (do not brown).

Combine soup and sour cream in a bowl. Add chicken, salt, Worcestershire sauce, pepper, 1 tblsp. milk, bacon and sautéed vegetables; mix well. Turn into greased 2-qt. casserole.

Combine biscuit mix, eggs, ½ c. milk, pimientos and cheese; mix until just blended. Drop by spoonfuls on top of chicken mixture.

Bake in moderate oven (350°) 45 minutes or until biscuits are golden brown. Makes 6 to 8 servings.

COMPANY CHICKEN BAKE

Refrigerate prepared casserole and bake until bubbly before serving

½ c. butter or regular margarine
½ c. flour
2 c. chicken bouillon
2 c. light cream
1 tsp. salt
½ tsp. pepper
3 c. cut up, cooked chicken
1 (8 oz.) can sliced mushrooms, drained
½ c. chopped ripe olives
2 c. soft bread crumbs
3 tblsp. grated Parmesan cheese
2 tblsp. melted butter or regular margarine
⅛ tsp. paprika

Melt ½ c. butter in medium saucepan. Stir in flour; blend well. Gradually stir in chicken bouillon and light cream. Cook over medium heat, stirring constantly, until mixture thickens. Add salt, pepper, chicken, mushrooms and olives. Heat well. Turn into greased 3-qt. casserole.

Combine bread crumbs, Parmesan cheese, 2 tblsp. melted butter and paprika. Sprinkle over mixture.

Bake in moderate oven (350°) 30 minutes or until hot and bubbly. Makes 6 to 8 servings.

BUSY DAY? BAKE A CHICKEN DISH

Crisp Oven-Fried Chicken that bakes to a golden goodness is a boon to a homemaker on days when she would like to shove her main dish in the oven and forget it. Sweet and Sour Chicken Wings, for instance, bake in a zippy sauce. All these dishes are "no watching necessary" recipes that will please the family and remove the pressure from the cook.

CRISP OVEN-FRIED CHICKEN

Children in one family choose this crispy chicken for birthday dinner

1 c. crushed saltine crackers	½ tsp. onion salt
¼ c. grated Parmesan cheese	¼ tsp. paprika
1 tblsp. minced fresh parsley	¼ tsp. pepper
½ tsp. salt	½ bay leaf, crushed
½ tsp. orégano leaves	2 (3 lb.) broiler-fryers, cut up
½ tsp. crushed basil leaves	½ c. evaporated milk
½ tsp. celery salt	⅓ c. cooking oil

Combine saltine crackers, Parmesan cheese, parsley, salt, orégano, basil, celery and onion salt, paprika, pepper and bay leaf. Dip chicken pieces in evaporated milk and coat with crumbs.

Place in shallow roasting pan, skin side up. Bake in moderate oven (375°) 30 minutes. Brush with oil; continue baking 30 minutes or until golden brown and tender. Makes 8 servings.

SWEET AND SOUR CHICKEN WINGS

Exceptionally good dish to bring to covered dish buffets or suppers

16 chicken wings	1½ c. sugar
¼ tsp. salt	1 c. cider vinegar
2 eggs, beaten	½ c. ketchup
½ c. cornstarch	½ c. chicken bouillon
½ c. cooking oil	2 tblsp. soy sauce

Bend wing tips behind large bone joints (wings will be easier to fry).

Season chicken with salt. Coat with egg and then with cornstarch. Brown in hot oil in large skillet. Remove as chicken browns and place in 13 × 9 × 2″ baking pan.

Combine sugar, vinegar, ketchup, chicken bouillon and soy sauce in medium saucepan. Bring mixture to a boil. Pour into baking pan.

Bake in moderate oven (350°) 45 minutes or until chicken is tender and golden brown. Let stand a few minutes before serving. Makes 6 to 8 servings.

CHICKEN-RICE PYRAMIDS

Round out the menu with hot, buttered corn on the cob and coleslaw

3 c. cooked rice	1 c. shredded Cheddar cheese
3 c. diced, cooked chicken	1 tsp. chili powder
½ c. chopped celery	½ tsp. orégano leaves
½ c. chopped onion	½ c. melted butter or regular
½ c. chopped walnuts	margarine
3 eggs, beaten	1 c. corn flake crumbs
1 tsp. poultry seasoning	

Mix together rice, chicken, celery, onion, walnuts, eggs, poultry seasoning, cheese, chili powder and orégano. Chill. Form into 12 cone-shaped mounds. Dip each cone into butter and then into crumbs.

Place on greased baking sheet. Bake in moderate oven (350°) 30 minutes or until golden brown. Serve with homemade or prepared chicken gravy. Makes 6 servings.

BULGARIAN CHICKEN

An unusual flavor combination that is especially good on a cold day

5 c. coarsely chopped cabbage	2 (1 lb.) cans tomatoes
1 (1 lb.) can sauerkraut	2 (2½ lb.) broiler-fryers, cut in
½ c. regular rice	serving pieces
¾ c. water	½ tsp. salt
1 c. chopped onion	⅛ tsp. pepper
3 tblsp. cooking oil	

Place cabbage in bottom of small roasting pan or 13 × 9 × 2″ baking dish. Top with layers of sauerkraut and rice. Pour over water.

Sauté onion in hot oil in skillet until tender (do not brown). Arrange layers of sautéed onion and tomatoes in baking dish.

Season chicken with salt and pepper. Place, skin side up, on vegetables.

Bake in moderate oven (375°) 1 hour 30 minutes until chicken is tender and golden brown. Makes 8 servings.

SPICY OVEN-BARBECUED CHICKEN

Marinated cucumbers and corn muffins are good accompaniments

½ c. chopped onion	3 tblsp. brown sugar
½ c. chopped celery	2 tblsp. vinegar
2 tblsp. cooking oil	2 tblsp. prepared mustard
1 (10½ oz.) can condensed	1½ tsp. salt
tomato soup	¼ tsp. pepper
1 c. ketchup	2 drops Tabasco sauce
½ c. water	2 (2½ lb.) broiler-fryers,
¼ c. lemon juice	quartered
3 tblsp. Worcestershire sauce	

Sauté onion and celery in hot oil in saucepan until tender (do not brown). Add tomato soup, ketchup, water, lemon juice, Worcestershire sauce, brown sugar, vinegar, mustard, salt, pepper and Tabasco sauce. Bring mixture to a boil; reduce heat. Simmer, uncovered, for 30 minutes.

Meanwhile, place chicken in shallow roasting pan. Bake in hot oven (400°) 40 minutes. Baste with barbecue sauce. Continue baking and basting with sauce until chicken is crisp and tender. Makes 8 servings.

CHICKEN AND STUFFING PIE

Just add a tossed green salad and pass a plate of crisp relishes

1 (8 oz.) pkg. herb-seasoned stuffing mix
¾ c. chicken broth
½ c. melted butter or regular margarine
1 egg, beaten
1 (4 oz.) can mushrooms
2 tsp. flour
½ c. chopped onion
1 tblsp. butter or regular margarine

1 (10½ oz.) can chicken giblet gravy
3 c. cubed, cooked chicken
1 c. peas
2 tblsp. diced pimientos
1 tblsp. parsley flakes
1 tsp. Worcestershire sauce
½ tsp. thyme leaves
4 slices process American cheese

Mix together stuffing mix, chicken broth, ½ c. butter and egg. Press into greased 10″ pie plate.

Drain mushrooms. Combine mushroom liquid with flour; set aside.

Sauté mushrooms and onion in 1 tblsp. melted butter in saucepan until tender (do not brown). Stir in chicken giblet gravy, chicken, peas, pimientos, parsley flakes, Worcestershire sauce, thyme and mushroom liquid. Heat thoroughly.

Turn into crust. Bake in moderate oven (375°) 20 minutes. Cut each cheese slice into 4 strips. Place in lattice design on pie. Bake 5 more minutes. Makes 6 servings.

CHICKEN DISHES TO SIMMER

These chicken dishes bubble gently in a succulent sauce until the flavors mingle together and the chicken is meltingly tender. Every recipe starts out with chicken but it's the sauce that makes the difference. And we have an intriguing selection of sauces: rich robust tomato sauces, tart orange sauce laced with ginger, and velvety smooth sour cream sauce. Serve these mouth-watering chicken creations over fluffy hot cooked rice or golden egg noodles.

CHICKEN CURRY

Pass bowls of coconut, peanuts, chutney and chopped raw vegetables

1 (3 lb.) broiler-fryer, cut in serving pieces
1 tsp. salt
¼ c. cooking oil
1 (4 oz.) can mushrooms
½ c. chopped onion
1 tblsp. curry powder
1 (10½ oz.) can condensed chicken broth
1 c. diced, pared apple
3 tblsp. flour
¼ c. water
¾ c. light cream
Hot, cooked rice

Season chicken with salt. Brown on all sides in hot oil in 10" skillet. Remove chicken from skillet as it browns.

Drain mushrooms and reserve liquid. Sauté mushrooms and onion until tender (do not brown). Stir in curry powder.

Add enough water to chicken broth to make 1½ c. Add chicken broth, reserved mushroom liquid, apple and chicken. Bring to a boil; reduce heat. Cover; simmer for 45 minutes or until chicken is tender.

Combine flour and ¼ c. water. Slowly stir into hot liquid. Bring to a boil; boil for 1 minute. Stir in cream and heat. (Do not boil.) Serve with rice. Makes 4 servings.

ORIENTAL-STYLE CHICKEN

Garnish serving platter with sprigs of parsley and orange segments

1 (3 lb.) broiler-fryer, cut in serving pieces
1 tsp. salt
¼ tsp. pepper
3 tblsp. cooking oil
2 c. reconstituted frozen orange juice
1 (6 oz.) can water chestnuts, drained and sliced
½ tsp. ground ginger
1 tblsp. cornstarch
2 tblsp. water
¼ c. sliced ripe olives
Hot, cooked rice

Season chicken with salt and pepper. Brown on all sides in hot oil in skillet. Add orange juice, water chestnuts and ginger. Bring to a boil; reduce heat. Cover; simmer for 45 minutes or until tender.

Remove chicken to serving platter. Combine cornstarch and water. Slowly stir into hot liquid. Bring to a boil; boil for 1 minute. Stir in olives. Spoon over chicken. Serve with rice. Makes 4 servings.

CHICKEN PAPRIKA

Serve with hot, fluffy rice and green beans with toasted almonds

1 (3½ lb.) broiler-fryer, cut up
¼ c. flour
½ tsp. salt
¼ tsp. pepper
⅓ c. cooking oil
3 c. sliced onion
1 tblsp. paprika

1 (10½ oz.) can condensed
  chicken broth
6 medium carrots, cut in strips
3 tblsp. flour
¼ c. water
1 c. dairy sour cream
Fresh parsley

Coat chicken with mixture of ¼ c. flour, salt and pepper. Brown chicken in hot oil in 12″ skillet, removing pieces as they brown. Sauté onion until tender (do not brown). Stir in paprika. Slowly stir in chicken broth; bring to a boil, stirring. Add chicken and carrots. Cover; simmer for 30 minutes or until chicken is tender.

Arrange chicken and carrots on platter and keep warm. Combine 3 tblsp. flour with water. Slowly stir into mixture in skillet; boil for 1 minute. Remove from heat; stir in sour cream. Pour ½ c. sauce over chicken and serve remaining sauce in bowl. Sprinkle chicken with parsley. Makes 4 servings.

SPAGHETTI CARUSO

New way to serve chicken livers that your family is sure to like

½ c. chopped onion
2 tblsp. butter or regular
  margarine
¼ c. flour
1 (10½ oz.) can condensed
  beef consommé
1 (8 oz.) can tomato sauce
⅓ c. water
1 (4 oz.) can mushrooms

½ lb. chicken livers, cut up
2 tblsp. butter
½ tsp. salt
⅛ tsp. pepper
1 bay leaf
Hot, cooked spaghetti
Minced fresh parsley
Grated Parmesan cheese

Sauté onion in 2 tblsp. melted butter in saucepan until tender (do not brown). Stir in flour, blending until smooth. Add consommé, tomato sauce and water. Drain mushrooms and add liquid to sauce mixture. Simmer, uncovered, until thickened, stirring occasionally.

Meanwhile, sauté mushrooms and chicken livers in 2 tblsp. melted butter in skillet until all liquid is absorbed (about 5 minutes). Add salt, pepper and bay leaf. Add chicken livers to sauce. Spoon over spaghetti; top with parsley and Parmesan cheese. Makes 4 to 6 servings.

CHILI CHICKEN STEW

A Texas farm woman shares a favored family heirloom recipe

1 (4½ lb.) stewing chicken, cut in pieces	⅓ c. parboiled rice
2 qts. water	2 tblsp. lemon juice
1 tsp. salt	1 tblsp. chili powder
1 (1 lb.) can tomatoes	2 tsp. salt
4 c. sliced pared potatoes	1 tsp. pepper
1 c. diced pared carrots	1 tsp. Worcestershire sauce
1 c. chopped onion	1 tsp. marjoram leaves
1 c. ketchup	1 bay leaf

Cook chicken in water and 1 tsp. salt in Dutch oven until tender (about 2 hours). Chicken can also be cooked in pressure cooker according to manufacturer's directions.

Add tomatoes, potatoes, carrots, onion, ketchup, rice, lemon juice, chili powder, 2 tsp. salt, pepper, Worcestershire sauce, marjoram and bay leaf. Simmer, covered, for 1 hour or until vegetables are tender. Makes 6 servings.

CHICKEN CACCIATORE

Complete the meal with crisp garden salad and crusty garlic bread

1 (3½ lb.) broiler-fryer, cut in serving pieces	1 clove garlic, minced
¼ c. flour	½ c. chopped green pepper
½ tsp. salt	1 (4 oz.) can mushrooms
¼ tsp. pepper	1 (15 oz.) can tomato sauce
¼ c. cooking oil	1 c. water
½ c. chopped onion	½ tsp. orégano leaves
	½ bay leaf

Coat chicken with combined flour, salt and pepper.

Brown chicken on all sides in hot oil in skillet. Remove from skillet.

Add onion and garlic; sauté until tender (do not brown). Add green pepper, undrained mushrooms, tomato sauce, water, orégano, bay leaf and chicken. Bring mixture to a boil; reduce heat. Simmer, covered, for 45 minutes or until chicken is tender. Skim off excess fat. If you wish, serve with rice or noodles. Makes 4 servings.

CHICKEN IN SPICY SAUCE

Fluffy mashed potatoes or spaghetti are also delicious with this

1 (3½ lb.) broiler-fryer, cut in serving pieces
½ c. flour
1 tsp. salt
⅛ tsp. pepper
¼ c. cooking oil
1 c. chopped celery
½ c. chopped onion
1 clove garlic, minced

1 (1 lb.) can stewed tomatoes
1 (8 oz.) can tomato sauce
1 tblsp. brown sugar
2 tsp. Worcestershire sauce
½ tsp. marjoram leaves
2 drops Tabasco sauce
½ c. water
Hot, cooked rice

Moisten chicken with water. Shake several pieces at a time in a bag with flour, salt and pepper. Brown chicken on all sides in hot oil. Remove from skillet.

Add celery, onion and garlic; sauté until tender (do not brown). Add stewed tomatoes, tomato sauce, brown sugar, Worcestershire sauce, marjoram, Tabasco sauce and ½ c. water. Place chicken back in sauce. Bring to a boil; reduce heat. Simmer, covered, for 50 minutes or until chicken is tender. Serve with rice. Makes 4 servings.

Chapter 3

CASSEROLES...
WELCOME AT THE
FAMILY TABLE

Fixing the main part of a meal in one dish is a great timesaver for busy women. These dishes need little watching and can simmer slowly to a delicious goodness for several hours with little or no attention. And an extra bonus—casserole or one-pot dishes will wait for tardy family or guests.

Because of the unpredictable nature of farm work, rural women depend on meals-in-one-dish, and they originate some excellent combinations. So, most country kitchens include a collection of all types of casseroles, large skillets and pots of metal, ovenproof ceramic, and enameled cast iron. They come in handsome colors and artistic shapes and, as serving dishes, actually add to the attractiveness of a table or buffet setting.

Experience has taught the farm woman not to overcook casseroles, especially rice or pasta, as they will continue cooking after being removed from the oven (or while waiting for a husband overdue from the field). She has also learned from experience that this is a good way to add valuable vitamins, minerals and protein into the diet of her family. Many of these bubbling casseroles use a wide variety of ingredients and help to achieve a balanced diet.

Casserole becoming too dry? Heat some water or bouillon and add to the dish. Never add a cold liquid as it throws off the total baking time. Casserole too liquid? Simply remove the cover and let the dish bake until some of the liquid is reduced, then pop on the cover and continue baking.

Good country cooks have one-dish dinners for every situation, because this type of cooking fits their busy days. We have their choicest recipes . . . the hearty casseroles that always bring requests for seconds from their men . . . casseroles that the youngsters beg Mother to "make again, please" and ask to have served at their birthday dinners . . . meals-in-a-dish that star at family reunions and carry well to church suppers.

As one farm homemaker says, "I love casseroles because when unexpected guests drop in, I can say 'Stay for supper' and all I have to do is take my specialty from the freezer, bake it, toss a salad, heat frozen rolls and dinner is ready."

COMPANY COMING?
CREATE A SPECIAL CASSEROLE

A good casserole can make a party dinner a spectacular success. We have several such splendid selections that farm women have been serving to appreciative guests for years. And, as they tell us, they welcome these versatile one-step main dishes that can be readied ahead of time—gives them more opportunity to visit with their guests.

TAMALE CASSEROLE

"I make one for the church supper and a second for the family"

1 lb. ground beef	1 (1 lb.) can cream-style corn
½ c. chopped onion	2 (8 oz.) cans tomato sauce
½ c. chopped green pepper	4 oz. wide noodles, cooked and
1 (15 oz.) can tamales, cut in	drained
1″ chunks	2 tblsp. Worcestershire sauce
1 (1 lb.) can red kidney beans,	1 tblsp. chili powder
drained	½ c. shredded Cheddar cheese

Brown ground beef in large skillet. When meat begins to turn color, add onion and green pepper. Sauté until meat is well browned. Combine tamales, kidney beans, corn, tomato sauce, noodles,

Worcestershire sauce, chili powder and meat mixture in a large bowl. Mix well. Turn into 3-qt. casserole. Top with cheese.

Bake in moderate oven (375°) 35 minutes or until hot and bubbly. Makes 6 to 8 servings.

HAM AND BROCCOLI ROYALE

Use leftover holiday ham for this creamy, nutritious casserole

3 c. cooked rice	½ tsp. salt
2 (10 oz.) pkgs. frozen broccoli spears, cooked and drained	¼ tsp. pepper
	3 c. milk
6 tblsp. butter or regular margarine	4 c. cubed, cooked ham (about 1½ lb.)
2 c. soft bread crumbs	1 (8 oz.) pkg. sliced process American cheese
2 c. chopped onion	
3 tblsp. flour	

Spoon cooked rice into greased 3-qt. casserole. Layer broccoli over rice.

Melt butter in saucepan; remove 2 tblsp. and sprinkle over bread crumbs in a bowl; set aside.

Sauté onion in remaining butter. Blend in flour, salt and pepper. Slowly stir in milk. Cook over medium heat, stirring constantly, until thickened. Add ham; heat until bubbly. Pour into casserole. Layer cheese over ham mixture.

Sprinkle on buttered crumbs. Bake in moderate oven (350°) 45 minutes or until top is golden brown. Makes 8 to 10 servings.

HAM AND SWEET POTATO CASSEROLE

A marvelous way to use leftover ham . . . apple juice adds tang

1½ tblsp. cornstarch	2 lbs. cooked ham, cut in slices
1½ c. apple juice	2 (1 lb. 7 oz.) cans sweet potatoes or yams, drained
¼ c. golden raisins	
2 tblsp. brown sugar	3 tblsp. melted butter or regular margarine
1 tblsp. lemon juice	
1 tsp. prepared mustard	1 c. crushed corn flakes
⅛ tsp. pepper	Butter or regular margarine

Combine cornstarch and apple juice in small saucepan; mix well. Add raisins. Cook over medium heat, stirring constantly, until thickened. Add brown sugar, lemon juice, mustard and pepper; stir until smooth.

Arrange ham slices in 13 × 9 × 2″ baking dish. Pour sauce over ham slices.

Mash sweet potatoes. Add 3 tblsp. melted butter; mix until smooth. Spread half of potato mixture over ham. Top with corn flakes. Spread remaining potato mixture on top. Dot with butter.

Bake in moderate oven (350°) 30 minutes or until hot. Makes 6 to 8 servings.

MEATBALL AND CHEESE BAKE

For children's parties, substitute cut-up hot dogs for the meatballs

1 lb. ground beef	1 clove garlic, minced
½ c. dry bread crumbs	3 (8 oz.) cans tomato sauce
2 tblsp. chopped fresh parsley	1 tsp. sugar
1 tblsp. grated Parmesan cheese	1 c. water
1 clove garlic, minced	1 (8 oz.) pkg. cream cheese
1 tsp. salt	¾ c. dairy sour cream
½ tsp. orégano leaves	1 tblsp. chopped fresh parsley
⅛ tsp. pepper	⅛ tsp. salt
2 eggs, beaten	8 oz. wide noodles, cooked and
⅓ c. milk	drained
3 tblsp. cooking oil	1 c. shredded Cheddar cheese
3 tblsp. chopped onion	

Combine ground beef, bread crumbs, 2 tblsp. parsley, Parmesan cheese, 1 clove garlic, 1 tsp. salt, orégano, pepper, eggs and milk. Mix lightly; but well. Shape into 20 meatballs. Brown, a few at a time, in hot oil in medium skillet. Remove meatballs as they brown.

Remove all but 3 tblsp. oil. Add onion and 1 clove garlic; sauté until tender (do not brown). Stir in tomato sauce, sugar and water. Add meatballs; simmer, uncovered, for 20 minutes.

Combine softened cream cheese, sour cream, 1 tblsp. parsley and ⅛ tsp. salt; blend well.

Spoon some sauce into bottom of 13 × 9 × 2″ baking dish. Top with noodles. Spread cream cheese mixture over noodles. Top with sauce, placing meatballs in rows. Sprinkle with cheese. Cover loosely with aluminum foil.

Bake in moderate oven (350°) 30 minutes or until hot and bubbly. Makes 8 to 10 servings.

NEAPOLITAN LASAGNA

So easy on the budget . . . yet attractive and flavorful buffet choice

2 tblsp. finely chopped onion
½ tsp. minced garlic
⅓ c. cooking oil
1 (2 lb. 3 oz.) can plum tomatoes, sieved
2 beef bouillon cubes
1 c. water
1 (6 oz.) can tomato paste
½ bay leaf
2 whole cloves
½ tsp. basil leaves
½ tsp. orégano leaves
½ tsp. salt
¼ tsp. pepper

¼ tsp. sugar
1 lb. cream-style cottage cheese
1 (10 oz.) pkg. frozen spinach, cooked, drained and chopped
2 eggs, slightly beaten
½ c. grated Parmesan cheese
¼ tsp. salt
¼ tsp. ground nutmeg
⅛ tsp. pepper
1 (1 lb.) pkg. lasagna noodles, cooked and drained
¼ lb. mozzarella cheese, shredded
Grated Parmesan cheese

Sauté onion and garlic in hot oil in large saucepan until tender (do not brown). Stir in tomatoes, bouillon cubes, water, tomato paste, bay leaf, cloves, basil, orégano, ½ tsp. salt, pepper and sugar. Bring to boil; reduce heat. Simmer for 1 hour. Stir occasionally. Remove bay leaf and cloves.

Blend together cottage cheese, spinach, eggs, Parmesan cheese, ¼ tsp. salt, nutmeg and pepper. Set aside.

Spread 1 c. sauce in 13 × 9 × 2″ baking dish. Lay ⅓ of noodles in single layer on top. Spread with sauce; spoon on ½ spinach mixture; sprinkle with ⅓ of mozzarella cheese. Repeat layers, topping with sauce. Add remaining noodles; cover with remaining sauce. Sprinkle with mozzarella and Parmesan cheeses. Cover loosely with aluminum foil. Bake in moderate oven (350°) 40 minutes. Makes 12 servings.

AMERICAN-STYLE ENCHILADAS

Makes two large dishes—one to serve and one to store in freezer

6 eggs, well beaten
3 c. milk
2 c. sifted flour
¾ tsp. salt
1 lb. ground beef
1 lb. bulk pork sausage
1 c. chopped onion
½ c. chopped green pepper
2 cloves garlic, minced
1⅔ tblsp. chili powder

1 tsp. salt
1 (10 oz.) pkg. frozen spinach, cooked, drained and chopped
1 (29 oz.) jar or 2 (15 oz.) cans meatless spaghetti sauce
1 (8 oz.) can tomato sauce
1 c. water
1 tblsp. chili powder
2 c. shredded Cheddar cheese

Combine eggs and milk. Add flour and ¾ tsp. salt; beat until smooth. Pour about ¼ c. batter into hot greased 6 to 7″ skillet, tilting skillet so batter covers surface. Batter can also be spread into 6″ rounds on greased griddle. Turn pancakes when the surface looks dry. Pancakes can be stacked while remaining pancakes are baked. Makes 30.

Brown ground beef and pork sausage in large skillet. Pour off all but 1 tblsp. fat. Add onion, green pepper, garlic, 1⅔ tblsp. chili powder and 1 tsp. salt. Simmer for 10 minutes. Add spinach; mix well. Let cool.

Combine spaghetti sauce, tomato sauce, water and 1 tblsp. chili powder; set aside.

Spoon scant ¼ c. meat mixture across center of each pancake. Fold sides over about ½″. Starting at end closest to you, roll up each pancake. Place in two 13 × 9 × 2″ baking dishes. Pour half of the sauce over the rolled pancakes in each baking dish. Top each with half of shredded cheese.

Bake in slow oven (325°) 30 minutes or until hot and bubbly. Makes 15 servings.

Note: Prepared Enchiladas can be frozen. To reheat: Bake in moderate oven (375°) 45 minutes or until hot and bubbly.

TIMBALLO WITH CHEESE SAUCE

Refrigerate timballo . . . pop into the oven when guests arrive

1 lb. spaghetti (break strands in half)

⅓ c. butter or regular margarine

1 lb. pork sausage

1 (4 oz.) can sliced mushrooms, drained

3 tblsp. finely chopped onion

⅓ c. sliced stuffed olives

½ c. grated Parmesan cheese

2 tblsp. chopped fresh parsley

½ tsp. salt

¼ tsp. pepper

¼ c. dry bread crumbs

2 eggs, well beaten

¼ lb. mozzarella cheese, shredded

Cheese Sauce (recipe follows)

Cook spaghetti for 10 minutes in boiling salted water. Drain; toss with butter; coat well.

Sauté sausage in skillet until almost done. Pour off all fat except 2 tblsp. Add mushrooms and onion. Sauté in fat until tender (do not brown).

Toss together spaghetti, sausage mixture, olives, Parmesan cheese, parsley, salt and pepper.

Coat a buttered 9″ spring-form pan with bread crumbs; reserve some for top. Place half the spaghetti mixture in pan; pour eggs evenly over all. Sprinkle with mozzarella cheese; put remaining mixture on top. Sprinkle with remaining crumbs. Cover with aluminum foil; bake in moderate oven (375°) 40 minutes. Let stand for 5 minutes. Serve with Cheese Sauce. Makes 6 to 8 servings.

Cheese Sauce: Stir ¼ c. Parmesan cheese and 1 tblsp. chopped fresh parsley into 2 c. of medium white sauce.

BRING A BUBBLING CASSEROLE

Even though farm women have jam-packed days, they like to get together with friends for an evening of good food and lively conversation. It's then that they turn to the "everyone bring a dish." That means twice as much fun sampling everyone's good cooking . . . and half the work when everyone pitches in and contributes.

Take your pick of any one of these dishes for your next neighborhood get-together.

COMPANY BEAN POT

A Colorado cook often substitutes ground elk or venison for beef

1 lb. ground beef	½ tsp. garlic salt
1 c. chopped onion	3 (1 lb.) cans red kidney beans
2 (8 oz.) cans tomato sauce	1 (15½ oz.) can chick peas
2 tblsp. Worcestershire sauce	1 (12 oz.) can mexicorn
1 tsp. Tabasco sauce	2 (15 oz.) cans tamales, cut in
1½ tsp. chili powder	1″ chunks

Brown ground beef in skillet. When meat begins to change color, add onion. Sauté until meat is well browned.

Add tomato sauce, Worcestershire sauce, Tabasco sauce, chili powder and garlic salt. Simmer, uncovered, for 5 minutes.

Drain kidney beans, chick peas and mexicorn; reserve liquid. Add enough water to liquid to make 1 c.

Combine meat mixture, kidney beans, chick peas, mexicorn, tamales and 1 c. reserved liquid in a large bowl; mix well. Turn into greased 15 × 10½ × 2″ roasting pan. Cover with aluminum foil.

Bake in moderate oven (350°) 1 hour or until hot and bubbly. Makes 15 to 20 servings.

TRI-BEAN BAKE

Double tomato flavor bubbles through this bake . . . easy to fix

4 strips bacon	1 c. cubed, cooked ham
1 c. chopped onion	½ c. ketchup
1 (1 lb.) can lima beans, drained	⅓ c. brown sugar, firmly packed
	2 tblsp. vinegar
1 (1 lb.) can red kidney beans	1 tsp. dry mustard
1 (1 lb.) can pork and beans in tomato sauce	1 clove garlic, minced

Fry bacon until crisp in small skillet. Remove and drain on paper towels. Crumble.

Sauté onion in bacon fat until tender (do not brown).

Combine lima beans, undrained kidney beans and pork and beans in a large bowl. Add ham, ketchup, brown sugar, vinegar, dry mustard, garlic, bacon and sautéed onion; mix well. Turn into greased 3-qt. casserole.

Bake in moderate oven (350°) 1 hour or until hot and bubbly. Makes 6 to 8 servings.

GOLDEN NOODLE BAKE

Tasty accompaniment for ham, roast beef or barbecued chicken

¼ c. finely chopped onion

3 tblsp. melted butter or regular margarine

1 c. dairy sour cream

1 lb. cream-style cottage cheese

½ c. milk

2 tblsp. sugar

1 tsp. salt

8 oz. wide noodles, cooked and drained

1 c. crushed corn flakes

3 tblsp. melted butter or regular margarine

Chopped fresh parsley

Sauté onion in 3 tblsp. melted butter in small skillet until tender (do not brown).

Combine sour cream, cottage cheese, milk, sugar, salt and sautéed onion; mix well. Toss with noodles. Turn into greased 11 × 7 × 1½″ baking dish.

Combine corn flakes and 3 tblsp. melted butter. Sprinkle over noodle mixture.

Bake in moderate oven (350°) 50 minutes or until hot and bubbly. Cut into squares. Serve sprinkled with parsley. Makes 12 servings.

BEEF AND CABBAGE SCALLOP

This hot, bubbling casserole is good during the cold winter months

1 lb. ground beef

1 c. chopped celery

½ c. chopped onion

2 tblsp. flour

1 (1 lb. 12 oz.) can tomatoes

1 (8 oz.) can tomato sauce

1½ tsp. salt

1 tsp. orégano leaves

¼ tsp. pepper

4 c. coarsely chopped cabbage

2 c. thinly sliced pared potatoes

2 c. bread cubes (½″)

2 tblsp. melted butter or regular margarine

Brown ground beef in large skillet. When meat begins to turn color, add celery and onion. Cook for 5 minutes. Stir in flour, tomatoes, tomato sauce, salt, orégano and pepper. Bring mixture to a boil; remove from heat.

Place alternate layers of meat mixture, cabbage and potatoes in 3-qt. casserole. Combine bread and butter; sprinkle on top. Cover.

Bake in moderate oven (375°) 1 hour or until vegetables are tender. Makes 6 to 8 servings.

ALPINE BEEF CASSEROLE

Busy-day helper to assemble ahead and refrigerate

1 lb. round steak, about ½" thick
½ tsp. salt
¼ tsp. pepper
3 tblsp. cooking oil
1 c. green pepper strips
½ c. sliced onion
½ tsp. basil leaves

2 tblsp. diced pimientos
3½ c. bread cubes (½")
1½ c. shredded Swiss cheese
1 (10½ oz.) can condensed cream of celery soup
½ c. water
Paprika

Pound meat with meat mallet or edge of heavy plate. Cut into 2 × ¼" strips. Season meat with salt and pepper. Brown meat in hot oil in skillet. Add green pepper and onion; sauté until tender (do not brown). Stir in basil and pimientos.

Place 1 c. bread cubes in bottom of greased 2-qt. casserole. Top with ½ of meat mixture. Repeat layers. Place layer of cheese over meat mixture.

Combine soup and water in skillet. Heat well, scraping up browned particles in skillet. Pour soup over all. Top with remaining 1½ c. bread cubes. Sprinkle with paprika.

Bake in moderate oven (350°) 25 minutes or until top is golden. Makes 6 servings.

CARRY-ALONG CASSEROLE

Nutritious with dairy products, this is a big favorite with children

2 lbs. ground beef
2 tblsp. butter or regular margarine
1 c. chopped onion
¼ c. chopped green pepper
2 tblsp. flour
2 (8 oz.) cans tomato sauce
1 tsp. marjoram leaves
¾ tsp. salt

¼ tsp. pepper
½ c. water
2 c. cream-style cottage cheese
1 c. dairy sour cream
1 tblsp. chopped fresh parsley
1 egg, slightly beaten
½ tsp. onion salt
8 oz. large elbow macaroni, cooked and drained

Brown ground beef in melted butter in 10″ skillet. When meat begins to turn color, add onion and green pepper. Sauté until meat is well browned.

Stir in flour. Add tomato sauce, marjoram, salt, pepper and water. Simmer, uncovered, for 5 minutes.

Combine cottage cheese, sour cream, parsley, egg and onion salt; mix well. Toss with cooked noodles.

Alternate layers of meat mixture and noodle mixture in 3-qt. casserole, ending with meat mixture.

Bake in moderate oven (375°) 30 minutes or until hot and bubbly. Makes 6 to 8 servings.

DO STAY FOR SUPPER

Farm women are known for their instant hospitality. They urge drop-in guests to stay for a quick supper: "No trouble at all—we'll have a hot dish and a salad."

For just these last-minute situations they have a repertoire of hot and hearty one-dish dinners. We've tested them all in our FARM JOURNAL Countryside Test Kitchens and pronounced each one—delicious!

SWEET AND SOUR BAKED BEANS

Stars at church suppers and is a favorite dish at family reunions

1 c. chopped onion
1 clove garlic, minced
½ c. bacon drippings
1 c. chopped celery
¼ c. dark brown sugar, firmly packed
¼ c. dark molasses
1 (15 oz.) can tomato sauce
½ c. chili sauce
1 tsp. salt

¼ tsp. pepper
2 dashes Tabasco sauce
1 lb. navy beans, cooked and drained
1 (13½ oz.) can pineapple chunks, drained and cut in half
½ c. chopped sweet pickles
¼ c. sliced stuffed olives

Sauté onion and garlic in bacon drippings in skillet until tender (do not brown). Stir in celery, brown sugar, molasses, tomato sauce, chili sauce, salt, pepper and Tabasco sauce. Simmer, uncovered, for 20 minutes.

Combine with cooked navy beans, pineapple, pickles and olives. Turn into 3-qt. casserole; cover. Bake in moderate oven (350°) 1 hour. Uncover; bake 15 more minutes. Makes 8 to 10 servings.

BARLEY HOT DISH

A rib-sticking hot dish that's popular with the field crew

1½ lbs. ground beef	2 (1 lb.) cans tomatoes
1 c. chopped onion	1 (10½ oz.) can condensed
½ c. chopped celery	cream of mushroom soup
3 tblsp. cooking oil	2½ c. water
2½ tsp. salt	¾ c. barley
¼ tsp. pepper	½ c. chopped green pepper
1 tsp. dried marjoram leaves	1 (1 lb.) can peas
½ bay leaf	

Sauté ground beef, onion and celery in hot oil in Dutch oven until well browned. Stir in salt, pepper, marjoram, bay leaf, tomatoes, soup, water, barley, green pepper and undrained peas; mix well. Bring to a boil.

Turn into 15 × 10⅝ × 2″ shallow roasting pan (4-qt.). Cover with lid or aluminum foil. Bake in moderate oven (375°) 1 hour 15 minutes or until barley is tender. Makes 10 to 12 servings.

MEAT AND SPAGHETTI MEAL

Can be prepared early in the day . . . great to fix for a family reunion

1½ lbs. ground beef	1 (1 lb.) jar meatless spaghetti
⅓ c. chopped onion	sauce
1 clove garlic, minced	8 oz. spaghetti, cooked and
½ tsp. orégano leaves	drained
½ tsp. salt	½ c. dairy sour cream
¼ tsp. pepper	1 c. cream-style cottage cheese
1 (4 oz.) can sliced mushrooms	½ c. grated Parmesan cheese

Sauté ground beef, onion, garlic, orégano, salt and pepper in skillet until meat is well browned.

Brew a big pot of coffee and pass these extra special yeast breads, *Triple Fruit Kuchen* (page 119) and *Pineapple Cinnamon Buns* (page 120). Both these sweet dough breads are scrumptious to look at and to eat—good for brunch.

Light and tangy *Lemon Pudding Cake* (page 228) is a great dessert any time of the year. Just spoon it warm-from-the-oven into individual serving dishes. For a special treat, top each with a puff of country-fresh whipped cream.

Subtly spiced *American-Style Enchiladas* (page 50) can be made ahead and frozen for unexpected company. A perfect main dish for buffet suppers. Complete the menu with tossed green salad and scoops of ice cream topped with fresh fruit.

Serve *Spicy Sugar Loaf* (page 133) with mugs of frothy hot chocolate for a great evening snack or yummy breakfast treat. In minutes you can transform an ordinary loaf of white bread into a piping hot, attractive cinnamon bread.

Stir in undrained mushrooms and spaghetti sauce. Simmer, uncovered, for 10 minutes.

Place half of spaghetti in bottom of greased 9″ square baking dish. Spoon on half of meat mixture.

Combine sour cream and cottage cheese. Spread over meat mixture. Add remaining spaghetti and top with remaining meat mixture. Sprinkle with Parmesan cheese.

Bake in moderate oven (375°) 35 minutes or until hot and bubbling. Let stand for 5 minutes. Cut in squares. Makes 6 servings.

MACARONI-SAUSAGE CASSEROLE

Nourishing combination . . . a favorite with children for supper

1 (8 oz.) pkg. elbow macaroni	3 tblsp. flour
1 lb. bulk pork sausage	½ tsp. salt
½ c. chopped onion	2 c. milk
½ c. green pepper strips	2 c. shredded Cheddar cheese

Cook macaroni in 3 qts. boiling salted water for 7 to 8 minutes; drain well.

Brown sausage in saucepan; remove and reserve ½ of sausage. Sauté onion and green pepper with remaining sausage in 2 tblsp. of fat. Stir in flour and salt. Slowly add milk. Cook over medium heat, stirring, until thick. Stir in 1½ c. cheese.

Combine macaroni and sauce; turn into greased 2-qt. casserole. Top with ½ c. cheese and reserved sausage. Bake in hot oven (400°) 25 minutes or until golden. Makes 6 servings.

JUST FOR THE FAMILY

"My husband always takes seconds when I make my Ground Beef Casserole—it tastes like a stew, he tells me." "My children always clean their plates whenever I fix Cheese/Beef Casserole." "The first time I prepared Hamburger/Lima Bean Casserole, the whole family said: 'Make this again, Mom!'"

These are a few of the comments about these sizzling casseroles that families like. Their dinners-in-a-dish have been winning top praise and satisfying appetites for many a meal. Try one on your family.

CHEESE / BEEF CASSEROLE

Cream cheese swirled into the sauce makes this especially smooth

1 lb. ground beef
½ c. chopped onion
1 (3 oz.) pkg. cream cheese, cubed
1 (10½ oz.) can condensed cream of mushroom soup
1 (12 oz.) can mexicorn
¼ c. milk

1 c. cooked peas, canned or frozen
½ tsp. thyme leaves
¼ tsp. salt
¼ tsp. pepper
1 tblsp. diced pimientos
Pastry for 1-crust pie
Milk

Sauté ground beef and onion in skillet until meat is well browned.

Add cream cheese, mushroom soup, mexicorn and ¼ c. milk; stir well. Cook over low heat, stirring constantly, until cream cheese melts.

Stir in peas, thyme, salt, pepper and pimientos. Turn into 2-qt. casserole.

Roll out pastry to fit top of casserole. Make slits in top. Brush with milk.

Bake in hot oven (425°) 25 minutes or until golden brown. Makes 6 servings.

HAMBURGER / LIMA BEAN CASSEROLE

With a base of hamburger and beans, this is double rich in protein

1 lb. ground beef
1 tsp. salt
1 tblsp. cooking oil
½ c. chopped onion
¼ c. chopped celery
¾ c. ketchup

2 tblsp. sugar
2 tblsp. Worcestershire sauce
½ tsp. chili powder
1 (1 lb.) can lima beans, drained
¾ c. water

Combine ground beef and salt. Form into small meatballs. Brown a few at a time in hot oil in skillet. Remove from skillet.

Add onion and celery; sauté until tender (do not brown). Stir in ketchup, sugar, Worcestershire sauce, chili powder, lima beans and water. Bring to a boil.

Combine lima bean mixture and meatballs. Turn into greased 2-qt. casserole.

Bake in moderate oven (350°) 45 minutes or until hot and bubbly. Makes 6 servings.

GROUND BEEF AND STUFFING CASSEROLE

Savory main dish with its own baked-on mushroom gravy topping

1 c. chopped celery
½ c. chopped onion
2 tblsp. butter or regular
   margarine
5 c. bread cubes (1")
1 tsp. salt
1 tsp. rubbed sage
¼ tsp. pepper
¼ tsp. ground nutmeg

1 (10½ oz.) can condensed
   cream of mushroom soup
1 c. milk
2 lbs. lean ground beef
1 tblsp. prepared mustard
2 tsp. Worcestershire sauce
1 (10½ oz.) can condensed
   cream of mushroom soup

Sauté celery and onion in melted butter in skillet until tender (do not brown).

Combine bread cubes, salt, sage, pepper, nutmeg, mushroom soup, milk and sautéed vegetables; mix well. Combine bread mixture with ground beef, mustard and Worcestershire sauce; mix lightly, but well. Press mixture in greased 13 × 9 × 2" baking dish.

Stir remaining mushroom soup until smooth. Spoon over meat mixture.

Bake in moderate oven (375°) 1 hour or until done. Cool for 10 minutes. Cut in squares. Makes 8 servings.

HEARTY BEEF AND POTATO CASSEROLE

Serve crisp cole slaw and a batch of hot popovers with this

1½ lbs. ground beef
1 c. chopped onion
½ c. chopped celery
1½ tsp. salt
1 tsp. marjoram leaves
¼ tsp. ground nutmeg

⅛ tsp. pepper
1 tblsp. flour
1 (1 lb.) can stewed tomatoes
6 medium potatoes, pared and
   sliced
1 c. sliced, pared carrots

Sauté ground beef, onion, celery, salt, marjoram, nutmeg and pepper in skillet until meat is well browned.

Stir in flour. Add tomatoes; mix well. Bring to a boil.

Place half of potatoes in greased 2-qt. casserole. Add half of carrots, then a layer of meat mixture. Repeat layers. Cover.

Bake in moderate oven (350°) 50 minutes. Uncover. Bake 10 more minutes. Makes 6 to 8 servings.

MACARONI AND CHEESE

An old-time favorite . . . the tomatoes add an imaginative note

2 c. sliced onion	¼ tsp. pepper
¼ c. butter or regular margarine	12 oz. elbow macaroni, cooked
3 (1 lb.) cans stewed tomatoes	and drained
1½ tsp. Worcestershire sauce	2 c. shredded Cheddar cheese
1 tsp. salt	

Sauté onion in melted butter in large skillet until tender (do not brown).

Add tomatoes, Worcestershire sauce, salt and pepper. Simmer, uncovered, for 5 minutes. Combine with macaroni; mix well.

Turn mixture into greased 3-qt. casserole, alternating layers of macaroni mixture and cheese. End with cheese layer.

Bake in moderate oven (375°) 30 minutes or until hot and bubbly. Makes 6 to 8 servings.

GROUND BEEF CASSEROLE

Even the smallest grandchildren like this—takes everyday ingredients

1 lb. lean ground beef	2 (8 oz.) cans tomato sauce
¾ c. parboiled rice	1 (1 lb.) can tomatoes
½ c. chopped onion	1 (4 oz.) can sliced mushrooms
1½ tsp. salt	1 (10½ oz.) can condensed
½ tsp. ground coriander	beef broth
¼ tsp. pepper	1 c. shredded Swiss cheese

Sauté ground beef, rice and onion in large skillet until meat is well browned.

Add salt, coriander, pepper, tomato sauce, tomatoes and undrained mushrooms; mix well. Add enough water to beef broth to make 1½ c. Stir into meat mixture. Bring to a boil. Turn into greased 3-qt. casserole. Cover.

Bake in moderate oven (350°) 55 minutes. Uncover. Top with cheese. Bake for 5 more minutes or until cheese melts. Makes 8 to 10 servings.

BEEF / CARROT CASSEROLE

Serve with marinated tomato wedges and baked apples for dessert

1 lb. ground beef
1 tblsp. butter or regular
  margarine
¼ c. minced onion
1 clove garlic, minced
2 (8 oz.) cans tomato sauce
1 tsp. salt
¼ tsp. pepper

1 c. dairy sour cream
1 c. cream-style cottage cheese
¼ c. chopped fresh parsley
1 c. sliced, cooked carrots
8 oz. medium noodles, cooked
  and drained
1 c. shredded Cheddar cheese

Brown beef in melted butter in skillet. When meat begins to turn color, add onion and garlic. Sauté until meat is well browned. Stir in tomato sauce, salt and pepper. Simmer, uncovered, for 5 minutes.

Combine sour cream, cottage cheese, parsley and carrots. Add to cooked noodles; mix well.

Alternate layers of the meat mixture and cottage cheese mixture in greased 3-qt. casserole, beginning and ending with noodles. Top with cheese.

Bake in moderate oven (350°) 30 minutes or until hot and bubbly. Makes 6 to 8 servings.

Chapter 4

VEGETABLES YOUR FAMILY WILL LIKE

Country cooks have a flair with vegetables. Their families are accustomed to red-ripe juicy tomatoes plucked right from the vine, fresh corn, tender green beans or young peas from the garden. And in the wintertime they continue to enjoy summer's bounty via home canned or frozen vegetables.

The first of the season's vegetables usually are served plain with a big pat of butter and a shake of salt and pepper. But farm women are famous for "dressing up" their vegetables, combining them with a sauce or featuring a trio of vegetables for attractive appearance and out-of-the-ordinary flavor.

They know the secrets of proper cooking to retain bright color and optimum flavor and texture of vegetables. They plunge fresh vegetables into boiling salted water—just enough to keep them from sticking—and then cook only until crisp-tender. At this stage, the flavor and the vitamin and mineral value are at their peak. Green vegetables are the most easily discolored by incorrect cooking. During the first few minutes, green vegetables release a gas which is harmless but does fade the color. To prevent this, cover the boiling vegetables for about a minute and then remove cover for a minute to allow the cooking vapor to escape. Repeat this process several times during the cooking period.

American diets are often low in vitamin A and vitamin C. A great many vegetables are rich in both vitamins. A wise homemaker will try to see that her family eats a good variety of green and yellow vegetables daily.

We have a tempting selection of vegetable recipes that we have collected and tested in our Countryside Test Kitchens—from excellent farm cooks who know how to present vegetables with flair and imagination so that their families pass their plates for seconds. Try the Skillet Cabbage, a pleasing medley of cabbage, onions, green pepper, celery and tomatoes all cooked together with a touch of bacon fat for added flavor. Serve Baked Carrot Loaf, a tasty concoction of mashed carrots, eggs, onions and cracker crumbs—a hearty favorite with farm husbands. A spinach dish so delicious that even those who are lukewarm toward spinach ask for more. To accompany a baked ham, serve our Asparagus Cheese Bake which has an egg-rich custard base.

Children will especially like the Vegetable Egg Combo—onions, tomatoes, green pepper, cheese, chives, and parsley all cooked together with six eggs for extra nourishment. They will also "lick their plates clean," as one farm woman testified, when you serve them Corn Scramble on Toast.

Then we have a fine crop of potato recipes that are big favorites with the men. Some plain, some fancy, but all delicious!

READY TO SERVE IN 15 MINUTES

A medley of vegetable dishes that can be fixed, cooked and on the table in minutes. Cucumbers with Celery cooks in chicken broth with a touch of basil—delightfully different way of serving the popular cucumber. For a colorful collection of everyday vegetables you'll want to make the Skillet Cabbage . . . it bubbles to tender-crisp perfection in 10 minutes.

CUCUMBERS WITH CELERY

Complete the menu with pork chops, potatoes and tomato slices

4 large cucumbers, peeled (about 2½ lbs.)	1 tblsp. cornstarch
1 c. diagonally sliced celery	2 tblsp. water
1 (10½ oz.) can condensed chicken broth	2 tblsp. butter or regular margarine
1 tsp. lemon juice	¼ tsp. basil leaves
	2 tblsp. diced pimientos

Slice cucumbers in half lengthwise; remove seeds. Cut into 1" pieces. Combine cucumbers, celery, chicken broth and lemon juice in saucepan. Cover and bring to a boil. Cook over low heat for 10 minutes or until vegetables are tender.

Combine cornstarch and water. Slowly stir into vegetable mixture. Add butter, basil and pimientos. Heat well. Makes 6 to 8 servings.

SKILLET CABBAGE

The short-cooking method assures the fresh-from-the-garden flavor

2 tblsp. cooking oil	2 c. chopped seeded tomatoes
3 c. chopped cabbage	1 tsp. sugar
1 c. chopped celery	¾ tsp. salt
¾ c. chopped green pepper	¼ tsp. pepper
½ c. chopped onion	

Heat oil in 10" skillet. Add cabbage, celery, green pepper, onion, tomatoes, sugar, salt and pepper; mix well. Cover and cook over medium heat for 10 minutes or until cabbage is tender but still crisp. Makes 6 servings.

SWEET AND SOUR BEANS

This recipe can easily be doubled or tripled for a large crowd

1 (9 oz.) pkg. frozen cut green beans	¼ c. water
	¼ c. vinegar
2 strips bacon	2 tblsp. sugar
¼ c. minced onion	½ tsp. salt
1 tblsp. flour	⅛ tsp. pepper

Cook beans in slightly salted water until tender. Drain and reserve ½ c. cooking liquid.

Fry bacon until crisp in medium saucepan. Remove from saucepan and drain on paper towels. Crumble.

Sauté onion in bacon fat until tender (do not brown). Stir in flour. Add reserved cooking liquid, water, vinegar, sugar, salt and pepper. Stirring constantly, bring mixture to a boil. Stir in beans; heat well. Serve topped with bacon bits. Makes 3 to 4 servings.

SAVORY GREEN BEANS AND RICE

Substitute 1½ cups of your own home canned or frozen green beans

1 (9 oz.) pkg. frozen cut green
   beans
1 (1 lb.) can stewed tomatoes
¼ c. butter or regular margarine

1 tsp. cornstarch
½ tsp. seasoned salt
⅛ tsp. pepper
1 c. cooked rice

Cook beans in boiling salted water according to package directions. Drain.

Combine tomatoes, butter, cornstarch, salt and pepper in medium saucepan. Cook over medium heat, stirring constantly, until thickened. Add beans and rice; heat well. Makes 6 to 8 servings.

GREEN BEANS WITH GOLDEN MUSHROOM SAUCE

This unusual vegetable combination can be ready to serve in no time

¼ c. chopped onion
2 tblsp. butter or regular
   margarine
1 (10¾ oz.) can condensed
   golden mushroom soup

½ c. chopped canned tomatoes
1 tsp. Worcestershire sauce
2 (9 oz.) pkgs. frozen cut green
   beans, cooked and drained

Sauté onion in melted butter in 2-qt. saucepan until tender (do not brown). Stir in soup, tomatoes, Worcestershire sauce and beans. Heat well; stirring occasionally. Makes 4 to 6 servings.

CANTONESE-STYLE VEGETABLES

A small can of drained mushrooms can be substituted for fresh ones

1 (10 oz.) pkg. frozen French-
   cut green beans
1 (6 oz.) can water chestnuts,
   thinly sliced
½ lb. fresh mushrooms, sliced
1 medium green pepper, cut in
   strips
1 c. diagonally sliced celery
¾ tsp. salt

½ tsp. garlic salt
¼ tsp. pepper
¼ c. cooking oil
1 (10½ oz.) can condensed
   chicken broth
2 tblsp. cornstarch
1 (4 oz.) jar pimientos, drained
   and diced
⅓ c. toasted slivered almonds

Add beans, water chestnuts, mushrooms, green pepper, celery, salt, garlic salt and pepper to hot oil in large skillet. Cook, stirring frequently, for about 10 minutes or until vegetables are tender crisp.

Add enough water to broth to make 1½ c. Combine broth and cornstarch. Add to vegetables and cook until thickened. Add pimientos. Serve topped with almonds. Makes 6 servings.

GO-ALONGS WITH THE HOLIDAY TURKEY

If creamed onions are a must on your Christmas menu, you might want to try our duo of Creamy Carrots and Onions for a slight change of pace. And the Nutty Yam Bake that a farm cook describes as "southern and rich" but a bit different from the usual candied yams. You'll like the bright green Company Broccoli, too, with its bright flecks of pimiento that add just the right touch of Christmas color.

CREAMY CARROTS AND ONIONS

An easy-to-fix vegetable which is delicious with poultry or pork

1 lb. carrots, cut in strips	2 tblsp. butter or regular
2 c. sliced onion	margarine
1 (10½ oz.) can condensed	⅛ tsp. pepper
cream of chicken soup	Fresh chopped parsley

Cook carrots and onions in boiling salted water in saucepan for 10 minutes or until tender. Drain and reserve ⅓ c. cooking water. Combine soup, reserved cooking water, butter and pepper. Combine soup mixture with cooked vegetables. Heat well, stirring occasionally. Garnish with parsley. Makes 6 servings.

COMPANY BROCCOLI

A colorful holiday vegetable that complements roast turkey or ham

3 (10 oz.) pkgs. frozen broccoli	⅛ tsp. pepper
spears	1 (13¾ oz.) can chicken broth
⅓ c. butter or regular margarine	¾ c. heavy cream
⅓ c. flour	¼ c. chopped ripe olives
¼ tsp. salt	2 tblsp. diced pimientos

Cook broccoli in boiling salted water according to package directions. Drain.

Melt butter in large saucepan. Stir in flour, salt and pepper. Gradually stir in chicken broth. Cook, stirring constantly, until mixture thickens. Slowly stir in heavy cream, olives and pimientos. Add broccoli and heat well. Do not boil. Makes 10 to 12 servings.

NUTTY YAM BAKE

Your guests will like this new variation of a holiday vegetable

3 large sweet potatoes or yams	2 eggs
1 c. sugar	½ c. flour
¼ c. butter or regular margarine	½ c. sugar
1 tsp. ground cinnamon	¼ c. butter or regular margarine
½ tsp. ground allspice	½ c. chopped walnuts
¼ tsp. ground nutmeg	½ tsp. ground cinnamon
2 c. milk	Butter or regular margarine

Cook sweet potatoes in boiling water until tender.

Mash sweet potatoes while hot. Add 1 c. sugar, ¼ c. butter, 1 tsp. cinnamon, allspice and nutmeg; mix well. Beat in milk and eggs; whip well with electric mixer. Turn into greased 3-qt. casserole.

Combine flour, ½ c. sugar and ¼ c. butter until crumbly. Mix in walnuts and ½ tsp. cinnamon. Sprinkle over top of sweet potato mixture. Dot with butter.

Bake in moderate oven (375°) 35 to 40 minutes. Makes 6 servings.

PUFFY CARROT SOUFFLÉ

Makes any company meal elegant . . . serve with roast beef or ham

2 tblsp. minced onion	⅛ tsp. ground nutmeg
¼ c. butter or regular margarine	1 c. milk
¼ c. flour	3 eggs, separated
¼ tsp. salt	¼ tsp. cream of tartar
	1 c. sieved, cooked carrots

Sauté onion in melted butter in 1-qt. saucepan until tender (do not brown). Stir in flour, salt and nutmeg. Gradually stir in milk. Cook, stirring constantly, until mixture thickens. Add some of the hot mixture to the egg yolks. Mix well. Pour all of egg mixture back into hot mixture. Cook for 2 minutes, stirring constantly.

Beat egg whites with cream of tartar until stiff peaks form. Fold in carrots and cooked mixture. Pour into well-buttered 1½-qt. casserole. Place casserole in pan of hot water.

Bake in moderate oven (350°) 50 minutes or until puffed and golden. Makes 4 to 6 servings.

PEAS WITH MUSHROOMS

A colorful vegetable combination—perfect for holiday entertaining

1 (10 oz.) pkg. frozen peas	1 (10½ oz.) can condensed
2 (4 oz.) cans sliced mush-	cream of mushroom soup
rooms, drained	⅓ c. milk
¼ c. slivered almonds	2 tblsp. chopped pimientos
2 tblsp. butter	

Cook peas in boiling water until tender. (Do not add salt.) Drain. Sauté mushrooms and almonds in melted butter in 2-qt. saucepan until almonds are golden brown. Combine soup and milk and stir into sautéed mixture. Add peas and pimientos. Heat well; stirring occasionally. Makes 6 servings.

HOLIDAY CAULIFLOWER

Festive vegetable with a creamy cheese sauce . . . guests like it

1 large head cauliflower	⅓ c. flour
1 (4 oz.) can sliced mushrooms,	2 c. milk
drained	1 tsp. salt
¼ c. diced green pepper	1 c. shredded Swiss cheese
¼ c. butter or regular	2 tblsp. chopped pimientos
margarine	

Break cauliflower into medium-size flowerettes; cook in boiling water until crisp-tender, for about 10 minutes. Drain well; set aside.

In 2-qt. saucepan, sauté mushrooms and green pepper in melted butter until tender (do not brown). Blend in flour. Gradually stir in milk. Cook over medium heat, stirring constantly, until mixture is thick. Stir in salt, cheese and pimientos.

Place half of the cauliflower in buttered 2-qt. casserole. Cover with half of the sauce; add remaining cauliflower. Top with sauce.

Bake in slow oven (325°) 15 minutes. Makes 8 servings.

SWEET POTATO BONBONS

Prepare bonbons and refrigerate. Just bake and serve hot from oven

3 lbs. sweet potatoes, peeled and
    cooked
¼ c. butter or regular margarine
½ c. brown sugar, firmly packed
1 tsp. salt
½ tsp. grated orange rind

6 marshmallows, halved
⅓ c. melted butter or regular
    margarine
4 c. corn flakes, crushed
12 pecan halves

Mash sweet potatoes until light and fluffy. Beat in ¼ c. butter, brown sugar, salt and orange rind. Let cool. Divide into 12 portions. Press potatoes around each marshmallow half, being careful to keep marshmallow in center. Shape into ovals.

Coat with ⅓ c. melted butter. Roll in crushed corn flakes, top with pecan half and place on lightly greased baking sheet.

Bake in very hot oven (450°) 7 to 8 minutes. Makes 6 to 8 servings.

VEGETABLES MEN REQUEST

"My husband really likes this," we hear again and again when women send in their favorite vegetable dishes. All these recipes have been favorites with farm men . . . in fact they often pass their plates and say "seconds, please."

CABBAGE HOT DISH

Serve with thin slices of corned beef and parsley-buttered carrots

2 medium cabbages, quartered
    (about 4 lbs.)
1 c. chopped onion
1 c. chopped celery
½ c. chopped green pepper
¼ c. melted butter or regular
    margarine
3 slices white bread, cut in 1"
    cubes

½ tsp. salt
¼ tsp. pepper
¼ c. chopped parsley
1 pt. half and half
2 c. bread cubes (½")
¼ c. melted butter or regular
    margarine
1 c. shredded Cheddar cheese
Paprika

Cook cabbage in boiling salted water in large saucepan until almost tender. Drain well. Cut each quarter in thirds.

Sauté onion, celery and green pepper in ¼ c. melted butter in skillet until tender (do not brown).

Arrange cabbage, sautéed vegetables, 1″ bread cubes, salt, pepper and parsley in 13 × 9 × 2″ baking pan. Pour half and half over all.

Combine 2 c. bread cubes, ¼ c. melted butter and cheese. Arrange on top of vegetables. Sprinkle with paprika.

Bake in moderate oven (350°) 35 to 40 minutes or until top is golden and cabbage is tender. Makes 6 to 8 servings.

CORN CUSTARD PUDDING

An old-fashioned vegetable that goes well with roast pork or ham

1 (1 lb.) can cream-style corn	1 tblsp. chopped pimientos
2 tblsp. flour	2 tblsp. sugar
2 tblsp. melted butter or regular margarine	1 tsp. salt
	3 eggs, slightly beaten
1 tblsp. minced onion	2½ c. milk

Combine corn, flour, butter, onion, pimientos, sugar and salt. Beat together eggs and milk. Stir into corn mixture. Turn into greased 9″ square baking dish.

Bake in slow oven (300°) 1 hour or until knife comes out clean. Place under broiler a few minutes to brown top. Makes about 9 servings.

LIMA BEAN BAKE

This vegetable dish is certain to be popular at potluck suppers

5 slices bacon	1 (1 lb.) can tomatoes
⅓ c. chopped onion	2 (1 lb.) cans cooked lima beans, drained
¼ c. chopped celery	
¼ c. chopped green pepper	1 bay leaf
2 tblsp. flour	1 c. soft bread crumbs
½ tsp. salt	2 tblsp. melted butter or regular margarine
⅛ tsp. pepper	

Fry bacon in skillet until crisp. Remove and drain on paper towels. Crumble.

Sauté onion, celery and green pepper in bacon fat until tender (do not brown).

Add flour, salt and pepper; stir until smooth. Stir in tomatoes, lima beans, bacon and bay leaf. Bring mixture to a boil. Pour into 2-qt. casserole and top with combined bread crumbs and butter.

Bake in moderate oven (350°) 30 to 35 minutes or until bubbly and golden. Makes 6 to 8 servings.

BAKED CARROT LOAF

"A favorite with our men folk," a Pennsylvania homemaker wrote

2 c. mashed, cooked carrots
1 c. milk
3 eggs, beaten
¼ c. melted butter or regular margarine

⅓ c. chopped onion
1 c. dry bread crumbs
1 tsp. salt
¼ tsp. pepper

Combine all ingredients. Turn mixture into greased 2-qt. casserole. Bake in moderate oven (350°) about 1 hour or until golden. Makes 6 servings.

SWEET AND SOUR KRAUT

Its sweet and sour flavor enhances roast pork and whipped potatoes

1 (32 oz.) can sauerkraut
1 c. water
2 tblsp. minced onion
1 medium potato, pared and shredded

1 medium apple, pared and shredded
2 tblsp. sugar
½ tsp. caraway seeds

Combine all ingredients in 2-qt. saucepan. Bring to a boil; reduce heat and simmer for 30 minutes. Makes 4 servings.

BRAISED RED CABBAGE

This dish is traditionally served with duckling and potato dumplings

¼ c. chopped onion
3 tblsp. butter or regular
  margarine
1 medium red cabbage, shredded
  (about 2 lbs.)

¼ c. water
¼ c. vinegar
2 apples, pared and sliced
1 tsp. sugar
1 tsp. salt

Sauté onion in melted butter in 10″ skillet until tender (do not brown). Add cabbage, water, vinegar, apples, sugar and salt. Cover and simmer for 30 minutes or until cabbage is tender. Makes 4 servings.

BAKE ALONG WITH THE MEAT

When you are busy, it's best to plan to serve a vegetable that can be put in the oven and then forgotten until it's time to pull it out piping hot and serve with the main dish. All these recipes travel well to church suppers and potlucks too! They team beautifully with any kind of meat or poultry.

CELERY PARMESAN

Especially good with ham, baked potatoes and tart red apple rings

½ c. chopped onion
2 c. chopped celery leaves
4 slices bacon, cubed
1 bunch celery, cut in 1″
  diagonal slices (about 6 c.)
1 (10½ oz.) can condensed
  chicken broth
1 whole clove
1 (8 oz.) can tomato sauce

¼ tsp. basil leaves
¼ tsp. orégano leaves
⅛ tsp. garlic powder
½ c. grated Parmesan cheese
1 (10 oz.) pkg. frozen peas,
  thawed
½ c. crushed rice cereal
1 tblsp. melted butter or regular
  margarine

Sauté onion, celery leaves and bacon in large skillet until onion is tender (do not brown). Add celery, broth and clove; bring mixture to a boil. Reduce heat and simmer for 10 minutes or until celery is tender.

Combine tomato sauce, basil, orégano, garlic powder and cheese. Toss with celery mixture. Turn mixture into 2-qt. casserole.

Bake in moderate oven (350°) 25 minutes. Stir in peas. Top with combined rice cereal and butter. Bake an additional 20 minutes or until top is golden. Makes 6 to 8 servings.

TOMATO AND CORN SCALLOP

Complete the meal with broiled salmon steaks and tossed green salad

1 (1 lb.) can whole kernel corn
2 eggs
⅔ c. evaporated milk
¼ c. melted butter or regular margarine
¼ tsp. salt
⅛ tsp. pepper
⅛ tsp. ground nutmeg
1 (1 lb.) can cream-style corn
2 (1 lb.) cans stewed tomatoes
2 c. coarse saltine cracker crumbs

Drain whole kernel corn; reserve ¼ c. liquid.

Beat eggs slightly. Add reserved corn liquid, evaporated milk, butter, salt, pepper and nutmeg. Blend well. Stir in whole kernel corn, cream-style corn, tomatoes and cracker crumbs. Turn into greased 3-qt. casserole.

Bake in slow oven (325°) 1 hour 10 minutes or until golden brown and set around edges. Makes 8 to 10 servings.

VEGETABLE MELANGE

An ideal accompaniment to ham with mustard sauce, candied yams

1 (10 oz.) pkg. frozen Italian green beans
1 (10 oz.) pkg. frozen peas
1 (10½ oz.) can condensed cream of chicken soup
¼ lb. Cheddar cheese, shredded
1 (8 oz.) can small onions, drained
1 (4 oz.) jar pimientos, diced
1 (4 oz.) can sliced mushrooms
½ c. slivered almonds

Cook beans and peas in boiling water until almost tender. (Do not add salt.) Drain.

Heat together soup and cheese until cheese melts.

Combine beans, peas, onions, pimientos and undrained mushrooms with soup mixture. Turn into greased 2-qt. casserole. Top with almonds.

Bake in moderate oven (350°) 30 minutes or until golden. Makes 8 to 10 servings.

SAVORY VEGETABLE CASSEROLE

An applause-winning combination that's sure to please your family

1 c. diced, pared potatoes	2 tblsp. butter
1 c. coarsely chopped celery	1 tsp. salt
1 (10 oz.) pkg. frozen lima beans, cooked and drained	½ tsp. basil leaves
	⅛ tsp. pepper
¼ c. chopped onion	4 beef bouillon cubes, crumbled
¼ c. uncooked regular rice	1 c. boiling water
1 (1 lb.) can tomatoes	

Combine all ingredients. Turn into 2-qt. casserole and cover.

Bake in moderate oven (350°) 1 hour or until vegetables are tender. Makes 6 servings.

CRUNCHY VEGETABLE BAKE

A vegetable duo that is a hit served with barbecued chicken or ribs

1 (10 oz.) pkg. frozen French-cut green beans	½ c. toasted slivered almonds
1 c. chopped onion	1 (4 oz.) jar pimientos, drained and diced
½ c. butter or regular margarine	1 (10½ oz.) can condensed cream of mushroom soup
1 (10 oz.) pkg. frozen peas, thawed	1 c. dairy sour cream
	1 c. crushed potato chips

Cook green beans in boiling salted water until almost tender. Drain well.

Sauté onion in melted butter in large skillet until tender, but not brown. Add beans, peas, almonds and pimientos. Combine soup and sour cream. Add to vegetables; toss gently. Turn into greased 1½-qt. casserole. Top with potato chips.

Bake in slow oven (325°) 30 minutes. Makes 6 to 8 servings.

EASY SPINACH SOUFFLÉ

An Ohio homemaker says that this is a never-fail soufflé recipe

2 c. cream-style cottage cheese
½ c. shredded Cheddar cheese
3 eggs
⅓ c. flour
¼ c. melted butter or regular
   margarine

¾ tsp. salt
¼ tsp. ground nutmeg
⅛ tsp. pepper
2 (10 oz.) pkg. frozen chopped
   spinach, thawed and drained

Place cottage cheese, Cheddar cheese, eggs, flour, butter, salt, nutmeg and pepper in a blender. Blend at high speed for 1 minute. Mix with spinach. Turn into greased 2-qt. soufflé dish. Set dish in a pan of hot water.

Bake in moderate oven (350°) 1 hour or until mixture is set. Makes 6 to 8 servings.

MUSHROOM PILAF

Serve with roast Cornish hens or chicken, green beans, garden salad

1 (4 oz.) can mushrooms
1 c. chopped onion
¼ c. butter or regular
   margarine
¼ c. cooking oil
2 c. raw regular rice

3 (10½ oz.) cans condensed
   beef broth
½ tsp. salt
2 tsp. orégano leaves
Fresh chopped parsley

Drain mushrooms; reserve liquid. Add enough water to make 2 c.; set aside.

Sauté mushrooms and onion in melted butter and oil in large saucepan until tender, but not brown. Stir in rice and brown slightly, stirring occasionally. Stir in reserved liquid, beef broth, salt and orégano. Bring mixture to a boil. Pour into 3-qt. casserole; cover.

Bake in moderate oven (375°) 25 minutes or until rice is tender. Garnish with parsley. Makes 8 to 10 servings.

PRIZED POTATO RECIPES

Potatoes are a popular vegetable in most farm families and appear at least once a day on the menu. Farm women have shared a wonderful crop of potato recipes with us. Brown crusted Oven-Fried Potatoes that team well with most anything and are especially good with fried eggs and bacon for a hearty breakfast. The Golden Parmesan Potatoes bake in melted butter to a golden crisp. A spectacular for company dinners, Ham-Stuffed Potatoes, can be fixed ahead and refrigerated until ready to be baked.

OVEN-FRIED POTATOES

Serve with meat loaf, peas, salad and raisin-stuffed baked apples

2 eggs, beaten
¼ c. flour
½ tsp. baking powder
1 tsp. salt
¼ tsp. pepper
½ c. chopped onion

8 medium potatoes, pared and shredded
¼ c. melted butter or regular margarine
Paprika

Combine eggs, flour, baking powder, salt and pepper. Add onion, potatoes and butter; mix well. Turn mixture into greased 9″ square baking dish. Sprinkle with paprika.

Bake in moderate oven (350°) 1 hour or until potatoes are tender and top is brown and crisp. Makes 6 to 8 servings.

GOLDEN PARMESAN POTATOES

These crisp potatoes are delicious with baked chicken or roast pork

6 large potatoes (about 3 lbs.)
¼ c. sifted flour
¼ c. grated Parmesan cheese
¾ tsp. salt

⅛ tsp. pepper
⅓ c. butter or regular margarine
Chopped fresh parsley

Pare potatoes; cut into quarters. Combine flour, cheese, salt and pepper in a bag. Moisten potatoes with water and shake a few at a time in bag, coating potatoes well with cheese mixture.

Melt butter in 13 × 9 × 2″ baking pan. Place potatoes in a layer in pan.

Bake in moderate oven (375°) about 1 hour, turning once during baking. When golden brown, sprinkle with parsley. Makes 6 to 8 servings.

HAM-STUFFED POTATOES

The meal will be complete with cabbage salad and sliced fresh fruit

6 baking potatoes (about 5″ long)	½ tsp. salt
	¼ tsp. pepper
¾ c. diced ham	1¼ c. dairy sour cream
¼ c. chopped green pepper	½ c. finely shredded Swiss
2 tblsp. finely chopped onion	cheese

Bake potatoes in hot oven (400°) about 1 hour or until done.

Cut off top; scoop out hot potato with a spoon. Break up potato with fork. (Do not mash.) Combine hot potato, ham, green pepper, onion, salt and pepper. Add enough sour cream to moisten. Pile mixture into shells. Place on baking sheet. Top with Swiss cheese.

Bake in hot oven (400°) 15 to 20 minutes or until golden. Makes 6 servings.

CREAMED POTATO / EGG CASSEROLE

For a festive touch, sprinkle with paprika and chopped parsley

4 c. sliced, pared potatoes	1 c. evaporated milk
½ c. chopped onion	1 c. water
¼ c. chopped green pepper	1 c. shredded Cheddar cheese
3 tblsp. butter or regular margarine	1 tsp. salt
	¼ tsp. pepper
3 tblsp. flour	2 hard-cooked eggs, chopped

Cook potatoes in boiling water until tender. Drain well.

Sauté onion and green pepper in melted butter in saucepan until tender (do not brown). Stir in flour. Combine evaporated milk and water. Gradually add to flour mixture. Cook, stirring constantly, until mixture thickens. Stir in cheese, salt and pepper; heat until cheese melts. Combine drained potatoes, eggs and cheese sauce. Turn into greased 1½-qt. casserole.

Bake in moderate oven (375°) 20 minutes or until top is brown. Makes 6 servings.

BASQUE POTATOES

Delicious with golden fried chicken, tomato slices and fresh peas

½ c. finely chopped onion
½ c. chopped celery
½ c. shredded carrot
1 clove garlic, minced
2 tblsp. butter or regular
  margarine

1 (10½ oz.) can condensed
  chicken broth
2 lbs. potatoes, pared and cut in
  1″ cubes (about 4 c.)
½ tsp. salt
⅛ tsp. pepper
Chopped fresh parsley

Sauté onion, celery, carrot and garlic in melted butter in 10″ skillet until tender (do not brown). Combine chicken broth with enough water to make 2 c. Add chicken broth, potatoes, salt and pepper to sautéed vegetables. Cover; simmer for 10 minutes. Remove cover. Simmer, stirring occasionally, for 20 minutes or until broth is thickened. Sprinkle with parsley. Makes 4 to 6 servings.

SCALLOPED POTATOES SUPREME

A hearty meal with crisp cole slaw and buttered cornmeal muffins

4 c. thinly sliced, pared
  potatoes (about 6 medium)
1 c. coarsely diced ham
¾ c. chopped onion
1 (10½ oz.) can condensed
  cream of celery soup

¼ c. milk
¼ tsp. salt
⅛ tsp. pepper
1 c. shredded Cheddar cheese
Paprika

Combine potatoes, ham and onion in 2-qt. casserole.

Mix together soup, milk, salt and pepper. Pour over potato mixture. Cover and bake in moderate oven (350°) 1 hour.

Uncover and top with cheese. Sprinkle with paprika. Continue baking 30 more minutes or until potatoes are tender and top is golden brown. Makes 6 servings.

SOMETHING DIFFERENT FOR SUPPER

"What shall we have for supper?" is a question that farm women often ask. We would suggest a main dish of vegetables served along with either a salad or a platter of thickly sliced tomatoes. There are several recipes in this group that are rich in eggs and cheese so that they are nourishing and will provide a well-balanced meal . . . Asparagus Cheese Bake and Corn Scramble on Toast. Men like the Potato-Bacon Omelet.

ASPARAGUS CHEESE BAKE

Green beans or carrots can be substituted . . . use about 2 cups

2 (10 oz.) pkgs. frozen
  asparagus spears
3 eggs, beaten
½ c. milk
1 c. soft bread crumbs
¼ c. finely chopped onion

½ clove garlic, minced
3 tblsp. grated Parmesan cheese
½ tsp. salt
¼ tsp. orégano leaves
⅛ tsp. pepper

Cook asparagus in boiling salted water until almost tender. Drain well. Arrange in 8" square baking dish.

Combine eggs and milk. Stir in bread crumbs, onion, garlic, Parmesan cheese, salt, orégano and pepper. Pour over asparagus.

Bake in slow oven (325°) 35 minutes or until mixture is set. Makes 6 to 8 servings.

CORN SCRAMBLE ON TOAST

Makes a hearty breakfast served with sausage links and fresh fruit

6 slices bacon
1 (10 oz.) pkg. frozen whole
  kernel corn, thawed
¼ c. milk
6 eggs, slightly beaten

½ tsp. salt
⅛ tsp. pepper
6 slices buttered toast
6 tblsp. shredded Cheddar
  cheese

Fry bacon until crisp in 10" skillet. Remove and drain on paper towels. Crumble. Reserve 2 tblsp. bacon fat in skillet. Add corn; cook for 5 minutes or until golden brown, stirring occasionally. Add milk; simmer for 2 to 3 minutes.

Combine eggs, salt and pepper. Add to corn mixture. Cook over low heat, gently lifting from bottom and sides with spatula as mixture sets, so liquid can flow to bottom. (Avoid constant stirring.) Cook until set but still moist and remove from heat.

Spoon egg mixture onto toast slices. Top each serving with cheese. Place under broiler and broil until cheese melts (about 2 to 3 minutes). Garnish with bacon. Makes 6 servings.

POTATO-BACON OMELET

Place omelet on heated platter and garnish with sprigs of parsley

6 slices bacon	1 tblsp. cooking oil
1 c. diced, pared potatoes	8 eggs, well beaten
2 tblsp. chopped onion	1 tblsp. water
¼ tsp. salt	½ tsp. salt
2 tblsp. chopped fresh parsley	⅛ tsp. pepper
1 tblsp. chopped pimientos	

Fry bacon until crisp in small skillet. Remove and drain on paper towels. Crumble. Reserve 2 tblsp. bacon fat. Add potato, onion and ¼ tsp. salt; cook until potatoes are tender and golden. Stir in parsley, bacon and pimientos; set aside.

Heat oil in 10″ skillet over medium heat. Beat together eggs, water, ½ tsp. salt and pepper. Stir in vegetable mixture; pour into skillet. With fork, lift cooked edges so uncooked portion flows underneath. Slide pan back and forth to avoid sticking. Cook until mixture is set, but top is creamy. Fold in half and slide onto serving platter. Makes 4 servings.

POTATO / CHEESE PUFF

An Italian heirloom recipe that has been a family favorite for years

3 c. hot, mashed potatoes	2 tblsp. chopped fresh parsley
2 eggs, well beaten	1 tblsp. butter or regular
1½ c. milk	margarine
⅓ c. grated Parmesan cheese	½ tsp. salt
1 (4 oz.) pkg. mozzarella cheese, shredded	⅛ tsp. pepper
	Parmesan cheese
1 c. finely chopped ham	

Mix together potatoes and eggs. Gradually blend in milk. Add ⅓ c. Parmesan cheese, mozzarella cheese, ham, parsley, butter, salt and pepper. Turn into greased 8″ square baking dish. Sprinkle with Parmesan cheese.

Bake in moderate oven (350°) about 1 hour or until firm in center and golden brown. Cut into squares. Makes 6 to 8 servings.

SPINACH / RICE BAKE

A creamy rice casserole that is ideal for company buffet suppers

1 (4 oz.) can mushrooms	2 eggs, beaten
½ c. chopped onion	1 (14½ oz.) can evaporated
1 clove garlic, minced	milk
¼ c. butter or regular	½ tsp. salt
margarine	½ tsp. seasoned salt
1 (10 oz.) pkg. frozen leaf	¼ tsp. pepper
spinach, cooked and drained	3 tblsp. lemon juice
3 c. cooked regular rice	Paprika
½ c. shredded Cheddar cheese	

Drain mushrooms; reserve liquid.

Sauté mushrooms, onion and garlic in melted butter in small skillet until tender (do not brown).

Chop spinach. Combine spinach, rice, cheese and sautéed vegetables.

Beat together eggs, milk, reserved mushroom liquid, salt, seasoned salt, pepper and lemon juice. Pour over rice mixture; toss gently. Turn into greased 2-qt. casserole and sprinkle with paprika.

Bake in moderate oven (350°) 30 minutes or until mixture is set. Makes 6 to 8 servings.

VEGETABLE / EGG COMBO

Fresh vegetable dish suitable for brunch, luncheon or supper

½ c. chopped onion	¼ tsp. ground nutmeg
¼ c. butter or regular	2 tblsp. vinegar
margarine	½ c. grated Parmesan cheese
3 c. diced fresh tomatoes	2 tsp. chopped chives
⅓ c. chopped green pepper	2 tsp. chopped fresh parsley
1 tblsp. sugar	6 eggs, slightly beaten
2 tsp. salt	6 slices buttered toast
¼ tsp. pepper	Chopped fresh parsley

Sauté onion in melted butter in large skillet until tender (do not brown). Add tomatoes, green pepper, sugar, salt, pepper, nutmeg and vinegar. Cook until tender, for about 8 minutes, stirring occasionally. Blend in cheese, chives and parsley; cook for 2 minutes. Stir in eggs. Cook slowly, for about 2 to 3 minutes; stirring occasionally. Do not overcook. Serve on buttered toast. Garnish with parsley. Makes 6 servings.

FAMILY REUNION PICNICS

At country-style picnics or family gatherings you are bound to find a big bowl of creamy potato salad and a casserole of beans. Every family has a member noted for a recipe for either one. These recipes have been toted to family outings for years and have been rated tops by everyone who has sampled a helping.

HOT FRANK POTATO SALAD

A complete meal-in-a-dish that is sure to please potato salad fans

½ lb. bacon	¾ c. cider vinegar
¾ c. chopped onion	1½ c. water
3 tblsp. sugar	6 c. sliced, cooked potatoes
3 tblsp. flour	8 frankfurters, sliced
1½ tsp. salt	2 hard-cooked eggs, chopped
1 tsp. celery seeds	Chopped fresh parsley

Fry bacon until crisp in skillet. Remove and drain on paper towels. Crumble. Sauté onion in ⅓ c. bacon drippings until tender (do not brown). Add sugar, flour, salt and celery seeds. Stir in vinegar and water. Cook over medium heat, stirring constantly, until thick. Combine with bacon, potatoes, frankfurters and eggs. Turn into greased 3-qt. casserole.

Bake, covered, in moderate oven (350°) 20 minutes or until heated. Garnish with parsley. Makes 8 servings.

CREAMY POTATO SALAD

"A salad is only as good as its dressing," a Michigan woman says

4 c. diced, cooked potatoes	1 tsp. prepared mustard
½ c. chopped onion	¼ tsp. paprika
4 hard-cooked eggs, sliced	2 eggs
½ c. chopped celery	½ c. vinegar
½ c. diced cucumber	½ c. water
6 radishes, thinly sliced	2 tblsp. butter or regular
¼ c. sugar	margarine
2 tblsp. flour	Chopped fresh parsley
1 tsp. salt	

Combine potatoes, onion, eggs, celery, cucumber and radishes in a large bowl.

Combine sugar, flour, salt, mustard and paprika in double boiler top. Add eggs and beat until smooth. Stir in vinegar and water. Cook over hot water until mixture is smooth and thick, stirring constantly. Stir in butter and remove from heat. Cool slightly. Pour over potato mixture and toss gently. Chill well. Garnish with parsley. Makes 6 servings.

LIMA BEANS AU GRATIN

Crisp garden relish and hot rolls complete this protein-rich meal

1 lb. dried large lima beans, cooked	1 c. evaporated milk
	1 c. shredded Cheddar cheese
¼ c. chopped onion	3 tblsp. diced pimientos
¼ c. chopped celery	½ tsp. salt
¼ c. butter or regular margarine	¼ tsp. thyme leaves
	½ c. shredded Cheddar cheese
¼ c. flour	Paprika
1 c. milk	

Drain lima beans, reserving ¼ c. cooking liquid.

Sauté onion and celery in melted butter in saucepan until tender (do not brown). Stir in flour. Gradually add milk, evaporated milk and reserved cooking liquid. Cook until thick, stirring constantly. Stir in 1 c. cheese; stir until melted. Add pimientos, salt and thyme.

Place beans and sauce in alternate layers in greased 2-qt. casserole, ending with sauce. Top with ½ c. shredded cheese. Sprinkle with paprika.

Bake, uncovered, in moderate oven (350°) 1 hour or until golden. Makes 6 servings.

COLD BEAN CASSEROLE

Serve this refreshing summer salad with sliced cold luncheon meats

3 (1 lb. 4 oz.) cans white kidney beans, drained
1 c. sliced scallions or green onions
½ c. chopped green pepper
¼ c. chopped fresh parsley
1 (4 oz.) jar pimientos, drained and chopped
½ c. salad oil
¼ c. red wine vinegar
1 clove garlic, minced
½ tsp. salt
¼ tsp. pepper
2 bay leaves
2 tomatoes, quartered

Mix together kidney beans, scallions, green pepper, parsley and pimientos in a large bowl. Combine oil, vinegar, garlic, salt and pepper; pour over vegetables and toss gently. Place bay leaves in mixture. Refrigerate overnight. Remove bay leaves, and garnish with tomatoes. Makes 8 servings.

PATIO BAKED BEANS

Treat your relatives to this dish at your annual reunion

5 strips bacon
½ c. chopped onion
⅓ c. brown sugar, firmly packed
1 tblsp. vinegar
¼ c. water
1 tsp. dry mustard
1 tsp. instant coffee powder
2 (1 lb. 12 oz.) cans pork and beans in tomato sauce

Fry bacon until almost crisp in saucepan. Remove and drain on paper towels. Cut into 1″ pieces.

Sauté onion in 2 tblsp. bacon fat until tender (do not brown).

Add brown sugar, vinegar, water, mustard, coffee powder, beans and bacon. Bring to a boil. Turn into 2-qt. casserole.

Bake in moderate oven (350°) 1 hour. Makes 8 servings.

PRESSURE-COOKER BAKED BEANS

Delicious served with creamy cole slaw and golden cornmeal sticks

1 lb. dried navy beans	½ c. chopped onion
⅓ lb. bacon, cut in pieces	1½ tsp. salt
3 tblsp. brown sugar	½ tsp. prepared mustard
3 tblsp. molasses	2 c. water
3 tblsp. ketchup	

Wash beans. Soak overnight in water to cover. Rinse and drain.

Sauté bacon in 4-qt. pressure cooker. Add beans, brown sugar, molasses, ketchup, onion, salt, mustard and water. Close cover securely. Cook beans at 15 lbs. pressure (following manufacturer's directions for your pressure cooker) for 50 minutes. Let pressure drop of own accord. Makes about 6 servings.

Oven Method: Soak beans (as above) overnight. Rinse and drain. Add enough water to cover beans. Bring to a boil; reduce heat. Cook for 20 minutes.

Put beans and liquid in 2-qt. bean pot or casserole. Add remaining ingredients. Cover. Bake in slow oven (300°) 6 to 8 hours, adding more water as needed to keep beans moist. Uncover for last 30 minutes of baking. Beans should be tender and not mushy.

Chapter 5

SALADS THAT APPEAL TO EVERYBODY

Salads are given special attention in country meals and menus. Farm cooks have their salad specialties for every occasion whether it be a holiday meal, a family dinner, potluck or picnic, or family reunion.

Along with the salads we have collected from throughout the country, we share comments telling us why this salad is extra special. For example:

"Everyone just naturally expects me to bring this to all picnics; it's a third generation heirloom to which I've added my own extras," an Iowa woman says of her Homefront Sauerkraut Salad. Bright-colored, crispy, with a delicious tang, this salad will spark up any menu any time of the year.

Reaping the bounty of her vegetable garden, a Kansas woman schedules Molded Cucumber Delight often during the month of August—it's chock-full of home grown onions, green peppers and cucumbers along with protein-rich cottage cheese. All the ingredients are folded into lime-flavored gelatin—a refreshing dish on a hot summer night.

A crunchy slaw from North Carolina sparkles with color and flavor: "My family loves this with all kinds of meat, and it keeps at least 6 weeks in the refrigerator." For the men in the family we have rib-sticking Tuna and Lima Bean Salad—with lots of hot rolls it is a meal in itself.

For the holiday season, there's a selection of tart salads featuring the bright red cranberry: Cranberry Crunch Salad, Frosted Cranberry Squares and Cottage Cheese Cranberry Salad.

Many salads double as desserts in the country. Fruit salads that have ice cream or sherbet folded into fruits are examples, as are many molded gelatin beauties. Women tell us they are popular for carry-in dinners or potluck suppers—they make a big hit with everyone.

MAIN DISH SALADS

Here we present some substantial hearty salads that really are meals in themselves. They are easy to prepare and can be served with a minimum of fuss and bother. All the following make satisfying summer night suppers. Pile some potato chips in a bowl. Make a batch of homemade biscuits and a pitcher of iced tea. You're all set to serve an appetizing meal.

TUNA AND LIMA BEAN SALAD

Protein-rich hearty salad to serve for supper on a hot summer night

1 lb. dried large lima beans, cooked and drained
2 (7 oz.) cans tuna, drained and flaked
6 hard-cooked eggs, chopped
2 c. chopped celery
½ c. chopped green pepper
½ c. chopped onion
¼ c. diced pimientos
1 c. dairy sour cream
¾ c. mayonnaise
1 tblsp. lemon juice
1 tsp. salt
¼ tsp. pepper

Combine lima beans, tuna, eggs, celery, green pepper, onion and pimientos in a large bowl.

Mix together sour cream, mayonnaise, lemon juice, salt and pepper. Pour over salad mixture; toss gently. Chill until serving time. Makes 12 to 14 servings.

SPECIAL CHEF'S SALAD

A main dish salad supper that always makes a big hit with the men

2 c. bite-size pieces lettuce
2 c. bite-size pieces spinach
½ c. chopped green pepper
½ c. shredded carrot
½ c. halved cucumber slices
½ lb. ham, cut in strips (1 c.)
1 (3 oz.) pkg. cream cheese, cubed
2 hard-cooked eggs, chopped
1 small onion, sliced
Oil and Vinegar Dressing (recipe follows)

Combine lettuce, spinach, green pepper, carrot, cucumber, ham, cream cheese, eggs and onion in a large bowl.

Prepare Oil and Vinegar Dressing. Pour over salad ingredients. Toss gently. Makes 4 to 6 servings.

Oil and Vinegar Dressing: Combine ½ c. salad oil, ¼ c. vinegar, 1 tblsp. ketchup, ¾ tsp. sugar, ¾ tsp. salt, ½ tsp. garlic salt and ⅛ tsp. pepper in jar or bottle. Cover tightly and shake well.

CHICKEN SALAD HAWAIIAN

Best in the salad division was awarded to this different chicken salad

1 (8½ oz.) can crushed pineapple
2 c. cut-up, cooked chicken
1 c. chopped celery
1 c. diced, unpared apples
¼ c. diced, canned peaches
½ c. dairy sour cream
½ tsp. grated lemon rind
1 tsp. salt
1 banana, diced
½ c. coarsely chopped walnuts
Lettuce leaves

Drain pineapple, reserving 1 tblsp. juice.

Combine pineapple, chicken, celery, apples and peaches. Chill well.

Just before serving, combine sour cream, reserved pineapple juice, lemon rind and salt. Pour over fruits. Add banana and walnuts; toss gently. Serve on lettuce leaves. Makes 4 to 6 servings.

TUNA CARROT SALAD

Children will pass their plates for seconds when you serve this salad

1 (7 oz.) can tuna, drained and flaked
1 c. coarsely grated carrots
1 c. chopped celery
¼ c. finely chopped onion
½ c. mayonnaise
½ c. milk
1 tsp. prepared mustard
¼ tsp. pepper
1 (1¾ oz.) can shoestring potatoes

Combine tuna, carrots, celery and onion.

Mix together mayonnaise, milk, mustard and pepper. Add to tuna mixture; toss gently. Chill until serving time.

Add shoestring potatoes and toss. Makes 6 servings.

HAM AND EGG MOLD

A medley of vegetables captured in a mold. Garnish with tomatoes

1 envelope unflavored gelatin	½ c. diced celery
¼ c. cold water	¼ c. diced sweet pickles
1¼ c. boiling water	¼ c. chopped green pepper
1 tblsp. lemon juice	¼ c. diced pimientos
½ c. salad dressing	1 tsp. horseradish
2 c. ground, cooked ham	¼ tsp. salt
2 hard-cooked eggs, chopped	⅛ tsp. dry mustard
1 c. cooked peas	⅛ tsp. onion salt

Soften gelatin in cold water. Stir in boiling water and lemon juice; stir until dissolved. Chill until thick and syrupy.

Fold in salad dressing; blend well. Add ham, eggs, peas, celery, pickles, green pepper, pimientos, horseradish, salt, dry mustard and onion salt; fold until blended. Pour into lightly oiled 4-cup mold. Chill until set. Makes 4 to 6 servings.

GOLDEN MACARONI SALAD

Zippy yellow mustard gives this macaroni salad flavor and color

1 (8 oz.) pkg. shell macaroni, cooked and drained	3 eggs, slightly beaten
	½ c. sugar
2 (1 lb.) cans red kidney beans, drained	1 (9 oz.) jar prepared mustard
	3 tblsp. butter or regular
6 c. chopped cabbage	margarine
½ c. chopped celery	½ tsp. salt
½ c. green pepper strips	¼ tsp. pepper
¼ c. minced onion	

Toss together macaroni, kidney beans, cabbage, celery, green pepper and onion in a large bowl.

Combine eggs, sugar, mustard, butter, salt and pepper in top part of double boiler. Cook over simmering water for about 5 minutes, stirring constantly, or until mixture thickens slightly. Cool. Pour over vegetable mixture; toss. Makes 10 to 12 servings.

FLYING FARMER CHICKEN SALAD

Delight your guests on a hot summer night and serve this for supper

5 c. cubed, cooked chicken
2 tblsp. salad oil
2 tblsp. orange juice
2 tblsp. vinegar
1 tsp. salt
3 c. cooked rice
1½ c. small green grapes

1½ c. sliced celery
1 (13½ oz.) can pineapple
   tidbits, drained
1 (11 oz.) can mandarin
   oranges, drained
1 c. toasted slivered almonds
1½ c. mayonnaise

Combine chicken, salad oil, orange juice, vinegar and salt; let stand while preparing remaining salad ingredients. (Or you may refrigerate mixture overnight.)

Combine rice, grapes, celery, pineapple, mandarin oranges, almonds and mayonnaise. Toss gently. Add marinated chicken mixture; toss well. Makes 12 servings.

DOUBLE-DUTY SALADS

A sparkling selection of salads that are sweet enough to pinch-hit for dessert. A delicious mix of fruit-flavored gelatins combined with sour cream, cream cheese or ice cream along with fruits. The end result—creamy molds that look cool and inviting.

CREAMY FRUIT MOLD

Serve as salad or a light refreshing dessert after a hearty meal

1 (3 oz.) pkg. lime flavor
   gelatin
1 c. boiling water
1 c. dairy sour cream

1 (8½ oz.) can crushed
   pineapple, drained
1 c. diced, canned peaches
1 c. flaked coconut

Dissolve gelatin in boiling water. Chill until thick and syrupy.

Fold in sour cream. Then fold in pineapple, peaches and coconut. Pour into lightly oiled 5-cup mold. Chill until set. Makes 4 to 6 servings.

LIME ICE CREAM MOLD

Garnish with almond-flavored whipped cream and a strawberry

2 tsp. unflavored gelatin
⅔ c. cold water
2 (3 oz.) pkgs. lime flavor
  gelatin
2 c. boiling water
1 qt. vanilla ice cream

1 (8½ oz.) can crushed
  pineapple, drained
2 c. miniature marshmallows
6 tblsp. milk
⅔ c. dairy sour cream
⅔ c. chopped walnuts

Soften unflavored gelatin in cold water.

Dissolve lime gelatin in boiling water. Add softened gelatin; stir until dissolved. While hot, stir in vanilla ice cream and pineapple.

Meanwhile, melt marshmallows with milk. Remove from heat. Fold in sour cream and walnuts. Add to gelatin mixture; blend well. Pour into lightly oiled 2-qt. mold. Chill until set. Makes 8 to 10 servings.

ORANGE SHERBET MOLD

Try also with lemon flavor gelatin, fruit cocktail and vanilla ice cream

1 (3 oz.) pkg. orange flavor
  gelatin
1 c. boiling water
1 pt. orange sherbet
1 (11 oz.) can mandarin
  oranges, drained

1 c. miniature marshmallows
1 (8½ oz.) can crushed
  pineapple, drained
½ c. chopped pecans
10 maraschino cherries, cut up

Dissolve gelatin in boiling water. While hot, stir in orange sherbet. Chill until thick and syrupy.

Fold in mandarin oranges, marshmallows, pineapple, pecans and maraschino cherries. Pour into lightly oiled 5-cup mold. Chill until set. Makes 4 to 6 servings.

FRUIT DELIGHT SALAD

Wonderful to serve at big parties . . . popular at church suppers

2 (3 oz.) pkgs. strawberry
flavor gelatin
2 c. boiling water
2 (8½ oz.) cans crushed
pineapple
2 (10 oz.) pkgs. frozen
strawberries, partially thawed

2 bananas, cut up
1 (3 oz.) pkg. cream cheese,
softened
1 c. dairy sour cream
2 tblsp. lemon juice
¼ tsp. vanilla

Dissolve gelatin in boiling water. Add undrained pineapple and strawberries; stir until strawberries are thawed. Chill until thick and syrupy.

Fold in bananas. Pour half of mixture into lightly oiled 13 × 9 × 2″ baking dish. Chill until set. (Keep remaining gelatin mixture at room temperature.)

Beat cream cheese until smooth. Add sour cream, lemon juice and vanilla; blend well. Spread on gelatin layer. Chill for 30 minutes. Top with remaining gelatin mixture. Chill until set. To serve, cut into squares. Makes 12 servings.

LEMON FLUFF MOLD

Cool and velvety dessert that is nourishing with eggs and milk

2 c. milk
½ c. sugar
4 eggs, separated

1 (3 oz.) pkg. lemon flavor
gelatin

Heat milk in the top of a double boiler over hot water.

Beat in sugar and egg yolks with rotary beater. Cook, stirring constantly, until mixture begins to coat a spoon. Remove from hot water.

Sprinkle gelatin over hot mixture and stir to dissolve. Cool well.

Beat egg whites until stiff peaks form. Fold into cooled mixture. Turn into lightly oiled 5-cup mold. Chill until set. Makes 4 to 6 servings.

WHIPPED STRAWBERRY DELIGHT

Decorate this lovely mold with whipped cream and a walnut half

1 (8½ oz.) can crushed
pineapple
1 (3 oz.) pkg. strawberry flavor
gelatin

1 c. boiling water
1 envelope whipped topping mix
½ c. milk
⅔ c. chopped nuts

Drain pineapple, reserving juice. Add enough water to juice to make 1 c. of liquid.

Dissolve gelatin in boiling water. Stir in juice and water. Chill until thick and syrupy.

Whip topping mix with milk until soft peaks form.

Whip gelatin until fluffy. Beat in whipped topping. Add pineapple and nuts. Turn into lightly oiled 5-cup mold. Chill until set. Makes 4 to 6 servings.

BLUEBERRY LIME IMPERIAL

A truly elegant gelatin mold fit for the most special dinner guests

1½ c. reconstituted frozen
  limeade
1 (3 oz.) pkg. lime flavor
  gelatin

1 c. heavy cream, whipped
1 c. frozen blueberries, thawed
  and drained

Bring 1 c. limeade to a boil. Dissolve gelatin in hot limeade. Stir in remaining ½ c. limeade. Chill until slightly thickened.

Beat with electric mixer until light and fluffy. Fold in cream and blueberries.

Turn into lightly oiled 5-cup mold. Chill until set. Makes 6 to 8 servings.

MOLDED FRUIT MEDLEY

Perfect choice for family gatherings such as reunions and picnics

2 (3 oz.) pkgs. lemon flavor
  gelatin
2 c. boiling water
1 c. cold water
1 (8½ oz.) can crushed
  pineapple
⅓ c. lemon juice
¼ c. sugar

2 tblsp. cornstarch
2 eggs, beaten
1 c. heavy cream, whipped
1 (1 lb. 14 oz.) can fruit
  cocktail, drained
12 marshmallows, cut in
  quarters

Dissolve gelatin in boiling water. Stir in cold water. Chill until slightly thickened.

Meanwhile, drain pineapple, reserving juice. Combine pineapple juice, lemon juice, sugar and cornstarch in a small saucepan. Cook over medium heat, stirring constantly, until mixture thickens. Stir some of the hot mixture into the eggs; then gradually stir into remaining hot mixture. Cook, stirring, for 1 minute. Remove from heat; let cool.

Whip gelatin until light and fluffy. Fold in cooled custard and cream. Add fruit cocktail, marshmallows and pineapple; fold in lightly.

Turn into lightly oiled 10-cup mold. Chill until set. Makes 10 to 12 servings.

RUSSIAN CREAM MOLD

Double for company and pour into lightly oiled loaf pan

1 (3 oz.) pkg. lemon flavor gelatin	1 (1 lb.) can sliced peaches, drained and diced
1 c. boiling water	⅓ c. flaked coconut
1 c. dairy sour cream	1 c. sliced strawberries

Dissolve gelatin in boiling water. Chill until thick and syrupy.

Add sour cream; beat until blended. Fold in peaches, coconut and strawberries. Turn into lightly oiled 4-cup mold. Chill until set. Makes 4 to 6 servings.

MINT MIST

Garnish the serving plate with sprigs of fresh, bright-green mint

1 (20 oz.) can crushed pineapple	⅓ c. mint-flavored apple jelly
1 envelope unflavored gelatin	1 c. heavy cream, whipped

Drain pineapple, reserve juice.

Soften gelatin in ½ c. of pineapple juice. Place over low heat, stirring constantly until gelatin dissolves. Remove from heat; add jelly; stir until melted. Add pineapple and remainder of juice. Chill until thick and syrupy.

Fold cream into gelatin mixture. Turn into lightly oiled 4-cup mold. Chill until set. Makes 4 to 6 servings.

SALADS TO SPOTLIGHT A MEAL

Bright-colored salads in crisp lettuce cups add color and interest to any menu. We have some tempting salads that combine vegetables with gelatin, such as our light Cabbage Soufflé Salad and Cucumber/Cabbage Mold. Others feature fruits or vegetables seasoned just right with their own dressing. For a change of pace, put your imagination to work—substitute different fruits and vegetables and add an artistic garnish to make the salad your very own creation.

BARBECUE SLAW

A spicy slaw that teams well with all meats . . . popular at picnics

1 medium cabbage, shredded (about 10 c.)	¼ c. chopped onion
	½ c. sugar
2 large green peppers, chopped	¼ c. vinegar
1 (1 lb.) can tomatoes	1 tblsp. salt
2 c. sweet mixed pickles, drained and chopped	¼ tsp. pepper

Combine cabbage, green pepper, tomatoes, pickles and onion.

Mix together sugar, vinegar, salt and pepper. Add to cabbage mixture; toss well. Chill until ready to serve. Makes 10 to 12 servings.

OLD-FASHIONED APPLE SALAD

This tastes so good with crusty baked ham and candied sweet potatoes

1 c. raisins	1 c. light cream
1 c. water	1 tblsp. lemon juice
¾ c. sugar	4 large apples, cut in wedges
2 tblsp. cornstarch	(about 4½ c.)
¼ tsp. ground nutmeg	¼ c. flaked coconut

Combine raisins and water in small saucepan. Cook until tender and water is absorbed. Combine sugar, cornstarch and nutmeg. Stir in light cream. Add to raisins. Cook, stirring constantly, until thickened. Stir in lemon juice. Cool slightly.

Toss cooled custard with apples. Sprinkle with coconut. Makes 8 servings.

ROSY SPRING SALAD

Make this tangy rhubarb mold for dinner as the first hint of spring

4 c. diced rhubarb	1 c. orange juice
1½ c. water	1 tsp. grated orange rind
½ c. sugar	1 c. sliced fresh strawberries
2 (3 oz.) pkgs. strawberry flavor gelatin	

Combine rhubarb, water and sugar in saucepan. Cook until tender, for about 4 to 5 minutes. Pour over gelatin, stirring until dissolved. Add orange juice and rind. Chill until thick and syrupy.

Fold in strawberries. Pour into lightly oiled 6-cup mold; chill until set. Makes 6 to 8 servings.

CHERRY / PINEAPPLE MOLD

Surround salad with small puffs of whipped cream and bright cherries

1 (3 oz.) pkg. cherry flavor gelatin	1 (8½ oz.) can crushed pineapple
½ c. boiling water	½ c. chopped walnuts
½ c. small curd cottage cheese	¼ c. flaked coconut
¼ c. mayonnaise	1 c. heavy cream, whipped

Dissolve gelatin in boiling water. Stir in cottage cheese and mayonnaise. Stir in undrained pineapple, walnuts and coconut. Fold in whipped cream; blend well. Pour into lightly oiled 5-cup mold. Chill until set. Makes 4 to 6 servings.

CABBAGE SOUFFLÉ SALAD

Goes well with a bubbling pot of homemade beef stew and hot biscuits

1 (3 oz.) pkg. lemon flavor gelatin	2 tblsp. vinegar
1 c. boiling water	¼ tsp. salt
½ c. mayonnaise	1½ c. finely shredded cabbage
½ c. cold water	¼ c. diced green pepper
	1 tblsp. minced onion

Dissolve gelatin in boiling water. Stir in mayonnaise; mix until blended. Add cold water, vinegar and salt; stir well. Chill until slightly thickened.

Beat gelatin mixture until thick and fluffy. Fold in cabbage, green pepper and onion. Pour into lightly oiled 4-cup mold. Chill until set. Makes 4 to 6 servings.

CUCUMBER / CABBAGE MOLD

For a spectacular party salad, spoon into scooped-out tomato halves

2 (3 oz.) pkgs. lime flavor
  gelatin
¼ tsp. salt
3 c. boiling water
1 c. mayonnaise
1½ c. finely shredded cabbage

¾ c. chopped, pared cucumber
3 tblsp. chopped green pepper
3 tblsp. minced onion
2 tblsp. shredded carrot
½ tsp. celery seeds

Dissolve gelatin and salt in boiling water. Chill until thick and syrupy.

Beat in mayonnaise with rotary beater. Then fold in cabbage, cucumber, green pepper, onion, carrot and celery seeds. Pour into lightly oiled 6-cup mold. Chill until set. Makes 4 to 6 servings.

BARBECUE AND PICNIC SALADS

The next time you offer to take the salad to a barbecue, picnic or potluck, do try one of these outstanding recipes. There's a good variety to choose from. For baked ham dinner, you might like to make the Marinated Cucumber Salad or Grandmother's Best Potato Salad. The Double Dairy Salad tastes delicious with all meats and chicken.

DANISH POTATO SALAD

The special dressing makes this extra creamy and flavorful

¼ c. vinegar
¼ c. water
¼ c. sugar
¼ tsp. salt
$\frac{1}{16}$ tsp. pepper
1 tsp. prepared mustard
2 eggs, well beaten

1 c. salad dressing
4 c. cubed, cooked potatoes
  (about 2 lbs.)
2 hard-cooked eggs, chopped
½ c. chopped cucumber
1 tblsp. minced onion
1 tblsp. chopped green pepper

Combine vinegar, water, sugar, salt, pepper and mustard in medium saucepan. Bring to a boil. Reduce heat; gradually beat in well-beaten eggs. Cook over medium heat, stirring constantly, until slightly thickened, for about 5 minutes. Beat in salad dressing.

Toss together potatoes, hard-cooked eggs, cucumber, onion and green pepper. Pour on dressing; toss gently. Adjust seasoning if it's necessary. Makes 6 servings.

To make a larger quantity: For dressing: Use 1 c. each vinegar, water and sugar; 1 tblsp. mustard; 1 tsp. salt; ½ tsp. pepper; 5 eggs; and 1 qt. salad dressing.

Toss with 10 lbs. diced, cooked potatoes; 6 hard-cooked eggs; 2 c. cucumber; ½ c. each onion and green pepper. Makes about 6 quarts.

GRANDMOTHER'S BEST POTATO SALAD

This salad has been served for four generations at family picnics

1½ tblsp. sugar	½ c. cider vinegar
1 tblsp. flour	2 eggs, separated
1¼ tsp. salt	4 c. diced, cooked potatoes
¼ tsp. celery seeds	(about 2 lbs.)
⅛ tsp. pepper	½ c. sliced celery
1 tblsp. butter or regular	2 tblsp. chopped onion
margarine	2 tblsp. sliced pimiento-stuffed
1 tsp. prepared mustard	olives
¾ c. milk	

Combine sugar, flour, salt, celery seeds and pepper in small saucepan. Stir in butter, mustard, milk, vinegar and beaten egg yolks. Cook, stirring constantly, until mixture thickens. Cool slightly.

Beat egg whites until stiff. Fold into cooled mixture.

Combine potatoes, celery, onion and olives in a large bowl. Pour dressing over vegetables; toss gently. Chill until serving time. Makes 4 to 6 servings.

HOMEFRONT SAUERKRAUT SALAD

Crisp colorful relish . . . the sauerkraut flavor is a subtle undertone

1¼ c. sugar	1 c. chopped celery
1¼ c. water	½ c. coarsely grated carrots
½ c. vinegar	½ c. chopped green pepper
½ c. salad oil	½ c. chopped onion
1 (27 oz.) can sauerkraut,	2 tblsp. diced pimientos
drained, rinsed and snipped	

Combine sugar, water, vinegar and oil in small saucepan; mix well. Bring mixture to a boil, stirring occasionally. Remove from heat. Cool thoroughly.

Combine sauerkraut, celery, carrots, green pepper, onion and pimientos. Pour dressing over vegetables; toss gently. Chill several hours or overnight. Makes 6 servings.

DOUBLE DAIRY SALAD

Pleasant contrast of creamy cottage cheese and crunchy vegetables

2 c. large curd cottage cheese	¼ c. sliced green onions
2 c. dairy sour cream	¾ tsp. salt
1 c. diced, pared cucumber	¼ tsp. pepper
½ c. sliced radishes	Lettuce wedges or tomato slices

Mix together cottage cheese, sour cream, cucumber, radishes, onions, salt and pepper. Chill well.

Serve over wedges of lettuce or tomato slices. Makes 6 to 8 servings.

MARINATED CUCUMBER SALAD

Old-fashioned favorite that stays ultra crisp and crunchy overnight

2 large cucumbers, pared and sliced	2 tblsp. brown sugar, firmly packed
1 medium onion, sliced	½ tsp. seasoned salt
½ c. cider vinegar	¼ tsp. celery seeds
¼ c. salad oil	⅛ tsp. pepper

Combine cucumbers and onion in a bowl.

Mix together vinegar, oil, brown sugar, seasoned salt, celery seeds and pepper. Pour over cucumber mixture. Chill several hours or overnight. Makes 4 to 6 servings.

MOLDED CUCUMBER DELIGHT

Never a bite left when I take this to a picnic, a Kansas cook says

1 (3 oz.) pkg. lime flavor gelatin	⅛ tsp. salt
1 c. boiling water	1 c. chopped, pared cucumber
1 c. salad dressing	1 c. chopped celery
1 c. small curd cottage cheese	½ c. chopped green pepper
	2 tblsp. minced onion

Dissolve gelatin in boiling water. Using rotary beater, beat in salad dressing. Add cottage cheese and salt; blend well. Chill until slightly thickened.

Fold in cucumber, celery, green pepper and onion. Pour into lightly oiled 5-cup mold. Chill until set. Makes 4 to 6 servings.

WALDORF VARIATION SALAD

Lemonade makes this refreshing . . . keeps apples snowy white too

4 oranges, peeled and cut into sections

4 red apples, cut into wedges

1 c. sliced celery

1 (13½ oz.) can pineapple chunks, drained

1 (6 oz.) can frozen lemonade, slightly thawed

Combine all ingredients in large bowl. Toss well. Chill thoroughly. Makes about 8 servings.

FROSTY TOMATO

A marvelous make-ahead vegetable that can also double as a salad

3 (1 lb. 12 oz.) cans tomatoes, drained or 5 fresh medium tomatoes, chopped

1½ c. green pepper strips

1 medium onion, cut into rings

⅓ c. salad oil

2 tblsp. vinegar

1 tsp. salt

¾ tsp. orégano leaves

¾ tsp. basil leaves

¼ tsp. pepper

Combine all ingredients in bowl. Mix well. Chill. Makes 8 servings.

CHRISTMAS SPARKLERS

Festive salads are a part of Christmas entertaining. When we ask farm women for their favorite holiday recipes, there's bound to be a handsome salad in the group. Crimson cranberries are a natural this time of year and we have several scarlet beauties in this collection along with tangy apple and cabbage salads.

FROZEN APPLE SALAD

Garnish each frosty square with unpared apple slices and pecan halves

1 (8½ oz.) can crushed
   pineapple
½ c. sugar
⅛ tsp. salt
3 tblsp. lemon juice

2 eggs, beaten
1 c. heavy cream, whipped
2 c. diced, unpared apples
1½ c. miniature marshmallows
½ c. chopped celery

Drain pineapple, reserving juice. Add enough water to juice to make ½ c.

Combine sugar, salt and lemon juice in small saucepan. Gradually stir in reserved pineapple juice and eggs. Cook, stirring constantly, over low heat until thickened. Cool thoroughly.

Fold in pineapple, whipped cream, apples, marshmallows and celery. Pour into 9″ square baking dish. Cover and freeze.

Cut in squares to serve. Makes 9 servings.

CHRISTMAS APPLE SALAD

A West Virginia cook uses ingredients her family likes for this salad

1 (13½ oz.) can pineapple
   tidbits
6 unpared red apples, cut in
   wedges (5 c.)
1 c. chopped walnuts
1 c. chopped celery
½ c. quartered maraschino
   cherries

¾ c. mayonnaise
2 tblsp. lemon juice
½ tsp. salt
½ tsp. grated onion
1 c. frozen whipped topping,
   thawed
Lettuce leaves

Drain pineapple, reserving ¼ c. juice. Combine pineapple, apples, walnuts, celery and maraschino cherries in large bowl.

Combine mayonnaise, lemon juice, salt, onion and reserved pineapple juice; blend well. Fold in whipped topping. Pour dressing over apple mixture; toss gently. Serve on lettuce leaves. Makes 8 to 10 servings.

CHRISTMAS CABBAGE SALAD

Put this salad in your prettiest crystal bowl and wreathe with parsley

½ c. sugar
1 tblsp. flour
1 tblsp. cornstarch
½ tsp. salt
⅛ tsp. pepper
⅛ tsp. dry mustard
1 (8½ oz.) can pineapple tidbits

¾ c. white vinegar
2 eggs, beaten
6 c. shredded cabbage
1 c. miniature marshmallows
1 unpared red apple, cut in wedges
Pecan halves

Combine sugar, flour, cornstarch, salt, pepper and mustard in saucepan. Drain pineapple; add enough water to make 1½ c. juice. Stir juice and vinegar into dry ingredients. Beat in eggs. Cook over medium heat, stirring constantly, until mixture thickens. Cool well.

Toss with cabbage, marshmallows, apple and pineapple. Garnish with pecans. Serve immediately. Makes about 8 servings.

CRUNCHY APPLE SALAD

Refreshing salad that is so easy to prepare and oh so good!

1 c. diced, unpared apples
1 c. diced bananas
1 tblsp. lemon juice
½ c. drained pineapple tidbits

½ c. raisins
½ c. coarsely chopped pecans
⅓ c. mayonnaise
Lettuce

Combine apples, bananas, lemon juice, pineapple, raisins and pecans in bowl. Toss well.

Add mayonnaise. Toss just until mayonnaise is mixed thoroughly. Spoon into individual lettuce cups or into salad dish. Makes 6 servings.

COTTAGE CHEESE / CRANBERRY MOLD

Attractive in small molds ringed with greens and sliced oranges

1 (3 oz.) pkg. raspberry flavor gelatin
¾ c. boiling water
2 tblsp. orange juice
1 tsp. grated orange rind

⅛ tsp. salt
1 (1 lb.) can whole cranberry sauce
1 c. large curd cottage cheese
½ c. dairy sour cream

Dissolve gelatin in boiling water. Stir in orange juice, orange rind and salt. Chill until thick and syrupy.

Blend in cranberry sauce, cottage cheese and sour cream. Pour into lightly oiled 4-cup mold. Chill until set. Makes 4 to 6 servings.

SPICY MIXED FRUIT MOLD

Pour into hollowed-out orange shells for a festive party salad

2 (3 oz.) pkgs. raspberry flavor gelatin
1 tsp. ground cinnamon
¼ tsp. salt
¼ tsp. ground ginger
¼ tsp. ground cloves
3 c. boiling water

⅔ c. raisins
1 c. chopped pecans
½ c. chopped mixed candied fruit
1 (1 lb. 4½ oz.) can crushed pineapple, drained

Dissolve gelatin, cinnamon, salt, ginger and cloves in boiling water. Add raisins. Chill until thick and syrupy.

Fold in pecans, candied fruit and pineapple. Pour into lightly oiled 5-cup mold. Chill until set. Makes 4 to 6 servings.

RUBY CRANBERRY CRUNCH SALAD

Serve with the holiday turkey instead of the usual cranberry sauce

2 (3 oz.) pkgs. cherry flavor gelatin
c. boiling water
1 c. cold water, *Cola or wine*
2 tblsp. lemon juice

1 (1 lb.) can whole cranberry sauce
1 c. finely diced celery
½ c. chopped walnuts

I can cr. pineapple

Dissolve gelatin in boiling water. Stir in cold water and lemon juice. Chill until thick and syrupy.

Fold cranberry sauce, celery and walnuts into gelatin mixture. Pour into lightly oiled 2-qt. mold. Chill until set. Makes 8 to 10 servings.

FROSTED CRANBERRY SQUARES

A very tasty combination of flavors in this pretty Christmas salad

2 (3 oz.) pkgs. strawberry flavor
gelatin
1½ c. boiling water
1 (1 lb.) can whole cranberry
sauce
1½ c. ginger ale
1 c. chopped walnuts
1 c. chopped, unpared apple

1 (8½ oz.) can crushed
pineapple, drained
1 small banana, diced
1 tblsp. grated orange rind
1 c. heavy cream
1 (3 oz.) pkg. cream cheese,
softened

Dissolve gelatin in boiling water. Add cranberry sauce, stirring until dissolved. Stir in ginger ale. Chill until thick and syrupy.

Fold in walnuts, apple, pineapple, banana and orange rind. Pour into lightly oiled 8″ square baking dish. Chill until set.

Combine heavy cream and cream cheese. Beat until cream is whipped and mixture is thick. Spread over gelatin. Chill at least 1 hour. To serve, cut in squares. Makes 9 servings.

OLIVE WREATH MOLD

Garnish this lovely gelatin mold with sprigs of fresh parsley

1 (3 oz.) pkg. lime flavor
gelatin
1 c. boiling water
⅔ c. cold water
2 tblsp. lemon juice
1 c. heavy cream, whipped
⅓ c. sliced pimiento-stuffed
olives
½ c. shredded American cheese

1 (8½ oz.) can crushed
pineapple, drained
½ pimiento, chopped
½ c. finely chopped celery
½ c. chopped walnuts
½ tsp. salt
24 slices of pimiento-stuffed
olives

Dissolve gelatin in boiling water. Add cold water and lemon juice. Chill until thick and syrupy. Fold in whipped cream. Add ⅓ c. sliced olives, cheese, pineapple, pimiento, celery, walnuts and salt, blend well.

Arrange the 24 olive slices in a circle around the bottom of oiled 9″ ring mold. Pour mixture into mold. Chill until set. Makes 6 to 8 servings.

Chapter 6

THERE'S NOTHING
LIKE HOMEMADE BREAD

Can anything compare with the aroma of homemade bread baking in the oven . . . and the taste of a warm piece of bread slathered with butter.

Farm families know the joy of homemade bread and farm women are masters in the art of fine baking. We have collected and tested their most prized recipes so you'll find a wealth of outstanding breads in this chapter. And a great variety too.

There's a Nebraska homemaker's velvet-textured Blue Ribbon winner. Another, First Prize Rye Bread is a Washington woman's favorite recipe for Christmas giving. Her friends look forward to receiving a plump round loaf of crusty rye bread every year. For special occasions, do try the Cinnamon Swirl Bread with its icicle glaze or the Sugar Plum Loaf stuffed with walnuts, raisins, candied cherries and pineapple.

You'll hear a chorus of praise when you present your family with Cheddar Cheese Snack Bread—deliciously different, its top is custard-like in consistency and rich in cheese flavor. Serve it while warm and don't count on leftovers. Another great favorite is the Onion and Caraway Bread—it's the cottage cheese in the dough that produces the fine texture.

There are muffins galore. Some are especially "good for you," such as Cinnamon Bran Rolls with sugar crackled tops, and Wheat Germ Molasses Muffins.

When you really want to impress your friends, bake up a batch of Raised Cornmeal Muffins, tender and puffy. For those who like bacon flavor, Bacon 'n' Onion Muffins with sesame seed tops will be a real treat—the onion flavor is oh so subtle.

For the holiday season there are pumpkin breads, a Holiday Date Loaf, a Pineapple Tea Loaf and many more festive breads.

To satisfy hearty appetites on a bitter cold winter morning, stir up a batch of Oatmeal Griddle Cakes. Next try the Spicy Country Pancakes or the Whole Wheat Pancakes; every one will brighten a breakfast.

Surprise the field crew with a batch of Raspberry-Filled Bismarcks, a light and tasty raised doughnut filled with bright red raspberry jelly. They will like the sugared potato doughnuts or Applesauce Doughnuts (these are dropped by tablespoonfuls into bubbling fat and turn into crusty brown balls that are light as a puff).

We think you will want to sample every single recipe—they are all outstanding.

YEAST BREADS AND ROLLS

A bread or roll to suit every fancy describes our collection of creative homemade breads and rolls . . . hearty round ryes, raisin-filled oatmeal, salt-crusted sticks, tasty Onion and Caraway Bread and a raised cornmeal roll that is spectacular in flavor, texture and lightness. You'll have a hard time deciding which one to make first.

ONION AND CARAWAY BREAD

This will be a best seller at bazaars . . . it's deliciously different

1 c. cream-style cottage cheese	¼ c. lukewarm water
1 tblsp. melted butter or regular margarine	2½ to 3 c. sifted flour
1 tblsp. sugar	2 tblsp. onion flakes
1 tsp. salt	1 tblsp. caraway seeds
¼ tsp. baking soda	Melted butter or regular margarine
1 pkg. active dry yeast	

Combine cottage cheese, butter, sugar, salt and baking soda.
Sprinkle yeast on lukewarm water; stir to dissolve. Add yeast to

cottage cheese mixture. Add enough flour to make a soft dough. Add onion flakes and caraway seeds. Turn onto lightly floured surface and knead until smooth and satiny, for about 8 to 10 minutes.

Place in lightly greased bowl; turn dough over to grease top. Cover and let rise in warm place until doubled, for about 1 to 1½ hours.

Knead again for 3 minutes. Shape into a round loaf and place in greased 10″ pie plate. Let rise for 20 minutes. Brush top lightly with melted butter.

Bake in moderate oven (350°) 35 minutes or until bread tests done. Remove from pan. Cool on rack. Makes 1 loaf.

BLUE RIBBON WHITE BREAD

Your friends will want the recipe for this fine-textured loaf of bread

2 c. milk	1 pkg. active dry yeast
2 tblsp. shortening	¼ c. lukewarm water
2 tblsp. sugar	6½ to 7 c. sifted flour
2 tsp. salt	

Scald milk. Stir in shortening, sugar and salt. Cool to lukewarm.

Sprinkle yeast on lukewarm water; stir to dissolve. Add yeast and 2 c. flour to milk mixture. Beat with electric mixer at medium speed until smooth, for about 2 minutes, scraping bowl occasionally. Or beat with spoon until batter is smooth.

Gradually add enough remaining flour, a little at a time, to make a soft dough that leaves the sides of the bowl. Turn onto lightly floured surface and knead until smooth and satiny, for about 8 to 10 minutes.

Place in lightly greased bowl; turn dough over to grease top. Cover and let rise in warm place until doubled, for about 1 to 1½ hours.

Divide dough in half. Shape into loaves and place in 2 greased 9 × 5 × 3″ loaf pans. Let rise until doubled.

Bake in hot oven (400°) 40 minutes or until bread tests done. Remove from pans. Cool on racks. Makes 2 loaves.

OATMEAL RAISIN BREAD

Cut into thin slices, butter and broil until bubbly for breakfast

2 c. quick-cooking rolled oats	2 c. water
½ c. molasses	2 pkgs. active dry yeast
1 tsp. salt	½ c. lukewarm water
¼ c. melted butter or regular margarine	5½ c. sifted flour
	1 c. raisins

Combine oats, molasses, salt and butter. Stir in 2 c. water.

Sprinkle yeast on ½ c. lukewarm water; stir to dissolve. Add yeast and 2 c. flour to oat mixture. Beat with electric mixer at medium speed until smooth, for about 2 minutes, scraping bowl occasionally. Or beat with spoon until batter is smooth. Stir in raisins.

Gradually add enough remaining flour, a little at a time, to make a soft dough that leaves the sides of the bowl. Turn onto lightly floured surface and knead until smooth and satiny, for about 8 to 10 minutes.

Place in lightly greased bowl; turn dough over to grease top. Cover and let rise in warm place until doubled, for about 1 to 1½ hours.

Divide dough in half. Shape into loaves and place in 2 greased 9 × 5 × 3″ loaf pans. Let rise until doubled.

Bake in moderate oven (375°) 35 to 40 minutes or until bread tests done. Remove from pans. Cool on racks. Makes 2 loaves.

FIRST PRIZE RYE BREAD

This recipe turns out a trio of plump rounds of great-tasting bread

2 c. rye flour	½ c. lukewarm water
¾ c. molasses	6½ c. sifted flour
⅓ c. shortening	1 egg white, slightly beaten
2 tsp. salt	1 tblsp. water
2 c. boiling water	Caraway seeds
1 pkg. active dry yeast	

Combine rye flour, molasses, shortening and salt. Stir in 2 c. boiling water. Cool to lukewarm.

Sprinkle yeast on ½ c. lukewarm water; stir to dissolve. Add yeast and 1 c. flour to rye mixture. Beat with electric mixer at medium speed until smooth, for about 2 minutes, scraping bowl occasionally. Or beat with spoon until batter is smooth.

Gradually add remaining flour, a little at a time, to make a soft dough that leaves the sides of the bowl. Turn onto lightly floured surface and knead until smooth and satiny, for about 8 to 10 minutes.

Place in lightly greased bowl; turn dough over to grease top. Cover and let rise in warm place until doubled, for about 1 to 1½ hours.

Divide dough in thirds. Shape into round loaves and place on greased baking sheets. Let rise until doubled. Brush with combined egg white and water. Sprinkle with caraway seeds.

Bake in moderate oven (350°) 40 minutes or until bread tests done. Remove from baking sheets. Cool on racks. Makes 3 loaves.

SWEDISH RYE BREAD

Snack idea . . . slice and spread thickly with cream cheese and olives

1 c. milk	1 tsp. caraway seeds
¼ c. brown sugar, firmly packed	1 pkg. active dry yeast
3 tblsp. shortening	1 c. lukewarm water
2 tblsp. molasses	2 c. rye flour
1½ tsp. bottled sauce for gravy	4 c. sifted flour

Scald milk. Add brown sugar, shortening, molasses, bottled sauce for gravy and caraway seeds. Cool to lukewarm.

Sprinkle yeast on lukewarm water; stir to dissolve. Add yeast and rye flour to milk mixture. Beat with electric mixer at medium speed until smooth, for about 2 minutes, scraping bowl occasionally. Or beat with spoon until batter is smooth.

Gradually add enough flour, a little at a time, to make a soft dough that leaves the sides of the bowl. Turn onto lightly floured surface and knead until smooth and satiny, for about 8 to 10 minutes.

Place in lightly greased bowl; turn dough over to grease top. Cover and let rise in warm place until doubled, for about 1 to 1½ hours.

Divide dough in half. Shape each half into a ball and flatten slightly. Place on greased baking sheet. Repeat with remaining dough. Let rise until doubled.

Bake in moderate oven (375°) 25 to 30 minutes or until bread tests done. Remove from baking sheet. Cool on racks. Makes 2 loaves.

CHEDDAR CHEESE SNACK BREAD

Snappy cheese-flavored bread that goes so well with chef's salad

¾ c. milk	2½ c. sifted flour
2 tblsp. sugar	½ lb. Cheddar cheese, shredded
2 tblsp. shortening	(about 2 c.)
1 tsp. salt	5 tblsp. milk
1 pkg. active dry yeast	¾ tsp. grated onion
¼ c. lukewarm water	¼ tsp. salt
1 egg	Paprika

Scald ¾ c. milk. Stir in sugar, shortening and 1 tsp. salt. Cool to lukewarm.

Sprinkle yeast on lukewarm water; stir to dissolve. Add yeast, egg and 1 c. flour to milk mixture. Beat with electric mixer at medium speed until smooth, for about 2 minutes, scraping bowl occasionally. Or beat with spoon until batter is smooth.

Gradually add remaining flour, a little at a time. (Dough will be sticky.) Turn onto lightly floured surface and knead for 3 minutes.

Place in lightly greased bowl; turn dough over to grease top. Cover and let rise in warm place until doubled, for about 1 to 1½ hours.

Press dough into greased 13 × 9 × 2″ baking pan. Let rise until doubled. Combine cheese, 5 tblsp. milk, onion and ¼ tsp. salt. Spread evenly over dough. Sprinkle with paprika.

Bake in moderate oven (375°) 25 minutes or until top is golden. Cut in squares and serve warm. Makes 18 squares.

HONEY OATMEAL BREAD

Serve warm from the oven with honey drizzled over each slice

1 c. quick-cooking rolled oats	2 pkgs. active dry yeast
¼ c. butter or regular	1 c. lukewarm water
margarine	8 c. sifted flour
⅓ c. honey	Melted butter or regular
1 tblsp. salt	margarine
2 c. boiling water	

Combine oats, ¼ c. butter, honey and salt. Stir in 2 c. boiling water. Cool to lukewarm.

Sprinkle yeast on 1 c. lukewarm water; stir to dissolve. Add yeast and 2 c. flour to oat mixture. Beat with electric mixer at medium speed until smooth, for about 2 minutes, scraping bowl occasionally. Or beat with spoon until batter is smooth.

Gradually add enough remaining flour, a little at a time, to make a soft dough that leaves the sides of the bowl. Turn onto lightly floured surface and knead until smooth and satiny, for about 8 to 10 minutes.

Place in lightly greased bowl; turn dough over to grease top. Cover and let rise in warm place until doubled, for about 1 to 1½ hours.

Divide dough in thirds. Shape into loaves and place in 3 greased 9 × 5 × 3″ loaf pans. Let rise until doubled.

Bake in hot oven (400°) 10 minutes. Reduce heat to (350°) 30 to 35 minutes or until bread tests done. Remove from pans. Brush with melted butter. Cool on racks. Makes 3 loaves.

WHOLE WHEAT BREAD

Nourishing and nutritious . . . one of the best breads we've tasted

2 c. unseasoned mashed potatoes	3 c. boiling water
1 c. whole bran cereal	2 pkgs. active dry yeast
½ c. molasses	½ c. lukewarm water
¼ c. butter or regular margarine	9 c. sifted flour
	3 c. whole wheat flour
2 tblsp. salt	¾ c. yellow cornmeal

Combine mashed potatoes, bran cereal, molasses, butter and salt. Stir in boiling water. Cool to lukewarm.

Sprinkle yeast on ½ c. lukewarm water; stir to dissolve. Add yeast and 4 c. flour to bran mixture. Beat with electric mixer at medium speed until smooth, for about 2 minutes, scraping bowl occasionally. Or beat with spoon until batter is smooth.

Gradually add whole wheat flour, cornmeal and enough remaining flour to make a soft dough that leaves the sides of the bowl. Turn onto lightly floured surface and knead until smooth and satiny, for about 8 to 10 minutes.

Place in lightly greased bowl; turn dough over to grease top. Cover and let rise in warm place until doubled, for about 1 to 1½ hours.

Divide dough in fourths. Shape into loaves and place in 4 greased 9 × 5 × 3″ loaf pans. Let rise until doubled.

Bake in moderate oven (350°) 45 minutes or until bread tests done. Remove from pans. Cool on racks. Makes 4 loaves.

BACON / ONION STICKS

Split and fill with thinly sliced ham for special lunch box treats

2 pkgs. active dry yeast	5½ to 6 c. sifted flour
2 c. lukewarm milk	1 lb. lean bacon, diced
1 tsp. salt	1¼ c. chopped onion
1 tsp. sugar	¼ tsp. salt
½ c. melted butter or regular	¼ tsp. pepper
margarine	1 egg, beaten
1 tsp. ground cardamom	Salt crystals

Sprinkle yeast on milk; stir to dissolve. Stir in 1 tsp. salt, sugar, butter and cardamom. Add 2 c. flour. Beat with electric mixer at medium speed until smooth, for about 2 minutes, scraping bowl occasionally. Or beat with spoon until batter is smooth.

Gradually add enough remaining flour, a little at a time, to make a soft dough that leaves the sides of the bowl. Turn onto lightly floured surface and knead until smooth and satiny, for about 8 to 10 minutes.

Place in lightly greased bowl; turn dough over to grease top. Cover and let rise until doubled, for about 1¼ hours.

Meanwhile, sauté bacon and onion until cooked, but not crisp. Drain well. Add ¼ tsp. salt and pepper. Cool thoroughly.

Knead bacon mixture into dough. Roll dough into a 14″ square. Brush with egg. Sprinkle with salt crystals. Cut in half from top to bottom of square. Cut in thirds crosswise, making 6 sections. Cut each section into 6 sticks. Place on greased baking sheet and let rise for 30 minutes.

Bake in moderate oven (375°) 15 minutes or until golden brown. Remove from pans. Cool on racks. Makes 36 sticks.

RAISED CORNMEAL MUFFINS

Light as a whisper, these rolls taste every bit as good when reheated

2 c. milk	¼ c. lukewarm water
1 c. yellow cornmeal	2 eggs
½ c. sugar	5¼ c. sifted flour
½ c. shortening	Melted butter or regular
1 tsp. salt	margarine
1 pkg. active dry yeast	

Scald milk. Stir in cornmeal, sugar, shortening and salt. Cool to lukewarm.

Sprinkle yeast on lukewarm water; stir to dissolve. Add yeast, eggs and 2 c. flour to cornmeal mixture. Beat with electric mixer at medium speed until smooth, for about 2 minutes, scraping bowl occasionally. Or beat with spoon until batter is smooth.

Gradually add enough remaining flour, a little at a time, to make a thick batter. Let rise until doubled.

Stir down batter and spoon into greased 2½″ muffin-pan cups, filling one-half full. Let rise until doubled.

Bake in hot oven (400°) 15 minutes or until golden brown. Brush with melted butter. Makes 36 muffins.

REFRIGERATOR ROLLS

Prize-winning rolls that a Minnesota woman bakes for gatherings

1¾ c. milk	¼ c. lukewarm water
½ c. shortening	3 eggs
½ c. sugar	6½ c. sifted flour
2 tsp. salt	Melted butter or regular
1 pkg. active dry yeast	margarine

Scald milk. Stir in shortening, sugar and salt. Cool to lukewarm.

Sprinkle yeast on lukewarm water; stir to dissolve. Add yeast, eggs and 2 c. flour to milk mixture. Beat with electric mixer at medium speed until smooth, for about 2 minutes, scraping bowl occasionally. Or beat with spoon until batter is smooth.

Gradually add enough remaining flour, a little at a time, to make a soft dough that leaves the sides of the bowl.

Place in lightly greased bowl; turn dough over to grease top. Cover with plastic wrap. Refrigerate overnight.

Divide dough into fourths. Divide each portion into 10 equal pieces. Roll each into a ball. Place in 4 greased 9″ round cake pans, letting balls just touch each other. Let rise until doubled (about 1 hour).

Bake in moderate oven (350°) 15 minutes or until golden brown. Remove from pans. Brush with melted butter. Makes 40 rolls.

ONION / MUSTARD BUNS

Split and toast. Spread with cream cheese for a different snack

2 c. milk	¼ c. lukewarm water
2 tblsp. sugar	1 egg, slightly beaten
1 tblsp. prepared mustard	6 c. sifted flour
1½ tsp. salt	2 tblsp. instant minced onion
½ tsp. pepper	¼ c. water
2 tblsp. instant minced onion	1 egg, beaten
2 tblsp. oil	2 tblsp. water
1 pkg. active dry yeast	Instant minced onion

Scald milk. Stir in sugar, mustard, salt, pepper, 2 tblsp. instant minced onion and oil. Cool to lukewarm.

Sprinkle yeast on ¼ c. lukewarm water; stir to dissolve. Add yeast, egg and 2 c. flour to milk mixture. Beat with electric mixer at medium speed until smooth, for about 2 minutes, scraping occasionally. Or beat with spoon until batter is smooth.

Gradually add enough remaining flour to make a soft dough that leaves the sides of the bowl.

Turn onto floured surface; knead until smooth, for about 5 to 8 minutes. Place in greased bowl. Cover; let rise until doubled, for about 1½ hours.

Punch down. Divide dough into 2 equal parts. Let rest for 10 minutes. Pat each portion of dough into a 9″ square. Cut each square into 9 portions. Tuck corners under to form buns. Flatten with palm of hand. Let rise until doubled, for about 30 minutes.

Meanwhile, combine 2 tblsp. instant minced onion and ¼ c. water; allow to stand for 5 minutes.

Brush rolls with a glaze using 1 beaten egg and 2 tblsp. water. Sprinkle with onion.

Bake in moderate oven (375°) 20 minutes or until golden brown. Makes 18 buns.

HOT DINNER ROLLS

Very light, puffy rolls that can be made ahead and frozen

1 pkg. active dry yeast	3 eggs
1 c. lukewarm water	1 c. sugar
1 tblsp. salt	1 c. cooking oil
1 tblsp. sugar	Melted butter or regular
3 c. water	margarine
14 c. sifted flour	

Sprinkle yeast on 1 c. lukewarm water; stir to dissolve. Stir in salt, 1 tblsp. sugar, 3 c. water and 4 c. flour. Beat thoroughly (mixture should be bubbly). Cover and let stand in a warm place for 3 hours.

Beat eggs, 1 c. sugar and oil into batter; blending well. Gradually add enough remaining flour to make a soft dough that leaves the sides of the bowl. Turn onto lightly floured surface and knead until smooth and satiny, for about 8 to 10 minutes.

Divide dough in fourths. Cut each fourth into 12 parts. Shape each part into 3 balls. Place 3 balls in each greased 2½" muffin-pan cups. Let rise until doubled.

Bake in moderate oven (375°) 18 minutes or until golden brown. Remove from pans. Brush with melted butter. Makes 4 dozen.

SWEET YEAST BREADS AND ROLLS

Yummy Sugar Strips that a North Dakota family can demolish in one sitting and a giant kuchen that has been served hundreds of times by popular request—these are just two examples of the excellent yeast breads that follow.

QUICK CINNAMON ROLLS

An Idaho farm wife streamlined a recipe and produced these rolls

2 pkgs. active dry yeast	1 c. chopped walnuts
3 tblsp. sugar	¼ c. melted butter or regular
1 tsp. salt	margarine
1 c. light cream	1½ tsp. ground cinnamon
1 c. water	⅛ tsp. salt
5 c. sifted flour	Vanilla Glaze (recipe follows)
1½ c. brown sugar, firmly	
packed	

Combine yeast, sugar and 1 tsp. salt. Add light cream and water. Gradually add enough flour, a little at a time, to make a soft dough that leaves the sides of the bowl. Turn onto lightly floured surface and knead for 5 minutes.

Combine brown sugar, walnuts, melted butter, cinnamon and ⅛ tsp. salt.

Divide dough in half. Roll each half into 15 × 8″ rectangle. Sprinkle with half of brown sugar mixture. Roll up like jelly roll, starting at long side. Cut into 12 slices. Arrange in 2 greased 9″ square baking pans. Let rise until doubled (about 1 hour).

Bake in hot oven (425°) 18 to 20 minutes or until golden brown. Remove from pans. Cool on racks. Frost with Vanilla Glaze. Makes 24 rolls.

Vanilla Glaze: Combine 1 c. sifted confectioners sugar, 1½ tblsp. milk and ½ tsp. vanilla; beat until smooth.

YUMMY SUGAR STRIPS

Simply heavenly strips of sugary goodness . . . make two batches

¾ c. milk	3 c. sifted flour
3 tblsp. shortening	½ c. melted butter or regular
2 tblsp. sugar	margarine
1½ tsp. salt	¾ c. sugar
1 pkg. active dry yeast	¼ c. brown sugar, firmly
¼ c. lukewarm water	packed
1 egg	1 tsp. ground cinnamon

Scald milk. Stir in shortening, 2 tblsp. sugar and salt. Cool to luke-warm.

Sprinkle yeast on lukewarm water; stir to dissolve. Add yeast, egg and 1 c. flour to milk mixture. Beat with electric mixer at medium speed until smooth, for about 2 minutes, scraping bowl occasionally. Or beat with spoon until batter is smooth.

Gradually add enough remaining flour, a little at a time, to make a soft dough that leaves the sides of the bowl. Turn onto lightly floured surface and knead until smooth and satiny, for about 8 to 10 minutes.

Place in lightly greased bowl; turn dough over to grease top. Cover and let rise in warm place until doubled, for about 1 to 1½ hours.

Roll dough on lightly floured surface to 12 × 9″ rectangle. Cut into 12 (1″) strips. Then cut these strips in half, making 24 (4½″) strips. Dip each strip in melted butter and then in combined ¾ c. sugar, brown sugar and cinnamon. Place strips with sides touching in greased 15½ × 10½ × 1″ jelly roll pan. Let rise until doubled.

Bake in moderate oven (375°) 15 minutes or until golden brown. Makes 24 rolls.

MOLASSES STICKY BUNS

Pecan-studded molasses bun that never fails to bring rounds of praise

¾ c. milk
⅓ c. sugar
⅓ c. butter or regular margarine
1 tsp. salt
2 pkgs. active dry yeast
⅓ c. lukewarm water
1 egg
4 c. sifted flour
¼ c. molasses

½ c. brown sugar, firmly packed
⅓ c. butter or regular margarine
½ c. chopped pecans
1 c. brown sugar, firmly packed
½ c. raisins
1 tsp. ground cinnamon

Scald milk. Stir in sugar, ⅓ c. butter and salt. Cool to lukewarm.

Sprinkle yeast on lukewarm water; stir to dissolve. Add yeast, egg and 1 c. flour to milk mixture. Beat with electric mixer at medium speed until smooth, for about 2 minutes, scraping bowl occasionally. Or beat with spoon until batter is smooth.

Gradually add enough remaining flour, a little at a time, to make a soft dough that leaves the sides of the bowl. Turn onto lightly floured surface and knead until smooth and satiny, for about 8 to 10 minutes.

Place in lightly greased bowl; turn dough over to grease top. Cover and let rise in a warm place until doubled, for about 1 to 1½ hours.

Meanwhile, combine molasses, ½ c. brown sugar and ⅓ c. butter. Heat until butter melts. Spread mixture in 2 greased 9" round cake pans. Sprinkle with pecans.

Combine 1 c. brown sugar, raisins and cinnamon.

Divide dough in half. Roll each half into 12 × 8" rectangle. Sprinkle with half of brown sugar mixture. Roll up like jelly roll, starting at long side. Cut into 12 slices. Arrange in prepared pans. Let rise until doubled (for about 30 minutes).

Bake in moderate oven (350°) 25 to 30 minutes or until golden brown. Invert pans on plates and remove pans. Cool. Makes 24 rolls.

CINNAMON BRAN ROLLS

Light and delicious . . . tops are rolled in melted butter and sugar

1 c. milk	1 egg
1 c. whole bran cereal	2¾ c. sifted flour
¼ c. shortening	¼ c. melted butter or regular
¼ c. sugar	margarine
1 tsp. salt	⅓ c. sugar
1 pkg. active dry yeast	1 tsp. ground cinnamon

Scald milk. Reserve ¼ c. and cool. Combine ¾ c. milk, bran cereal, shortening, ¼ c. sugar and salt. Cool to lukewarm.

Sprinkle yeast over cooled ¼ c. milk; stir to dissolve. Add yeast and egg to bran mixture; beat well. Gradually add enough flour to make a soft dough that leaves the sides of the bowl. Turn onto lightly floured surface and knead until smooth and elastic, for about 8 to 10 minutes.

Place in lightly greased bowl; turn dough over to grease top. Cover and let rise in warm place until doubled, for about 1 to 1½ hours.

Punch down. Cover and let rise for 10 minutes. Shape into 24 balls. Place in greased 2½" muffin-pan cups. Let rise until doubled.

Bake in moderate oven (375°) 20 minutes or until golden brown. Remove from pans. Dip tops of rolls in melted butter and then in combined ⅓ c. sugar and cinnamon. Makes 24 rolls.

GOLDEN WALNUT ROLLS

Crunchy with nuts and buttery to taste, a perfect roll to serve guests

6½ c. sifted flour
6 tblsp. sugar
1½ tsp. salt
1 c. butter or regular margarine
2 pkgs. active dry yeast
½ c. lukewarm water
3 eggs

1 c. milk, scalded
1 c. chopped walnuts
1 c. sugar
¼ c. soft butter or regular margarine
1½ tsp. ground cinnamon
1 tsp. vanilla

Combine flour, 6 tblsp. sugar and salt in a large mixing bowl. Cut in 1 c. butter until mixture resembles coarse meal.

Sprinkle yeast on lukewarm water; stir to dissolve. Combine eggs and milk. Add yeast and milk mixture to dry ingredients. Mix well. Turn onto lightly floured surface and knead until smooth and satiny, for about 8 to 10 minutes.

Place in lightly greased bowl; turn dough over to grease top. Cover and let rise in warm place until doubled, for about 1 to 1½ hours.

Combine walnuts, 1 c. sugar, ¼ c. butter, cinnamon and vanilla.

Divide dough in fourths. Roll each portion into 9 × 8″ rectangle. Sprinkle with ¼ of walnut mixture. Roll up like jelly roll, starting at long side. Place on greased baking sheets. Let rise until doubled.

Bake in moderate oven (350°) 20 minutes or until golden brown. Remove from baking sheets. Cool on racks. Makes 4 coffee cakes.

TRIPLE FRUIT KUCHEN

This luscious fruit-filled coffee cake is shaped like a pizza

2 (13¾ oz.) pkgs. hot roll mix
1½ c. warm water
2 eggs
1 (1 lb. 8 oz.) jar cherry pie filling
1 (1 lb. 8 oz.) jar apple pie filling

Cream Cheese Mixture (recipe follows)
½ c. drained, sliced peaches
Brown Sugar Crumbs (recipe follows)

Pour water into a large bowl. Sprinkle in both packets of yeast from mixes; stir until dissolved. Add eggs and the flour mixture from mixes; blend well. Cover. Let rise in a warm place until doubled, for about 30 to 45 minutes.

Toss dough on floured surface until no longer sticky. Divide dough in half. Roll each into a 12" circle. Place in greased 13" pizza pans, pressing dough to sides. Make a rim around edge of pan.

Spoon cherry and apple pie fillings alternately with Cream Cheese Mixture over dough, using half for each pan. Decorate each with peach slices and Brown Sugar Crumbs. Let rise until doubled, for about 30 minutes.

Bake in moderate oven (350°) 25 to 30 minutes or until golden brown. Can be served warm or cold. Makes 2 kuchens, 6 to 8 servings each.

Cream Cheese Mixture: Beat 1 (8 oz.) pkg. cream cheese with electric mixer until smooth. Add 1 egg, ¼ c. sugar, ⅛ tsp. salt and 1 tsp. vanilla; beat well.

Brown Sugar Crumbs: Combine ⅓ c. brown sugar, firmly packed, ¼ c. sugar, ¼ c. unsifted flour, 2 tblsp. melted butter or regular margarine, ⅛ tsp. salt and ½ tsp. vanilla. Mix until crumbly.

Note: If disposable aluminum pizza pans are used, place them on baking sheets for easier handling.

PINEAPPLE CINNAMON BUNS

These large, puffy pineapple rolls are real family pleasers

½ c. milk	½ tsp. ground cinnamon
⅓ c. sugar	1 (8½ oz.) can crushed
¼ c. shortening	pineapple, drained
¾ tsp. salt	⅓ c. toasted, slivered almonds
1 pkg. active dry yeast	¼ c. chopped maraschino
½ c. lukewarm water	cherries
1 egg	2 tblsp. melted butter or regular
3¼ c. sifted flour	margarine
¼ c. sugar	

Scald milk. Stir in ⅓ c. sugar, shortening and salt. Cool to luke-warm.

Roast Chickens with Sausage Dressing (page 33) will become a family favorite the first time served. For guests, garnish serving platter with the slightly tangy *Spiced Fruit* (page 243), buttered broccoli spears, twisted lemon slices.

Light and delicate *Raspberry/Vanilla Cloud* (page 221) is a real "show-off" dessert and it tastes as good as it looks. Elegant and yet easy to prepare ahead for that very special occasion. Just refrigerate until serving time.

Rich *Cream of Potato Soup* (page 251) is the perfect choice for Christmas Eve supper. Make the soup the day before and reheat just before serving. Soup looks so festive topped with fresh parsley sprigs and shredded Cheddar cheese.

A great choice of cookies. At rear: *French Bars* (page 213) and *Party Whirls* (page 209). Foreground: *Fruit Blossom Cookies* (page 214) and *Pecan Lace Roll-Ups* (page 210). In stacks. *Six-in-One Refrigerator Cookies* (page 189).

Sprinkle yeast on lukewarm water; stir to dissolve. Add yeast, egg and 1 c. flour to milk mixture. Beat with electric mixer at medium speed until smooth, for about 2 minutes, scraping bowl occasionally. Or beat with spoon until batter is smooth.

Gradually add enough remaining flour, a little at a time, to make a soft dough that leaves the sides of the bowl. Turn onto lightly floured surface and knead until smooth and satiny, for about 8 to 10 minutes.

Place in lightly greased bowl; turn dough over to grease top. Cover and let rise in warm place until doubled, for about 1 to 1½ hours.

Combine ¼ c. sugar, cinnamon, pineapple, almonds and cherries; set aside. Roll dough into 15 × 10″ rectangle. Brush with butter. Sprinkle with pineapple mixture. Roll up like jelly roll, starting at narrow side. Cut into 12 slices. Place in greased 13 × 9 × 2″ cake pan. Let rise until doubled (for about 30 minutes).

Bake in moderate oven (350°) 25 minutes or until golden brown. Frost while warm with your favorite confectioners sugar frosting, if you wish. Makes 12 rolls.

DANISH CHRISTMAS RINGS

Blue Ribbon winner at a Wisconsin fair; makes four coffee cakes

4¼ c. sifted flour	1 c. milk, scalded
1 tsp. sugar	2 c. chopped pecans
1 tsp. salt	1 c. brown sugar, firmly packed
1 c. butter or regular margarine	½ c. soft butter or regular
2 pkgs. active dry yeast	margarine
½ c. lukewarm water	1 egg white, beaten
2 egg yolks	Vanilla Icing (recipe follows)

Combine flour, sugar and salt in a large mixing bowl. Cut in 1 c. butter until mixture resembles coarse meal.

Sprinkle yeast on lukewarm water; stir to dissolve. Combine egg yolks and milk. Add yeast and milk mixture to dry ingredients. Mix well.

Place in lightly greased bowl. Cover with plastic wrap or aluminum foil. Refrigerate for at least 2 hours. (Dough will keep well for 48 hours.)

Combine pecans, brown sugar and ½ c. butter.

Divide dough in fourths. Roll each portion into 18 × 6″ rectangle. Brush 3″ center strip with egg white. Spread ¼ of pecan mixture over egg white. Fold sides over filling, making three layers. Shape into ring; seal edges. Place on greased baking sheets. Let rise until doubled.

Bake in hot oven (400°) 20 to 30 minutes or until golden brown. Remove from baking sheets. Cool on racks. Frost with Vanilla Icing. Makes 4 coffee rings.

Vanilla Icing: Combine 2 c. sifted confectioners sugar, 1 tblsp. milk and ½ tsp. vanilla. Beat until smooth.

CINNAMON SWIRL BREAD

Handsome loaf to serve friends with pride during the holidays

1 c. milk	2 eggs
¼ c. butter or regular margarine	5 to 5½ c. sifted flour
¼ c. sugar	Melted butter or regular margarine
1 tsp. salt	⅓ c. sugar
1 pkg. active dry yeast	1 tblsp. ground cinnamon
¼ c. lukewarm water	Glaze (recipe follows)

Scald milk. Stir in butter, ¼ c. sugar and salt. Cool to lukewarm.

Sprinkle yeast on lukewarm water; stir to dissolve. Add yeast, eggs and 2 c. flour to milk mixture. Beat with electric mixer at medium speed until smooth, for about 2 minutes, scraping bowl occasionally. Or beat with spoon until batter is smooth.

Gradually add enough remaining flour, a little at a time, to make a soft dough that leaves the sides of the bowl. Turn onto lightly floured surface and knead until smooth and satiny, for about 8 to 10 minutes.

Place in lightly greased bowl; turn dough over to grease top. Cover and let rise in warm place until doubled, for about 1 to 1½ hours.

Divide dough in half. Roll each half into a 10 × 8″ rectangle. Brush lightly with melted butter. Sprinkle with half of combined ⅓ c. sugar and cinnamon. Roll up like jelly roll, starting at narrow end. Seal long edge. Place seam side down in greased 9 × 5 × 3″ loaf pan. Repeat with remaining dough. Let rise until doubled.

Bake in moderate oven (350°) 30 minutes or until bread tests done. Remove from pans. Cool on racks. Drizzle with Glaze. Makes 2 loaves.

Glaze: Combine 1 c. sifted confectioners sugar, 4 tsp. milk and ½ tsp. vanilla; blend well.

STREUSEL KUCHEN

Treasured recipe from Germany . . . a regular at family reunions

2 c. milk	1 c. dairy sour cream
½ c. sugar	1¾ c. unsifted flour
½ c. butter or regular margarine	½ c. melted butter or regular margarine
1¼ tsp. salt	½ c. sugar
1 pkg. active dry yeast	¼ tsp. salt
¼ c. lukewarm water	1 tsp. vanilla
3 eggs	½ tsp. almond extract
5 to 6 c. sifted flour	Confectioners sugar
1 tsp. vanilla	

Scald milk. Stir in ½ c. sugar, ½ c. butter and 1¼ tsp. salt. Cool to lukewarm.

Sprinkle yeast on lukewarm water; stir to dissolve. Add yeast, eggs, 2 c. flour and 1 tsp. vanilla to milk mixture. Beat with electric mixer at medium speed until smooth, for about 2 minutes, scraping bowl occasionally. Or beat with spoon until batter is smooth.

Gradually add enough flour to make a stiff batter. Cover and let rise in a warm place until doubled, for about 45 minutes. Stir down. Let rise for 20 more minutes; stir down. Repeat second rising procedure.

Divide dough in half. Press each half into greased 15½ × 10½ × 1″ jelly roll pan. Spread with half of sour cream. Combine 1¾ c. flour, ½ c. melted butter, ½ c. sugar, ¼ tsp. salt, 1 tsp. vanilla and almond extract; mix until crumbly. Sprinkle half over sour cream layer. Repeat with remaining dough. Let rise until doubled, for about 30 minutes.

Bake in moderate oven (375°) 25 minutes or until golden brown. Cool in pans on racks. Sprinkle with confectioners sugar. Makes 2 coffee cakes.

SUGAR PLUM LOAF

Once you make this for the holidays, you'll repeat it every year

1 c. milk, scalded	¾ c. seedless raisins
¼ c. sugar	¼ c. chopped candied cherries
¼ c. shortening	¼ c. chopped candied
1½ tsp. salt	pineapple
2 pkgs. active dry yeast	1 tsp. chopped candied lemon
2 eggs, beaten	peel
4 c. sifted flour	1 tsp. ground cardamom
1 c. chopped walnuts	

Combine milk, sugar, shortening and salt; cool to lukewarm. Stir in yeast. Add eggs; beat well. Add enough flour to make a soft dough.

Turn onto floured surface. Knead in walnuts, raisins, cherries, pineapple, lemon peel and cardamom; continue kneading dough until smooth. Place in a greased bowl and let rise until doubled. Punch down and let rest for 15 minutes. Divide dough in half.

Shape into 2 round loaves. Place on greased baking sheet. Let rise until doubled. Bake in moderate oven (350°) 25 minutes or until golden brown. Cool slightly; frost with your favorite confectioners sugar icing. Decorate with bits of candied fruit and walnuts, if you wish. Makes 2 loaves.

FINNISH COFFEE BRAID

These braided, light-textured loaves make handsome holiday presents

2 c. milk	2 pkgs. active dry yeast
1 c. sugar	½ c. lukewarm water
¼ c. butter or regular	2 eggs
margarine	1 tsp. cardamom seeds
1 tsp. salt	8½ to 9 c. sifted flour

Scald milk. Stir in sugar, butter and salt. Cool to lukewarm.

Sprinkle yeast on lukewarm water; stir to dissolve. Add yeast, eggs, cardamom seeds and 2 c. flour to milk mixture. Beat with electric mixer at medium speed until smooth, for about 2 minutes, scraping bowl occasionally. Or beat with spoon until batter is smooth.

Gradually add enough remaining flour, a little at a time, to make

From the
Desk of

CLARK V. CARRIKER

253 - ~~2141~~

255 - 4764

707 - 555 - 1212

a soft dough that leaves the sides of the bowl. Turn onto lightly floured surface and knead until smooth and satiny, for about 8 to 10 minutes.

Place in lightly greased bowl; turn dough over to grease top. Cover and let rise in warm place until doubled, for about 1 to 1½ hours.

Divide dough in fourths. Divide each portion in thirds. Roll each into a 10″ strip. Braid three strips together. Place on greased baking sheets. Let rise until doubled.

Bake in moderate oven (375°) 20 to 25 minutes or until golden. Remove from baking sheets and cool on racks. While warm, frost with your favorite glaze, if you wish. Makes 4 loaves.

TEA BREADS FOR HOLIDAY TIME

During the holidays fruit- and nut-filled tea breads are so good to have on hand. All these recipes can be made ahead and frozen for festive days ahead. They make wonderful gifts too; wrap in shiny colored foil and tie with a wide satin ribbon.

GRAND CHAMPION PUMPKIN BREAD

Twice honored with Grand Champion ribbon . . . superb bread

3⅓ c. sifted flour	⅔ c. cooking oil
4 tsp. pumpkin pie spice	4 eggs
2 tsp. baking soda	1 (1 lb.) can pumpkin (2 c.)
1½ tsp. salt	⅔ c. water
1 tsp. baking powder	⅔ c. chopped dates
2⅔ c. sugar	

Sift together flour, pumpkin pie spice, baking soda, salt and baking powder.

Beat together sugar and oil until light and fluffy. Add eggs, one at a time, beating well after each addition. Beat in pumpkin.

Add dry ingredients alternately with water, beating well after each addition. Stir in dates. Pour batter into 2 greased 9 × 5 × 3″ loaf pans.

Bake in slow oven (325°) 55 minutes or until bread tests done. Cool 10 minutes. Remove from pans. Cool on racks. Makes 2 loaves.

SPICY PUMPKIN BREAD

This bread is especially good spread with softened cream cheese

2 c. sifted flour	⅓ c. shortening
2 tsp. baking powder	1 c. brown sugar, firmly packed
½ tsp. salt	2 eggs
½ tsp. ground cinnamon	1 c. canned pumpkin
½ tsp. ground cloves	¼ c. milk
½ tsp. ground nutmeg	½ c. chopped walnuts
¼ tsp. baking soda	

Sift together flour, baking powder, salt, cinnamon, cloves, nutmeg and baking soda.

Cream together shortening and brown sugar until light and fluffy. Add eggs, one at a time, beating well after each addition. Beat in pumpkin and milk; blend well.

Gradually beat in flour mixture. Stir in walnuts. Turn batter into greased 9 × 5 × 3″ loaf pan.

Bake in moderate oven (350°) 55 to 60 minutes or until bread tests done. Cool for 10 minutes. Remove from pan. Cool on rack. Makes 1 loaf.

LUSCIOUS PUMPKIN BREAD

Rich, spicy bread that tastes so good with a big pot of hot cocoa

3½ c. sifted flour	½ tsp. ground cloves
2 tsp. baking soda	3 c. sugar
2 tsp. salt	1 c. cooking oil
1 tsp. baking powder	4 eggs
1 tsp. ground cinnamon	1 (1 lb.) can pumpkin (2 c.)
1 tsp. ground nutmeg	⅔ c. water
1 tsp. ground allspice	

Sift together flour, baking soda, salt, baking powder, cinnamon, nutmeg, allspice and cloves.

Beat together sugar, oil and eggs until light and fluffy. Add pumpkin; blend well.

Add dry ingredients alternately to pumpkin mixture with water, beating well after each addition. Pour batter into 2 greased 9 × 5 × 3″ loaf pans.

Bake in moderate oven (350°) 1 hour or until breads test done. Remove from pans. Cool on racks. Makes 2 loaves.

BANANA / LEMON LOAF

An Indiana woman combined two favorites and came up with this

2 c. sifted flour	2 eggs
3 tsp. baking powder	1 c. mashed bananas
½ tsp. salt	2 tblsp. lemon juice
½ c. shortening	1 c. chopped walnuts
1 c. sugar	1 tsp. grated lemon rind

Sift together flour, baking powder and salt.

Cream together shortening and sugar until light and fluffy. Add eggs, one at a time, beating well after each addition. Beat in bananas and lemon juice.

Gradually add dry ingredients; mix just until moistened. Stir in walnuts and lemon rind. Turn batter into greased 9 × 5 × 3″ loaf pan.

Bake in moderate oven (350°) 50 minutes or until bread tests done. Cool for 10 minutes. Remove from pan. Cool on rack. Makes 1 loaf.

PINEAPPLE TEA LOAF

Doubles as dessert when served with ice cream at a Minnesota farm

2 c. sifted flour	1 egg
¾ c. sugar	¼ c. melted butter or regular
3 tsp. baking powder	margarine
½ tsp. baking soda	¼ c. milk
½ tsp. salt	1 (8½ oz.) can pineapple
½ c. chopped walnuts	tidbits

Sift together flour, sugar, baking powder, baking soda and salt. Mix 1 tblsp. of flour mixture with walnuts; set aside.

Beat egg until light and fluffy. Add butter, milk and undrained pineapple. Combine with dry ingredients; stir to moisten. Stir in walnuts. Turn batter in greased 8 × 4 × 3″ ovenproof glass loaf pan.

Bake in moderate oven (350°) 50 minutes or until bread tests done. Remove from pan. Cool on rack. Wrap in aluminum foil. Let stand overnight. (Loaf slices better after standing.) Makes 1 loaf.

HOLIDAY DATE LOAF

Richly studded with all kinds of holiday ingredients . . . a beauty

2 c. sifted flour
2 tsp. baking powder
½ tsp. salt
1 c. chopped dates
½ c. raisins
12 maraschino cherries,
  quartered

¼ c. chopped walnuts
2 tsp. grated lemon rind
¼ c. butter or regular
  margarine
1 c. brown sugar, firmly packed
2 eggs
1 c. milk

Sift together flour, baking powder and salt. Mix ¼ c. flour mixture with dates, raisins, cherries, walnuts and lemon rind; set aside.

Cream together butter and brown sugar until light and fluffy. Add eggs, one at a time, beating well after each addition.

Add dry ingredients alternately to creamed mixture with milk, beating well after each addition. Stir in fruit-nut mixture. Turn batter into 2 greased 9 × 5 × 3″ loaf pans.

Bake in moderate oven (350°) 1 hour or until breads test done. Remove from pans. Cool on racks. Makes 2 loaves.

PINEAPPLE / PECAN LOAF

A light golden beauty that is so good to serve during the holidays

2 c. sifted flour
1 tsp. baking soda
¾ tsp. salt
½ c. brown sugar, firmly
  packed
¼ c. shortening
1 egg

⅓ c. frozen orange juice
  concentrate, thawed
3 tblsp. water
1 (8½ oz.) can crushed
  pineapple
1 tsp. vanilla
½ c. chopped pecans

Sift together flour, baking soda and salt.

Cream brown sugar and shortening until light and fluffy. Add egg; beat well.

Combine orange concentrate and water. Add alternately with dry ingredients to the creamed mixture, stirring well after each addition.

Stir in undrained crushed pineapple, vanilla and chopped nuts. Pour into a greased 9 × 5 × 3″ loaf pan.

Bake in moderate oven (350°) 40 to 50 minutes. Remove from pan immediately. Cool on rack. Makes 1 loaf.

SURPRISE DATE BREAD

Freeze several loaves for the busy holiday season ahead

¾ c. boiling water	½ c. sugar
½ lb. dates, finely chopped	1 egg, well beaten
1¾ c. sifted flour	1 c. shredded Cheddar cheese
1 tsp. baking soda	1 tsp. vanilla
½ tsp. salt	¾ c. chopped walnuts

Pour water over dates; let stand for 5 minutes.

Sift together flour, baking soda, salt and sugar into a bowl. Add date mixture, egg, cheese, vanilla and nuts; mix well. Pour into greased 9 × 5 × 3″ loaf pan.

Bake in moderate oven (350°) 45 to 50 minutes. Remove from pan. Cool on rack. Makes 1 loaf.

QUICK BREADS AND COFFEE CAKES

Farm cooks know that if you mix a quick bread or sweet coffee cake to serve with an everyday meal, that meal suddenly becomes special. They also have a great collection of quickies to whisk together for a neighborly coffee break or to surprise hungry men in the field at midafternoon snack time.

GRAHAM NUT BREAD

A lovely loaf with a nut-like flavor, velvety texture . . . keeps well

1¼ c. sifted flour	1 c. brown sugar, firmly packed
1 c. graham flour	1 egg
1 tsp. baking soda	1 c. buttermilk
½ tsp. salt	½ c. chopped walnuts
½ c. shortening	

Stir together flour, graham flour, baking soda and salt.

Cream together shortening and brown sugar until light and fluffy. Add egg; beat well.

Add dry ingredients alternately with buttermilk, beating well after each addition. Stir in walnuts. Turn batter into greased 9 × 5 × 3" loaf pan.

Bake in moderate oven (350°) 45 minutes or until bread tests done. Remove from pan. Cool on rack. Makes 1 loaf.

CORN BISCUIT STICKS

Stirred together in minutes, this bread makes a simple meal special

1 (8¾ oz.) can whole kernel corn	2½ c. biscuit mix
1 tblsp. finely chopped onion	1½ tblsp. chopped pimientos
1 tblsp. butter or regular margarine	¼ c. melted butter or regular margarine

Place corn in blender. Blend for a few seconds until smooth.

Sauté onion in 1 tblsp. melted butter in skillet until tender (do not brown).

Combine corn, onion, biscuit mix and pimientos; stir just until moistened. (Dough will be soft.) Knead mixture lightly on floured surface (about 10 times). Roll into a 10 × 6" rectangle. Cut into 3 × 1" strips. Coat strips in ¼ c. melted butter. Arrange on greased baking sheet or 15½ × 10½ × 1" jelly roll pan.

Bake in very hot oven (450°) 10 to 12 minutes or until golden. Makes 20 sticks.

QUICK BREAKFAST LOAF

Looks like corn bread with its yellow hue . . . tastes different

1 c. quick farina	1 egg, beaten
1 c. sifted flour	¼ c. cooking oil
¼ c. sugar	1 c. milk
4 tsp. baking powder	5 drops yellow food color
¼ tsp. salt	

Stir together farina, flour, sugar, baking powder and salt in bowl. Combine egg, oil and milk. Add to dry ingredients; stir just until moistened. Stir in yellow food color. Turn batter into greased 8½ × 4½ × 2½" loaf pan.

Bake in hot oven (425°) 25 minutes or until golden brown. Remove from pan. Cool on rack. Makes 1 loaf.

CINNAMON BRUNCH COFFEE CAKE

Cream cheese gives this an extra-velvety texture and taste

2 c. sifted flour	2 eggs
1 tsp. baking powder	1 tsp. vanilla
½ tsp. baking soda	⅓ c. milk
¼ tsp. salt	1 c. brown sugar, firmly packed
½ c. butter or regular margarine	½ c. sifted flour
1 (8 oz.) pkg. cream cheese	3 tblsp. softened butter or regular margarine
1¼ c. sugar	1 tsp. ground cinnamon

Sift together 2 c. flour, baking powder, baking soda and salt.

Cream together ½ c. butter, cream cheese and sugar until light and fluffy. Add eggs, one at a time, beating well after each addition. Beat in vanilla.

Add dry ingredients alternately with milk, beating well after each addition. Spread batter in greased and floured 13 × 9 × 2" cake pan.

Combine brown sugar, ½ c. flour, 3 tblsp. butter and cinnamon. Sprinkle over batter.

Bake in moderate oven (350°) 30 to 35 minutes or until done. Serve warm or cold. Makes 16 servings.

DELICIOUS HEALTH BREAD

A real stick-to-the-ribs kind of bread that men like for field lunches

1 c. raisins	1 c. quick-cooking rolled oats
1 c. boiling water	1 c. whole bran cereal
1 egg	1 tsp. baking soda
¾ c. sugar	1 c. buttermilk
½ tsp. salt	2 tblsp. wheat germ
1 c. graham flour	

Simmer raisins in boiling water for 5 minutes. Cool well.

Beat together egg, sugar and salt. Add graham flour, oats, bran cereal, baking soda and buttermilk. Stir just until mixture is moistened. Stir in raisins and liquid. Pour batter into 2 greased 8½ ×4½ × 2½″ loaf pans. Sprinkle tops with wheat germ.

Bake in moderate oven (350°) 1 hour or until breads test done. Remove from pans. Cool on racks. Makes 2 loaves.

QUICK ALMOND COFFEE CAKE

Bake and freeze several for the holidays . . . give some as gifts

2½ c. sifted cake flour	1 tsp. vanilla
1 tsp. baking powder	½ c. finely chopped almonds
½ tsp. baking soda	¼ c. brown sugar, firmly
½ c. butter or regular	packed
margarine	2 tblsp. butter
½ c. shortening	1 tsp. grated orange rind
1¼ c. sugar	½ tsp. ground cinnamon
3 eggs	1 tblsp. sugar
1 c. dairy sour cream	⅛ tsp. ground cinnamon

Sift together cake flour, baking powder and baking soda.

Cream together ½ c. butter, shortening and 1¼ c. sugar until light and fluffy. Add eggs, one at a time, beating well after each addition. Beat in sour cream and vanilla.

Gradually add dry ingredients; blend well.

Combine almonds, brown sugar, 2 tblsp. butter, orange rind and ½ tsp. cinnamon. Pour a third of the batter into greased 9″ tube pan. Top with half of almond mixture. Spread with another third of batter and top with remaining almond mixture. Spread remaining batter on top. Sprinkle with combined 1 tblsp. sugar and ⅛ tsp. cinnamon.

Bake in moderate oven (350°) 1 hour or until done. Cool for 15 minutes. Remove from pan. Serve warm. Makes 10 servings.

QUICK BREAD ROLLS

An old-fashioned favorite that is deliciously different and easy to fix

4 c. stale bread cubes (1")	3 tsp. baking powder
1¾ c. milk	2 tblsp. sugar
3 eggs, separated	¼ tsp. salt
2 tblsp. melted butter or regular margarine	½ c. dry bread crumbs
½ tsp. vanilla	¼ c. sugar
1 c. sifted flour	½ tsp. ground cinnamon

Soak bread cubes in milk for 15 minutes. Beat until smooth. Add egg yolks, butter and vanilla; beat until blended.

Sift together flour, baking powder, 2 tblsp. sugar and salt. Add to bread mixture; beat well.

Beat egg whites until stiff. Fold into batter.

Spoon batter into greased 2½" muffin-pan cups, filling two-thirds full. Combine bread crumbs, ¼ c. sugar and cinnamon. Sprinkle over tops.

Bake in hot oven (425°) 20 minutes or until done. Makes 18.

SPICY SUGAR LOAF

Keep all the ingredients for this on hand . . . so easy to make

1 (1 lb.) loaf white bread	1 tsp. ground cinnamon
¼ c. butter or regular margarine	½ c. sifted confectioners sugar
⅔ c. sugar	1½ to 2 tblsp. light cream
	2 tblsp. finely chopped nuts

Spread bread slices on one side with softened butter; sprinkle with combined sugar and cinnamon. Put back in shape of loaf and tie with string. Wrap loaf securely in foil.

Heat in moderate oven (375°) 20 to 25 minutes. Unwrap, cut and remove string.

Make glaze with confectioners sugar and cream; pour glaze over top and sprinkle with nuts. Serve piping hot. Makes 10 to 12 servings.

ORANGE SUGAR RING

A fast-fix hot bread that you'll want to make again and again

2 (8 oz.) pkgs. refrigerator
  biscuits
¼ c. melted butter or regular
  margarine
2 tblsp. orange juice

½ c. sugar
½ c. brown sugar, firmly
  packed
1 tsp. grated orange rind
¼ tsp. ground nutmeg

Separate biscuits. Combine butter and orange juice. Mix together sugars, orange rind and nutmeg. Dip biscuits in butter then sugar mixture. Stand upright in well-greased 1½ qt.-ring mold.

Bake in very hot oven (450°) 12 to 15 minutes. Turn out on plate. Makes 1 ring.

ALWAYS A HIT . . . HOT MUFFINS

Wonderful little gems to brighten a breakfast . . . take your pick of cranberry-swirled, spicy cinnamon, nutty wheat germ and others. Whatever recipe you decide to make, we think your family will say "Are these ever good!"

ORANGE DATE MUFFINS

A marvelous muffin that is easy to make when guests drop in

2 c. sifted flour
½ c. sugar
2½ tsp. baking powder
½ tsp. salt
½ c. chopped dates

1½ tsp. grated orange rind
1 egg, beaten
¾ c. milk
¼ c. melted butter or regular
  margarine

Sift together flour, sugar, baking powder and salt into bowl. Add dates and orange rind; coat with flour mixture.

Combine egg, milk and butter. Add to dry ingredients, stirring just enough to moisten.

Spoon batter into greased 2½" muffin-pan cups, filling two-thirds full.

Bake in hot oven (400°) 20 minutes or until done. Makes 16.

BACON 'N' ONION MUFFINS

There's just the right amount of bacon and onion in these muffins

½ lb. bacon, cut in 1" pieces	½ tsp. salt
¼ c. chopped onion	2 eggs, beaten
2¼ c. sifted flour	⅓ c. milk
2 tblsp. sugar	1 c. dairy sour cream
1 tblsp. baking powder	Sesame seeds
½ tsp. baking soda	

Fry bacon until crisp in skillet. Remove and drain on paper towels. Crumble.

Sauté onion in 1 tblsp. of bacon drippings until tender (do not brown). Set aside to cool.

Sift flour, sugar, baking powder, baking soda and salt into bowl.

Combine eggs, milk and sour cream. Add to dry ingredients, stirring just enough to moisten. Stir in bacon and onion.

Spoon batter into greased 2½" muffin-pan cups, filling two-thirds full. Sprinkle with sesame seeds.

Bake in moderate oven (375°) 18 to 20 minutes or until done. Makes 18.

CRANBERRY MUFFINS

A breakfast favorite of an Illinois family . . . piping hot muffins

2¼ c. sifted flour	¾ c. buttermilk
¼ c. sugar	¼ c. cooking oil
¾ tsp. baking soda	1 c. chopped cranberries
¼ tsp. salt	½ c. sugar
1 egg, beaten	

Sift together flour, ¼ c. sugar, baking soda and salt into a bowl.

Combine egg, buttermilk and oil. Add to dry ingredients, stirring just enough to moisten. Combine cranberries and ½ c. sugar; stir into batter.

Spoon batter into greased 2½" muffin-pan cups, filling two-thirds full.

Bake in hot oven (400°) 20 minutes or until done. Makes 12.

CINNAMON BRAN MUFFINS

Serve with lots of butter and orange marmalade at brunch

1 c. sifted flour
¼ c. sugar
2½ tsp. baking powder
½ tsp. salt
1½ c. bran flakes

1 c. milk
1 egg, beaten
¼ c. soft shortening
⅓ c. raisins
Sugar and cinnamon mixture

Sift together flour, sugar, baking powder and salt into a bowl.

Combine bran flakes, milk, egg and shortening. Add to dry ingredients, stirring just enough to moisten. Stir in raisins.

Spoon batter into greased 2½″ muffin-pan cups, filling two-thirds full. Sprinkle with sugar and cinnamon mixture.

Bake in hot oven (400°) 25 to 30 minutes or until done. Makes 12.

WHEAT GERM MOLASSES MUFFINS

Cinnamon-spiced wheat muffins that are tasty and good for you

1¾ c. sifted flour
1 c. toasted wheat germ
¼ c. sugar
1 tsp. salt
1 tsp. baking powder
½ tsp. baking soda

½ tsp. ground cinnamon
1 egg, beaten
½ c. milk
½ c. light molasses
¼ c. cooking oil

Combine flour, wheat germ, sugar, salt, baking powder, baking soda and cinnamon in a bowl.

Combine egg, milk, molasses and oil. Add to dry ingredients, stirring just enough to moisten.

Spoon batter into greased 2½″ muffin-pan cups, filling two-thirds full.

Bake in hot oven (400°) 15 to 18 minutes or until done. Makes 12.

SPECIAL CORNMEAL MUFFINS

Serve these corn muffins with big bowls of homemade chicken soup

1¼ c. sifted flour	1 egg, beaten
1 c. yellow cornmeal	1 c. milk
2 tblsp. sugar	¼ c. cooking oil
4 tsp. baking powder	1 tblsp. chopped pimientos
½ tsp. salt	1 tblsp. chopped green pepper

Sift together flour, cornmeal, sugar, baking powder and salt into a bowl.

Combine egg, milk and oil. Add to dry ingredients, stirring just until moistened. Stir in pimientos and green pepper.

Spoon batter into greased 2½″ muffin-pan cups, filling two-thirds full.

Bake in hot oven (425°) 20 to 25 minutes or until done. Makes 12.

DOWNRIGHT DELICIOUS DOUGHNUTS

The very finest doughnut recipes from farm women . . . every one so good that you simply must reach for a second one. All are light puffy beauties that you will be proud to serve.

RASPBERRY-FILLED BISMARCKS

Generously filled with raspberry jelly, these are outstanding

1 c. milk	¼ c. lukewarm water
½ c. sugar	2 eggs
⅓ c. shortening	5½ c. sifted flour
1½ tsp. salt	Raspberry jelly
1 pkg. active dry yeast	Sugar

Scald milk. Stir in sugar, shortening and salt. Cool to lukewarm.

Sprinkle yeast on lukewarm water; stir to dissolve. Add yeast, eggs and 2 c. flour to milk mixture. Beat with electric mixer at medium speed until smooth, for about 2 minutes, scraping bowl occasionally. Or beat with spoon until batter is smooth.

Gradually add enough remaining flour to make a soft dough that leaves the sides of the bowl. Turn onto lightly floured surface and knead until smooth and satiny, for about 8 to 10 minutes.

Place in lightly greased bowl; turn dough over to grease top. Cover and let rise in warm place until doubled, for about 1 to 1½ hours.

Roll dough on floured surface to ½" thick. Cut with floured 3" round cookie cutter. Place on waxed paper. Cover and let rise until doubled.

Fry a few doughnuts at a time in hot cooking oil (360°). Drain on absorbent paper. Cut a 2" slit in the side of each. Fill with raspberry jelly. Roll doughnuts in sugar. Makes 24 doughnuts.

GLAZED RAISED DOUGHNUTS

You'll have no trouble selling these at the next church bazaar

½ c. milk	½ c. lukewarm water
½ c. butter or regular	2 eggs
margarine	4 c. sifted flour
½ c. sugar	¾ tsp. ground nutmeg
1 tsp. salt	Vanilla Glaze (recipe follows)
2 pkgs. active dry yeast	

Scald milk. Stir in butter, sugar and salt. Cool to lukewarm.

Sprinkle yeast on lukewarm water; stir to dissolve. Add yeast, eggs, 2 c. flour and nutmeg to milk mixture. Beat with electric mixer at medium speed until smooth, for about 2 minutes, scraping bowl occasionally. Or beat with spoon until batter is smooth.

Gradually add remaining flour, blending well. (Dough will be soft.) Place in lightly greased bowl; turn dough over to grease top. Cover and let rise in warm place until doubled, for about 1 to 1½ hours.

Turn onto lightly floured surface and knead about 1 minute. Cover and let rest for 10 minutes. Roll out dough ¼" thick. Cut with floured doughnut cutter. Place on waxed paper. Cover and let rise until doubled, for about 45 minutes.

Fry a few doughnuts at a time in hot cooking oil (375°). Drain on absorbent paper. Coat warm doughnuts with Vanilla Glaze. Place on cooling rack to dry. Makes about 24 doughnuts.

Vanilla Glaze: Combine 2 c. sifted confectioners sugar, ¼ c. milk and 1 tsp. vanilla. Beat until smooth.

APPLESAUCE DOUGHNUTS

Serve with steaming cups of hot chocolate after the football game

4½ c. sifted flour	4 eggs
3 tsp. baking powder	1 c. sugar
1 tsp. ground cinnamon	1 c. brown sugar, firmly packed
1 tsp. ground nutmeg	3 tblsp. cooking oil
½ tsp. salt	1 tsp. vanilla
½ tsp. ground cloves	½ c. milk
1 tsp. baking soda	Sugar
1 (1 lb.) can applesauce (2 c.)	

Sift together flour, baking powder, cinnamon, nutmeg, salt and cloves. Set aside. Stir baking soda into applesauce.

Beat eggs well. Gradually add 1 c. sugar, brown sugar and oil, beating well. Beat in applesauce mixture and vanilla. Add dry ingredients alternately with milk, mixing well.

Drop by tablespoonfuls into hot oil (375°). Fry until golden brown. Drain on paper towels. Roll in sugar. Makes 5 dozen.

BUTTERMILK POTATO DOUGHNUTS

Sugar-dusted doughnut puffs spiced with nutmeg; men love them!

1½ c. hot unseasoned mashed potatoes	1 tsp. vanilla
	5½ c. sifted flour
⅓ c. melted butter or regular margarine	4 tsp. baking powder
	1½ tsp. baking soda
2 c. sugar	1 tsp. salt
3 eggs	1 tsp. ground nutmeg
1 c. buttermilk	Sugar

Combine potatoes, butter, 2 c. sugar, eggs, buttermilk and vanilla. Beat until well blended.

Sift together flour, baking powder, baking soda, salt and nutmeg. Gradually stir dry ingredients into potato mixture, blending well after each addition. Chill for 1 hour.

Drop rounded teaspoonfuls of dough into hot oil (360°). Brown on one side. Turn over and brown on other side. Drain on paper towels. Roll in sugar. Makes about 6 dozen.

GLAZED POTATO DOUGHNUTS

So good that you will find it hard to eat just one puffy doughnut

1 c. milk	¾ c. mashed potatoes
¼ c. shortening	2 eggs, beaten
¼ c. sugar	5 to 6 c. sifted flour
1 tsp. salt	1 lb. confectioners sugar
1 pkg. active dry yeast	6 tblsp. water
¼ c. lukewarm water	1 tblsp. vanilla

Scald milk. Stir in shortening, sugar and salt. Cool to lukewarm.

Sprinkle yeast on lukewarm water; stir to dissolve. Add yeast, mashed potatoes, eggs and 2 c. flour to milk mixture. Beat with electric mixer at medium speed until smooth, for about 2 minutes, scraping occasionally. Or beat with spoon until batter is smooth.

Gradually add enough remaining flour to make a soft dough that leaves the sides of the bowl. Turn onto lightly floured surface and knead until smooth and satiny, for about 8 to 10 minutes.

Place in lightly greased bowl; turn dough over to grease top. Cover and let rise in warm place until doubled, for about 1 to 1½ hours.

Roll dough to ½" thick. Cut with floured 3" doughnut cutter. Place on waxed paper. Cover and let rise until doubled.

Meanwhile, stir together confectioners sugar, water and vanilla. Stir until smooth. (Mixture will look like very thick cream.)

Fry a few doughnuts at a time in hot cooking oil (375°). Drain on absorbent paper. Drop hot doughnuts into glaze. Place on cooling rack until glaze is set. Makes about 3½ dozen.

GERMAN TWISTS

Downright delicious twists that will please the whole family

½ c. boiling water	¼ c. lukewarm water
½ c. shortening	½ c. evaporated milk
⅓ c. sugar	2 eggs, beaten
1 tsp. salt	5 to 6 c. sifted flour
1½ pkgs. active dry yeast	Sugar

Combine ½ c. boiling water, shortening, sugar and salt. Cool to lukewarm.

Sprinkle yeast on ¼ c. lukewarm water; stir to dissolve. Add yeast, evaporated milk, eggs and 2 c. flour to water mixture. Beat with electric mixer at medium speed until smooth, for about 2 minutes, scraping occasionally. Or beat with spoon until batter is smooth.

Gradually add enough remaining flour to make a soft dough that leaves the sides of the bowl. Turn onto lightly floured surface. Knead until smooth and satiny (about 7 minutes).

Place in lightly greased bowl; turn over to grease top. Cover. Let rise in a warm place until doubled, for about 1 to 1½ hours.

Turn dough onto floured surface. Roll to ½" thickness; cut into 8 × ½" strips. Place fingers on ends of each strip and gently roll back and forth to form evenly shaped 12" sticks. Fold in half; cross ends of stick over each other to form twist. Pinch to secure ends well. Cover; let rise until doubled (about 30 minutes).

Fry in deep hot cooking oil (375°). Drain on absorbent paper. Roll in sugar. Makes about 3 dozen.

LET'S HAVE PANCAKES

The always popular hot cake can be served in almost any situation. We have some that are luscious for dessert, as well as for supper. Next time you're wondering what to have, get out the griddle and make a batch of pancakes. For a change from the usual syrup, pass an assortment of homemade jams and jellies.

OATMEAL GRIDDLE CAKES

Real favorites with men . . . next morning pop in the toaster!

2 c. old-fashioned rolled oats	1 tsp. baking soda
2¾ c. sour milk	2 tblsp. water
1½ c. unsifted flour	2 eggs, beaten
2 tblsp. sugar	2 tblsp. melted butter or regular
1 tsp. baking powder	margarine
1 tsp. salt	

Soak oats in sour milk overnight.

Sift together flour, sugar, baking powder and salt into a bowl.

Dissolve baking soda in water.

Combine dry ingredients and oat mixture. Add eggs, butter and baking soda mixture; beat until smooth.

Bake on lightly greased hot griddle, using ¼ c. batter for each. Bake until top is bubbly and edges dry; turn and brown other side. Makes 18 (4″) pancakes.

WHOLE WHEAT PANCAKES

Serve these for Sunday night supper with bacon and cranberry sauce

1¾ c. whole wheat flour	1¾ c. milk
4 tsp. baking powder	2 tblsp. melted butter or
1 tsp. sugar	regular margarine
½ tsp. salt	½ tsp. vanilla
2 eggs, beaten	

Combine wheat flour, baking powder, sugar and salt in a bowl.

Combine eggs, milk, butter and vanilla; beat until smooth. Add to flour; stirring only until smooth.

Bake on lightly greased hot griddle, using ¼ c. batter for each. Bake until top is bubbly and edges dry; turn and brown other side. Makes 15 (4″) pancakes.

GOLDEN DELIGHT PANCAKES

A glorious dessert with cherry pie filling and country whipped cream

1 c. cream-style cottage cheese	¼ c. cooking oil
6 eggs	¼ c. milk
½ c. sifted flour	½ tsp. vanilla
¼ tsp. salt	

Put all ingredients into a blender. Cover. Blend at high speed for 1 minute, stopping to stir down once.

Bake on lightly greased hot griddle, using ¼ c. batter for each. Bake until top is bubbly and edges dry; turn and brown other side. Makes 20 (4″) pancakes.

SPICY COUNTRY PANCAKES

These are delicious with hot spicy applesauce or fried apple rings

1¾ c. milk
¼ c. brown sugar, firmly
   packed
1½ tsp. salt
¼ c. cooking oil
1 pkg. active dry yeast

¼ c. lukewarm water
2 eggs, beaten
2 c. sifted flour
1 tsp. ground cinnamon
½ tsp. ground nutmeg

Scald milk; add brown sugar, salt and oil. Cool to lukewarm.

Sprinkle yeast on lukewarm water; stir to dissolve. Add to milk with eggs; mix well.

Sift together flour, cinnamon and nutmeg. Combine with liquid ingredients; beat until smooth.

Cover and let stand for 1 hour in a warm place. The batter will be light and bubbly. Use at once or refrigerate. (Do not refrigerate longer than 24 hours.)

Stir down batter. Bake on lightly greased hot griddle, using ¼ c. batter for each. Bake until top is bubbly and edges dry; turn and brown other side. Makes 24 (4") pancakes.

Chapter 7

GREAT CAKES TO SERVE
FAMILY AND FRIENDS

This is a collection of irresistible cakes. Even the strictest dieter will say "Well, just a little piece, please."

You will find modern quick and easy cakes as well as towering beauties that have passed the test of three generations, and blue-ribbon reputation winners from State Fairs. We have deep-dark delicious fudge cakes for the chocolate fans, velvet-textured pound cakes, sturdy raisin-studded lunch box surprises and other everyday warm-from-the-oven varieties.

In Ohio we found a moist spicy Walnut Applesauce Cake crammed with raisins and walnuts—so good on a crisp fall day with a glass of apple cider. A Colorado family enjoys Tangy Cranberry Squares with hot butter sauce for Christmas dinner. Two light-as-air chiffons —Banana Chiffon and Cocoa Chiffon—are just right to serve at your next company dinner.

We have batches of cupcakes for the lunch box brigade. The youngsters in the family will feel extra special when they find a Creole Cupcake, or Black Walnut Cupcake in their lunch. The young ones especially will like the crunchy Special Peanut Cake and the No-Fail Cocoa Cream Cake—so good to serve with cold milk after school when everyone is hungry.

Pass big squares of Hot Milk Sponge Cake when friends drop in unexpectedly. No frosting is necessary . . . just a dusting of confectioners sugar (though it is delicious with a spoonful of sugared fresh strawberries or peaches).

When you want to present something spectacular to your guests, bring on Coffee Angel Roll or Pineapple Cream Roll . . . easy, but oh so elegant!

BLUE RIBBON POUND CAKES

A choice selection of moist rich pound cakes, buttery as can be— especially the Sour Cream Pound Cake. When a Maryland home-maker serves this for dessert, her youngsters say "Oh goody, that wonderful cake." Friends say "I would love the recipe." Cranberry/ Nut Pound Cake is a delicious holiday gift for someone very special.

SOUR CREAM POUND CAKE

"My children call this that wonderful cake," says a Maryland woman

3 c. sifted flour	6 eggs
1 tsp. salt	1 tsp. vanilla
¼ tsp. baking soda	1 tsp. almond extract
1 c. butter	1 c. dairy sour cream
3 c. sugar	

Sift together flour, salt and baking soda.

Cream together butter and sugar until light and fluffy. Add eggs, one at a time, beating well after each addition. Add vanilla and al-mond extract. (Total beating time: 10 minutes.)

Add dry ingredients alternately with sour cream, beating well after each addition. Pour batter into greased 10″ bundt pan.

Bake in slow oven (325°) 1 hour or until cake tests done. Cool for 10 minutes. Remove from pan. Cool on rack. Dust with confec-tioners sugar before serving, if you wish. Makes 12 servings.

CRANBERRY / NUT POUND CAKE

A lovely gift cake, especially when baked in a bundt pan

2¼ c. sifted flour	4 eggs
½ tsp. baking powder	1 tblsp. vanilla
¼ tsp. salt	½ c. evaporated milk
1 c. butter	1 c. chopped raw cranberries
2 c. sugar	1 c. chopped walnuts

Sift together flour, baking powder and salt.

Cream together butter and sugar until light and fluffy. Add eggs, one at a time, beating well after each addition. Add vanilla. (Total beating time: 10 minutes.)

Add dry ingredients alternately with evaporated milk, beating well after each addition. Stir in cranberries and walnuts. Pour batter into greased and floured 10″ tube pan.

Bake in slow oven (325°) 1 hour 10 minutes or until cake tests done. Cool for 10 minutes. Remove from pan. Cool on rack. Dust with confectioners sugar, if you wish. Makes 12 servings.

COCONUT POUND CAKE

Top cake with fresh strawberries and a scoop of vanilla ice cream

3 c. sifted flour	1 tsp. lemon extract
¼ tsp. salt	½ tsp. vanilla
1 c. butter	1 c. milk
2 c. sugar	1 (3½ oz.) can flaked coconut
5 eggs	(1⅓ c.)

Sift together flour and salt.

Cream together butter and sugar until light and fluffy. Add eggs, one at a time, beating well after each addition. Add lemon extract and vanilla. (Total beating time: 10 minutes.)

Add dry ingredients alternately with milk, beating well after each addition. Stir in coconut. Pour batter into greased and floured 10″ tube pan.

Bake in slow oven (325°) 1 hour 30 minutes or until cake tests done. Cool for 10 minutes. Remove from pan. Cool on rack. Makes 12 servings.

BASIC POUND CAKE

A buttery, rich cake that goes well with fresh sliced fruit and cream

3 c. sifted flour	2 c. sugar
1 tsp. baking powder	4 eggs
1 tsp. salt	2 tsp. vanilla
½ tsp. baking soda	1 c. buttermilk
1 c. butter	

Sift together flour, baking powder, salt and baking soda.

Cream together butter and sugar until light and fluffy. Add eggs, one at a time, beating well after each addition. Add vanilla. (Total beating time: 10 minutes.)

Add dry ingredients alternately with buttermilk, beating well after each addition. Pour batter into greased 10″ tube pan.

Bake in slow oven (325°) 1 hour or until cake tests done. Cool for 10 minutes. Remove from pan. Cool on rack. Makes 12 servings.

CHOCOLATE AND FUDGE FAVORITES

For all those folks that think a cake isn't a cake unless it's chocolate, we have a moist, tender-crumbed collection of the best-ever chocolate cakes.

Some are layers high while others bake to perfection in a square or oblong pan and are good with or without frosting. Aunt Hazel's Chocolate Cake, for instance, should be eaten hot-from-the-oven with butter, an Iowa farm woman recommends. Exquisite Chocolate Cake bakes in three layers and is filled with coffee-flavored whipped cream.

AUNT HAZEL'S CHOCOLATE CAKE

This luscious cake won a Blue Ribbon at the Iowa State Fair

2 c. sifted cake flour	3 eggs, separated
½ c. cocoa	1 tsp. vanilla
½ tsp. salt	1 tsp. baking soda
½ c. butter or regular	1 tblsp. hot water
margarine	1 c. cold water
1¾ c. sugar	

Sift together flour, cocoa and salt.

Cream together butter and sugar until light and fluffy. Beat in egg yolks and vanilla; beat well.

Dissolve baking soda in 1 tblsp. hot water. Stir into creamed mixture.

Add dry ingredients alternately with 1 c. cold water, beating well after each addition.

Beat egg whites until stiff but not dry. Fold into cake batter. Pour batter into greased 13 × 9 × 2″ cake pan.

Bake in moderate oven (350°) 30 minutes or until cake tests done. Cool in pan on rack. Frost with your favorite frosting. Makes 16 servings.

EXQUISITE CHOCOLATE CAKE

"A family heirloom cake recipe that is always praised by my friends"

2¼ c. sifted cake flour
2 tsp. baking soda
½ tsp. salt
½ c. butter or regular
    margarine
2½ c. brown sugar, firmly
    packed
3 eggs

3 (1 oz.) squares unsweetened
    chocolate, melted
2 tsp. vanilla
½ c. sour milk
1 c. boiling water
Coffee Cream Topping (recipe
    follows)

Sift together flour, baking soda and salt.

Cream together butter and brown sugar until light and fluffy. Add eggs, one at a time, beating well after each addition. Blend in cooled chocolate and vanilla.

Add dry ingredients alternately with sour milk, beating well after each addition. Gradually beat in water. (Batter will be thin.) Pour batter into 3 greased 8″ round cake pans.

Bake in moderate oven (375°) 30 minutes or until cakes test done. Cool for 10 minutes. Remove from pans. Cool on racks. Frost between layers and on top with Coffee Cream Topping. Decorate with chocolate curls, if you wish. Makes 12 servings.

Coffee Cream Topping: Combine 1½ c. heavy cream, 1½ tblsp. instant coffee powder, 1½ tblsp. sugar and 1 tsp. vanilla in medium bowl. Beat until thick enough to spread.

NO-FAIL COCOA CREAM CAKE

Dust with confectioners sugar; serve slices with scoops of ice cream

4 eggs
2 c. heavy cream
2 tsp. vanilla
2½ c. sifted flour

2 c. sugar
½ c. cocoa
3 tsp. baking powder
½ tsp. salt

Beat eggs thoroughly in a large mixing bowl (about 5 minutes). Gradually beat in cream and vanilla, mixing well.

Sift together flour, sugar, cocoa, baking powder and salt. Add to egg mixture; beat until smooth. Pour batter into 2 greased $9 \times 5 \times 3''$ loaf pans.

Bake in moderate oven (350°) 45 minutes or until cakes test done. Cool for 10 minutes. Remove from pans. Cool on racks. Makes 16 servings.

MOTHER'S BEST FUDGE CAKE

The perfect birthday cake for the chocolate fans in your family

3 (1 oz.) squares unsweetened
  chocolate, melted
½ c. milk
1 egg
⅔ c. sugar
2 c. sifted cake flour
1 tsp. baking soda
¼ tsp. salt

½ c. shortening
1 c. sugar
2 eggs
1 tsp. vanilla
⅔ c. milk
Chocolate Satin Frosting (recipe
  follows)

Combine chocolate, ½ c. milk, 1 egg and ⅔ c. sugar in a small heavy saucepan. Cook over low heat, stirring constantly, until thickened. Cool thoroughly.

Sift together flour, baking soda and salt 3 times.

Cream together shortening and 1 c. sugar until light and fluffy. Add eggs, one at a time, beating well after each addition. Beat in vanilla and chocolate mixture.

Add dry ingredients alternately with ⅔ c. milk, beating well after each addition. Pour batter into 2 waxed-paper-lined 9″ layer cake pans.

Bake in moderate oven (350°) 30 to 35 minutes or until cakes test done. Cool in pans on rack. Frost with Chocolate Satin Frosting. Makes 12 servings.

Chocolate Satin Frosting: Melt 6 (1 oz.) squares unsweetened chocolate in 2-qt. heavy saucepan. Gradually blend in 3 c. sifted confectioners sugar and 4 tblsp. hot water. Add 2 eggs, beating well. Beat in ½ c. butter, a tablespoon at a time, beating well after each addition. Add 2 tsp. vanilla. (Frosting will be thin.) Place in a bowl of iced water and beat until of spreading consistency.

EXTRA FANCY CAKES

Your reputation will soar when you serve these delicate, gossamer-light cakes. They will look spectacular for the most elegant party. Some of these cakes have won both blue and purple fair ribbons and when you taste them you'll know why!

COCOA CHIFFON CAKE

This elegant cake will dazzle your friends at your next special occasion

½ c. cocoa	1 tsp. salt
¾ c. boiling water	½ c. cooking oil
1¾ c. sifted cake flour	8 eggs, separated
1¾ c. sugar	2 tsp. vanilla
1½ tsp. baking soda	½ tsp. cream of tartar

Mix cocoa and boiling water.

Sift together flour, sugar, baking soda and salt into a large mixing bowl. Make a well in the center. Add oil, egg yolks, vanilla and cocoa mixture; beat well (about 3 minutes).

Beat egg whites and cream of tartar until stiff. Fold into batter. Pour batter into ungreased 10″ tube pan. Cut through batter with spatula.

Bake in slow oven (325°) 55 minutes. Increase temperature to moderate oven (350°); bake 10 minutes or until cake tests done. Invert cake to cool.

If you wish, frost with your favorite chocolate frosting. Decorate edges with a chocolate glaze made by melting together 2 (1 oz.) squares unsweetened chocolate and 2 tsp. butter or regular margarine over low heat. Cool slightly. Spoon along edge of frosted cake allowing chocolate to drip down sides. Makes 12 servings.

BANANA CHIFFON CAKE

Frost with your favorite butter cream icing for a company dessert

2 c. sifted cake flour
1 c. sugar
1 tsp. baking powder
1 tsp. baking soda
1 tsp. salt
⅓ c. cooking oil
1 c. mashed bananas

⅓ c. buttermilk
1 tsp. vanilla
2 eggs, separated
⅓ c. buttermilk
⅓ c. sugar
½ c. chopped walnuts

Sift together flour, 1 c. sugar, baking powder, baking soda and salt into large mixing bowl. Make a well in the center. Pour in oil, bananas, ⅓ c. buttermilk and vanilla. Beat for 1 minute, mixing well. Add egg yolks and ⅓ c. buttermilk; beat for 1 minute.

Beat egg whites until frothy. Gradually beat in ⅓ c. sugar. Beat until stiff peaks form. Fold into batter. Fold in walnuts. Pour batter into ungreased 9" tube pan.

Bake in slow oven (325°) 55 minutes or until cake tests done. Invert cake to cool. Makes 8 servings.

PINEAPPLE CREAM ROLL

"One of Grandmother's specialties that has won many local prizes"

¾ c. sifted cake flour
¾ tsp. baking powder
¼ tsp. salt
4 eggs
¾ c. sugar

1 tsp. vanilla
Confectioners sugar
Pineapple Cream Filling (recipe
    follows)

Sift together flour, baking powder and salt.

Beat eggs until light and lemon-colored (about 10 minutes). Gradually add sugar, beating well after each addition. Add vanilla.

Fold in dry ingredients. Spread batter in waxed-paper-lined 15½ × 10½ × 1" jelly roll pan.

Bake in moderate oven (375°) 13 minutes or until cake tests done. Turn out on dish towel dusted with confectioners sugar. Roll up, starting at long side. Cool for 10 minutes.

Unroll cake and spread with Pineapple Cream Filling to within ½″ of edges. Start rolling up cake from long end. Cool thoroughly. Refrigerate until serving time. Makes 8 to 10 servings.

Pineapple Cream Filling: Combine ½ c. sugar, 2 tblsp. cornstarch, 2 tblsp. flour and ¼ tsp. salt in small saucepan. Gradually stir in 2 c. milk. Cook, stirring constantly, until mixture thickens. Mix some of the hot mixture with 2 egg yolks. Then stir egg mixture into hot mixture. Cook for 1 minute. Add 1 (8½ oz.) can crushed pineapple, drained; 8 maraschino cherries, quartered; and 1 tsp. vanilla. Cool well.

COFFEE ANGEL ROLL

Also delicious filled with cooled vanilla pudding and pie filling

1¼ c. egg whites (10 to 12)	½ c. sugar
1¼ tsp. cream of tartar	1 tblsp. instant coffee powder
½ tsp. salt	Confectioners sugar
¾ c. sugar	1 c. heavy cream
1 tsp. vanilla	2 tblsp. sugar
1 c. sifted cake flour	1 tsp. vanilla

Combine egg whites, cream of tartar and salt in a large mixing bowl. Beat until foamy. Add ¾ c. sugar gradually, 2 tblsp. at a time, until stiff peaks form. Add vanilla.

Sift together flour, ½ c. sugar and coffee 3 times. Fold dry ingredients into beaten egg whites in four additions. Spread batter in ungreased 15½ × 10½ × 1″ jelly roll pan.

Bake in moderate oven (350°) 20 minutes or until cake tests done. Turn out on dish towel dusted with confectioners sugar. Roll up starting at long side. Cool for 10 minutes.

Whip cream until it begins to thicken. Slowly beat in 2 tblsp. sugar and vanilla. Beat until mixture is stiff. Unroll cake and spread with whipped cream to within ½″ of edges. Start rolling up cake from long end. Cool thoroughly. Refrigerate until serving time. Makes 12 to 16 servings.

A medley of main dishes that are easy on the budget. Clockwise from top: *Corn-meal/Bean Squares* (page 26), *Lima Beans au Gratin* (page 83), *Sweet and Sour Baked Beans* (page 55) and hearty *Meatball and Lentil Soup* (page 250).

Rich and spicy *Pumpkin Pie Squares* (page 197) are a perfect choice to serve for dessert after a hearty holiday meal. Topped with soft drifts of whipped cream and pecan halves, they provide just the right amount of sweetness.

Our selection of dishes from great country cooks includes: enticing *Amish Vanilla Pie* (page 176), hearty *Green Bean Soup* (page 251), succulent and sweet *Three-Fruit Jam* (page 239) and glazed *Cinnamon Swirl Bread* (page 122).

Welcome spring with tempting rhubarb and strawberry dishes: crumb-topped *Rhubarb Surprise Pie* (page 174), tart and sparkling *Rosy Spring Salad* (page 95) and *Elegant Strawberry Torte* (page 219) wreathed with strawberries.

PICNIC OR LUNCH BOX CAKES

All these cakes rate high with both men and children. Good snacking cakes with a glass of milk or mug of cocoa. Or for family dessert, dress up these cakes with a scoop of ice cream or whipped cream and a sprinkling of nuts. They are also the hearty variety that travel well.

MOCHA RAISIN CAKE

No need to frost this cake . . . just sprinkle with confectioners sugar

2 c. sifted flour	1 c. brown sugar, firmly packed
½ c. cocoa	½ c. sugar
1 tsp. baking soda	2 eggs
1 tsp. ground cinnamon	1 c. cold coffee
¼ tsp. salt	1 c. raisins
¾ c. shortening	

Sift together flour, cocoa, baking soda, cinnamon and salt.

Cream together shortening and sugars until light and fluffy. Add eggs, one at a time, beating well after each addition.

Add dry ingredients alternately with coffee, beating well after each addition. Stir in raisins. Spread batter in greased 13 × 9 × 2″ cake pan.

Bake in moderate oven (350°) 40 to 45 minutes or until cake tests done. Cool in pan on rack. Makes 16 servings.

LUSCIOUS BLUEBERRY CAKE

A lovely complement for your favorite homemade vanilla ice cream

3 c. sifted flour	⅔ c. milk
2 tsp. baking powder	½ c. sugar
½ tsp. salt	3 c. blueberries, fresh, frozen
1 c. shortening	or canned and drained
1½ c. sugar	1 tblsp. flour
4 eggs, separated	Confectioners sugar
2 tsp. vanilla	

Sift together 3 c. flour, baking powder and salt.

Cream together shortening and 1½ c. sugar until light and fluffy. Add egg yolks and vanilla; blend well.

Add dry ingredients alternately with milk, beating well after each addition.

Beat egg whites until stiff. Gradually beat in ½ c. sugar. Fold into batter. Combine blueberries and 1 tblsp. flour. Fold into batter. Pour batter into greased 13 × 9 × 2″ cake pan.

Bake in moderate oven (350°) 50 minutes or until cake tests done. Cool in pan on rack. Sprinkle with confectioners sugar. Makes 16 servings.

CINNAMON APPLE CAKE

A first-prize winner in a regional apple baking contest in Nebraska

2 c. sifted flour	2 eggs
2 c. sugar	1 c. cooking oil
2 tsp. ground cinnamon	1 tsp. vanilla
1 tsp. baking soda	4 c. chopped, pared apples
¼ tsp. salt	½ c. chopped walnuts

Sift together flour, sugar, cinnamon, baking soda and salt.

Beat eggs and oil until light and foamy. Add vanilla. Gradually blend in dry ingredients. Stir in apples and walnuts. Pour batter into greased 13 × 9 × 2″ cake pan.

Bake in moderate oven (350°) 1 hour or until cake tests done. Cool in pan on rack. Dust with confectioners sugar, if you wish. Makes 16 servings.

SHEILA'S APPLE CAKE

"My family can't wait for this to cool," a Connecticut woman says

2 c. sifted flour	2 eggs
1¼ c. sugar	1 tblsp. sugar
2½ tsp. baking powder	1 tblsp. ground cinnamon
1 tsp. salt	3 c. sliced, pared apples
⅓ c. shortening	Vanilla Pudding Sauce (recipe
¾ c. milk	follows)
1 tsp. vanilla	

Sift together flour, 1¼ c. sugar, baking powder and salt into a large mixing bowl. Add shortening, milk and vanilla; beat thoroughly (about 3 minutes). Add eggs, one at a time, beating well after each addition.

Combine 1 tblsp. sugar and cinnamon. Pour half the batter into greased 13 × 9 × 2″ cake pan. Cover with apples and half the sugar/cinnamon mixture. Spread remaining batter on top. Sprinkle with remaining sugar/cinnamon mixture.

Bake in moderate oven (350°) 40 minutes or until cake tests done. Cool slightly in pan on rack. Cut into squares. Serve warm with Vanilla Pudding Sauce. Makes 16 servings.

Vanilla Pudding Sauce: Combine 1 (3¼ oz.) pkg. vanilla pudding and pie filling and 2¾ c. milk in a medium saucepan. Bring mixture to a boil, stirring constantly.

FRESH APPLE CAKE

This dessert can also double as a breakfast or brunch coffee cake

1¾ c. sifted flour
1 c. sugar
1 tsp. baking soda
¼ tsp. salt
¼ tsp. baking powder
½ c. cooking oil
1 egg
½ c. milk
1 tsp. vanilla

2 c. chopped, pared apples
½ c. brown sugar, firmly packed
½ c. chopped walnuts
2 tblsp. butter or regular margarine
2 tblsp. flour
1 tsp. ground cinnamon

Sift together 1¾ c. flour, sugar, baking soda, salt and baking powder into a large bowl.

Combine oil, egg, milk and vanilla. Add to dry ingredients; stir until well blended. Stir in apples. Spread batter in greased 9″ square pan.

Combine brown sugar, walnuts, butter, 2 tblsp. flour and cinnamon. Sprinkle over the top of the batter.

Bake in moderate oven (350°) 45 minutes or until cake tests done. Cool in pan on rack. Makes 9 servings.

HOT MILK SPONGE CAKE

Dust with confectioners sugar and serve with fresh strawberries

1 c. sifted flour	1 tsp. vanilla
1½ tsp. baking powder	½ tsp. lemon extract
¼ tsp. salt	½ c. hot milk
2 eggs	1 tblsp. melted butter or regular
1 c. sugar	margarine

Sift together flour, baking powder and salt.

Beat eggs until foamy. Slowly beat in sugar; continue beating until thick and lemon-colored. Beat in vanilla and lemon extract.

At low speed, beat in dry ingredients. Slowly beat in hot milk and butter. Pour batter into ungreased 9″ square pan.

Bake in moderate oven (350°) 30 minutes or until cake tests done. Invert cake to cool. Makes 9 servings.

SPECIAL PEANUT CAKE

Children will be delighted to find this cake in their packed lunch

1½ c. sifted flour	1 tsp. vanilla
1 tsp. baking soda	1 c. sour milk
⅓ c. shortening	1 (6½ oz.) can salted Spanish
1 c. sugar	peanuts, chopped (1 cup)
1 egg	1 (6 oz.) pkg. chocolate pieces

Sift together flour and baking soda.

Cream together shortening and sugar until light and fluffy. Add egg; beat well. Add vanilla.

Add dry ingredients alternately with sour milk, beating well after each addition. Stir in peanuts. Pour batter into greased 9″ square pan.

Bake in moderate oven (350°) 30 minutes or until cake tests done. Sprinkle chocolate pieces over the top and place cake in the oven until they begin to melt. Remove and spread chocolate over top. Cool in pan on rack. Makes 9 servings.

SPICY SURPRISE CAKE

This unusual spice cake will keep moist and fresh for several days

2 c. sifted flour
½ c. cocoa
2 tsp. baking powder
1 tsp. ground cinnamon
1 tsp. ground nutmeg
1 tsp. ground cloves
½ tsp. salt
1 c. butter or regular margarine
2 c. sugar

4 eggs
1 c. unseasoned mashed
  potatoes
½ c. light cream
1 (8½ oz.) can crushed
  pineapple, drained
1 c. chopped pecans
Cream Cheese Frosting (recipe
  follows)

Sift together flour, cocoa, baking powder, cinnamon, nutmeg, cloves and salt.

Cream together butter and sugar until light and fluffy. Add eggs, one at a time, beating well after each addition. Beat in mashed potatoes.

Add dry ingredients alternately with light cream, beating well after each addition. Stir in pineapple and pecans. Pour batter into greased 13 × 9 × 2″ cake pan.

Bake in moderate oven (350°) 45 minutes or until cake tests done. Cool in pan on rack. Frost with Cream Cheese Frosting. Makes 16 servings.

Cream Cheese Frosting: Beat together 1 (8 oz.) pkg. cream cheese and ¼ c. butter or regular margarine. Slowly beat in 2 c. sifted confectioners sugar and 2 tsp. vanilla; beat until light and fluffy.

OATMEAL / SPICE CAKE

Popular with men and with young people who like to "eat hearty"

1½ c. boiling water
1 c. quick rolled oats
1½ c. sifted flour
1 tsp. baking soda
1 tsp. ground cinnamon
1 tsp. ground nutmeg
½ tsp. salt
¼ tsp. ground allspice

½ c. shortening
1 c. brown sugar, firmly packed
½ c. sugar
2 eggs
1 tsp. vanilla
½ c. chopped walnuts
Lemon Butter Frosting (recipe
  follows)

Pour water over oats; let stand until cool.

Sift together flour, baking soda, cinnamon, nutmeg, salt and allspice.

Cream together shortening and sugars until light and fluffy. Beat in eggs, one at a time, beating well after each addition. Stir in oat mixture and vanilla. Mix in dry ingredients and walnuts; blend well. Spread mixture in greased and floured 9" square pan.

Bake in moderate oven (350°) 45 to 50 minutes or until cake tests done. Cool in pan on rack. Frost with Lemon Butter Frosting. Makes 9 servings.

Lemon Butter Frosting: Cream together ¼ c. butter or regular margarine and ¼ c. shortening. Gradually beat in 2 c. sifted confectioners sugar. Add 1 tblsp. milk, 1 tsp. grated lemon rind, ½ tsp. lemon extract and dash salt. Whip until light and creamy. If necessary, add a little more milk for proper consistency.

CINNAMON COFFEE SQUARES

Pile a platter high with these spicy squares and serve with hot coffee

3 c. sifted flour	1 c. butter or regular margarine
2 tsp. baking powder	2 c. brown sugar, firmly packed
2 tsp. ground cinnamon	2 eggs
½ tsp. baking soda	1 c. hot coffee
½ tsp. salt	Vanilla Icing (recipe follows)

Sift together flour, baking powder, cinnamon, baking soda and salt.

Cream together butter and brown sugar until light and fluffy. Add eggs, one at a time, beating well after each addition. Alternately add dry ingredients and coffee, beating after each addition.

Pour into greased 13 × 9 × 2" baking pan. Bake in moderate oven (350°) 35 minutes or until cake tests done.

Cool in pan on rack. Frost with Vanilla Icing and cut into squares. Makes 18.

Vanilla Icing: Combine 2 c. sifted confectioners sugar, ⅓ c. butter or regular margarine, 1½ tsp. vanilla, 1/16 tsp. salt and 2 tblsp. milk. Mix until smooth.

MARSHMALLOW / BANANA BARS

A yummy snack food served with hot coffee or icy cold lemonade

1½ c. sifted flour	1 tsp. vanilla
1 tsp. baking powder	1⅓ c. mashed bananas
½ c. shortening	1 (7 oz.) jar marshmallow
1 c. sugar	creme
1 egg	Vanilla Icing (recipe below)
1 tsp. baking soda dissolved in 1	
tblsp. water	

Sift together flour and baking powder.

Cream together shortening and sugar until light and fluffy. Add egg; beat well. Stir in soda mixture and vanilla. Add dry ingredients alternately with bananas, beating well after each addition. Spread into a greased 15½ × 10½ × 1" jelly roll pan.

Bake in moderate oven (350°) 25 to 30 minutes. Remove from oven. Drop spoonfuls of marshmallow creme on bars. Let stand for 2 minutes. Spread gently over surface of cake. Cool in pan on rack. Frost with Vanilla Icing. Cut into 3 × 1" bars. Makes 50 bars.

Vanilla Icing: Combine 2 c. sifted confectioners sugar, 1 tblsp. butter or regular margarine, 2 tblsp. milk, 1 tsp. vanilla and a few drops yellow food color. Blend until smooth.

'TIS THE SEASON TO BAKE
CHRISTMAS CAKES

Cakes that are chock-full of nuts, cranberries, spices, raisins and candied fruits will age and mellow for several weeks. Perfect for Christmas giving as well as for serving to neighbors who drop in to say "Merry Holidays!"

WALNUT APPLESAUCE CAKE

"I usually make several of these and give them for Christmas gifts"

2 c. sifted flour	½ c. shortening
1 tsp. baking soda	1 c. sugar
1 tsp. baking powder	1 egg
1 tsp. ground cinnamon	1 c. applesauce
1 tsp. ground nutmeg	1 tsp. vanilla
½ tsp. ground cloves	¾ c. raisins
½ tsp. salt	1 c. chopped walnuts

Sift together flour, baking soda, baking powder, cinnamon, nutmeg, cloves and salt.

Cream together shortening and sugar until light and fluffy. Add egg, applesauce and vanilla; blend well.

Gradually blend in dry ingredients. Stir in raisins and walnuts. Pour batter into greased 9 × 5 × 3″ loaf pan.

Bake in moderate oven (350°) 55 minutes or until cake tests done. Cool for 10 minutes. Remove from pan. Cool on rack. Makes 8 to 10 servings.

FRUIT PRESERVES CAKE

This holiday cake is ideal for morning or afternoon coffee breaks

3 c. sifted flour	4 eggs, separated
1 tsp. baking soda	1 tsp. vanilla
½ tsp. ground cinnamon	½ c. buttermilk
½ tsp. ground nutmeg	⅔ c. cherry preserves
½ tsp. ground cloves	⅔ c. apricot preserves
¾ c. butter or regular	⅔ c. pineapple preserves
margarine	1 c. chopped walnuts
2 c. brown sugar, firmly packed	

Sift together flour, baking soda, cinnamon, nutmeg and cloves.

Cream together butter and brown sugar until light and fluffy. Add egg yolks; beat well. Add vanilla.

Add dry ingredients alternately with buttermilk, beating well after each addition. Stir in preserves and walnuts.

Beat egg whites until stiff. Fold into batter. Pour batter into greased 10″ tube pan.

Bake in moderate oven (350°) 1 hour 30 minutes or until cake tests done. Cool for 10 minutes. Remove from pan. Cool on rack. Makes 12 servings.

TANGY CRANBERRY SQUARES

A cranberry-studded cake that is similar to a steamed holiday pudding

2 c. sifted cake flour	1 tsp. vanilla
3 tsp. baking powder	1 c. milk
½ tsp. salt	2 c. raw cranberries
2 tblsp. butter or regular margarine	Hot Butter Sauce (recipe follows)
1 c. sugar	

Sift together flour, baking powder and salt.

Cream together butter and sugar until light and fluffy. Add vanilla.

Add dry ingredients alternately with milk, beating well after each addition. Stir in cranberries. Pour batter into greased 9″ cake pan.

Bake in hot oven (400°) 30 to 35 minutes or until cake tests done. While warm, cut into squares and serve topped with Hot Butter Sauce. Makes 9 servings.

Hot Butter Sauce: Melt ½ c. butter or regular margarine in small saucepan. Stir in 1 c. sugar. Slowly stir in ½ c. light cream. Cook over low heat, stirring constantly, 3 to 4 minutes or until mixture thickens.

CRANBERRY ORANGE CAKE

Wrap with colored cellophane and tie with a bow for holiday gifts

1 c. cut-up dates	½ c. butter or regular margarine
1 c. chopped walnuts	
1 c. halved cranberries	1 c. sugar
½ c. sifted flour	2 eggs
2 c. sifted flour	2 tblsp. grated orange rind
1 tsp. baking powder	1 c. buttermilk
1 tsp. baking soda	⅔ c. orange juice
¼ tsp. salt	⅔ c. sugar

Combine dates, walnuts, cranberries and ½ c. flour.

Sift together 2 c. flour, baking powder, baking soda and salt.

Cream together butter and 1 c. sugar until light and fluffy. Add eggs, one at a time, beating well after each addition. Add orange rind.

Add dry ingredients alternately with buttermilk, beating well after each addition. Stir in fruit-nut mixture. Turn batter into greased 9″ spring form tube pan.

Bake in moderate oven (350°) 1 hour or until cake tests done. Cool for 10 minutes. Remove from pan. Cool on rack. Heat together orange juice and ⅔ c. sugar until sugar is dissolved. Pour over cake. Let cake stand for 12 hours before slicing. Makes 10 servings.

HOLIDAY CRANBERRY CAKE

Run berries through food chopper while still frozen—saves mess

1 (1 lb. 3 oz.) pkg. lemon cake mix	4 eggs
1 (3 oz.) pkg. cream cheese, softened	1¼ c. ground cranberries
	½ c. ground walnuts
¾ c. milk	¼ c. sugar
	1 tsp. ground mace

Blend cake mix, cream cheese and milk; beat with mixer for 2 minutes at medium speed. Add eggs, one at a time, beating for 2 additional minutes.

Thoroughly combine cranberries, walnuts, sugar and mace; fold into cake batter. Pour into a well-greased and floured 10″ tube or bundt pan. Bake in moderate oven (350°) 1 hour or until done. Cool for 5 minutes. Remove from pan. Cool on rack. Dust with confectioners sugar, if you wish. Makes 12 servings.

CUPCAKES

We give you here a choice of creative cupcakes that span the four seasons. For those who are watching their weight, there are some that aren't frosted or are just lightly dusted with sugar. Black walnut fans will love the Black Walnut Cupcakes frosted with buttery caramel icing.

BLACK WALNUT CUPCAKES

Take these light cupcakes to your next family reunion or picnic

3 c. sifted flour	4 eggs
1 tsp. baking soda	2 tsp. vanilla
1½ tsp. salt	¾ c. milk
1 c. shortening	1 c. chopped black walnuts
1¾ c. sugar	

Sift together flour, baking soda and salt.

Cream together shortening and sugar until light and fluffy. Add eggs, one at a time, beating well after each addition. Add vanilla.

Add dry ingredients alternately with milk, beating well after each addition. Stir in black walnuts. Pour batter into paper-lined 2½" muffin-pan cups, filling two-thirds full.

Bake in moderate oven (350°) 20 to 25 minutes or until done. Remove from pans. Cool on racks. Makes 3 dozen.

CHRISTMAS FRUIT CUPCAKES

Attractive miniature fruitcakes that will appeal to your guests

2¼ c. sifted flour	¼ c. finely chopped candied orange peel
1 tsp. ground cinnamon	
½ tsp. baking soda	½ c. butter or regular margarine
½ tsp. ground nutmeg	
½ tsp. ground cloves	1 c. dark brown sugar, firmly packed
¼ tsp. salt	
1 c. chopped figs	2 eggs, separated
1 c. chopped dates	½ c. dark corn syrup
1 c. raisins	1 c. grape juice
1 c. currants	½ c. buttermilk
½ c. chopped walnuts	Chopped candied fruits
¼ c. finely chopped candied lemon peel	Chopped walnuts

Sift together flour, cinnamon, baking soda, nutmeg, cloves and salt; reserve ¼ c.

Combine figs, dates, raisins, currants, ½ c. walnuts, lemon peel, orange peel and reserved ¼ c. flour mixture.

Cream together butter and brown sugar until light and fluffy. Add egg yolks and corn syrup; blend well.

Add dry ingredients alternately with grape juice and buttermilk, beating well after each addition. Stir in fruit/nut mixture.

Beat egg whites until stiff. Fold into batter. Pour batter into paper-lined 2½" muffin-pan cups, filling two-thirds full. Decorate tops with candied fruit and walnuts.

Bake in slow oven (300°) 45 minutes or until done. Remove from pans. Cool on racks. Makes 3 dozen.

CREOLE CUPCAKES

Decorate frosted cupcakes with gumdrop flowers for a special party

2 c. sifted flour	½ c. cooking oil
2 tblsp. cocoa	2 eggs
1 tsp. baking soda	1 tsp. vanilla
½ tsp. salt	½ c. buttermilk
2 c. sugar	1 c. boiling water

Sift together flour, cocoa, baking soda and salt.

Cream together sugar and oil until light. Add eggs, one at a time, beating well after each addition. Add vanilla.

Add dry ingredients alternately with buttermilk, beating well after each addition. Gradually beat in water. (Batter will be thin.) Pour batter into paper-lined 2½" muffin-pan cups, filling two-thirds full.

Bake in moderate oven (350°) 25 minutes or until done. Remove from pans. Cool on racks. Makes 24.

BROWNIE CUPCAKES

Youngsters say that these are even better than square brownies!

4 oz. semi-sweet chocolate	1¼ c. sifted flour
1 c. butter or regular margarine	4 eggs, beaten
1½ c. broken pecans	1 tsp. vanilla
1¾ c. sugar	¼ tsp. salt

Melt chocolate and butter in a heavy saucepan. Add pecans, stirring until well coated.

Combine sugar, flour, eggs, vanilla and salt; mix until blended. (Do not beat.) Combine mixtures, blending well. Spoon mixture into paper-lined 2½″ muffin-pan cups, filling about two-thirds full.

Bake in slow oven (325°) 35 minutes or until done. Remove from pans. Cool on racks. Makes 21.

ORANGE CUPCAKES

Serve these with frosty orange sherbet for a double flavor treat

2 c. sifted cake flour	1 egg
1 tsp. baking soda	1 tsp. grated orange rind
½ tsp. baking powder	⅔ c. buttermilk
¼ tsp. salt	1 c. sugar
1 c. sugar	½ c. orange juice
½ c. shortening	

Sift together cake flour, baking soda, baking powder and salt.

Cream together 1 c. sugar and shortening until light and fluffy. Add egg and orange rind; blend well.

Add dry ingredients alternately with buttermilk, beating well after each addition. Pour batter into paper-lined 2½″ muffin-pan cups, filling two-thirds full.

Bake in moderate oven (350°) 20 to 25 minutes or until done.

Meanwhile, combine 1 c. sugar and orange juice. Stir over medium heat until sugar dissolves. Remove cupcakes from pans. Spoon hot syrup over each. Cool on racks. Makes 18 cupcakes.

SPICY RAISIN CUPCAKES

"A family heirloom recipe that is always a favorite with our men"

1 lb. raisins	¼ tsp. salt
2 c. water	1½ c. sugar
2⅓ c. sifted flour	1 c. butter or regular margarine
2 tsp. baking soda	2 eggs
2 tsp. ground nutmeg	1 c. chopped walnuts
2 tsp. ground cinnamon	

Combine raisins and water in a small saucepan. Bring to a boil, reduce heat and simmer for 10 minutes. Drain and reserve cooking liquid. If necessary, add enough water to make 1 c.

Sift together flour, baking soda, nutmeg, cinnamon and salt.

Cream together sugar and butter until light and fluffy. Add eggs, one at a time, beating well after each addition.

Add dry ingredients alternately with cooking liquid, beating well after each addition. Stir in raisins and walnuts. Pour batter into paper-lined 2½″ muffin-pan cups, filling two-thirds full.

Bake in moderate oven (375°) 20 to 25 minutes or until done. Remove from pans. Cool on racks. Makes 3 dozen.

LEMON CRUNCH CUPCAKES

These easy-to-make cupcakes need no frosting . . . great for picnics

2 c. sifted flour	3 eggs
1 c. sugar	1 tblsp. grated lemon rind
2½ tsp. baking powder	¼ c. sugar
½ tsp. salt	1 tblsp. grated lemon rind
⅔ c. shortening	½ tsp. ground nutmeg
⅔ c. milk	

Sift together flour, 1 c. sugar, baking powder and salt into large mixing bowl. Add shortening and milk; beat thoroughly (about 3 minutes). Add eggs, one at a time, beating well after each addition. Add 1 tblsp. lemon rind.

Combine ¼ c. sugar, 1 tblsp. lemon rind and nutmeg. Pour batter into paper-lined 2½″ muffin-pan cups, filling two-thirds full. Sprinkle tops with sugar mixture.

Bake in moderate oven (375°) 20 to 25 minutes or until done. Remove from pans. Cool on racks. Makes 24.

Chapter 8

MOTHER MAKES THE BEST PIE

Ask any family to name their favorite pie and they'll usually answer in a second. Every family member can quickly go down the list of Mom's best and come up with *his* first choice.

Our pie chapter is full of favorite pies. There's Apple Macaroon Pie from an Illinois farm wife—she developed the recipe because her husband loves coconut and went on to win a Blue Ribbon and a $100 bond for her efforts. A prized Apple/Raisin Pie comes from Texas where the recipe was discovered scribbled on a scrap of paper when the family homestead was dismantled. It is a delicious combination of unpared chopped apples, raisins, pecans and spices baked to perfection.

You'll want to whip up the light and airy Date Chiffon Pie for company—or the 3-Layer Lemon Meringue Pie for a grand ending to a meal. A farm woman from Pennsylvania shared the Oatmeal Pie recipe with us and commented that the four men in her family request it often and she usually makes four at a time! A crunchy Peanut/Coconut Pie from New Mexico has won family accolades for years, as well as several Blue Ribbons at County Fairs.

For holiday treats, you'll want to make the Pecan Meringue Pie that's chock-full of ground pecans and topped with a golden meringue.

You'll discover unusual pies and everyday favorites with a new touch or flavor surprise. For instance, the men will beg for seconds when you serve the Deep Fudge Pie. The youngsters will love the Peanut Butter Cream Pie and Raspberry Parfait Pie. There's a pie for every season and every situation and each one good to the last flaky crumb!

The pastry is as important as the filling. It's easy to make perfect pastry every time. Successful pastry that is flaky and tender and practically melts on the tongue depends on how well the flour particles separate so that when the water is added the gluten in the flour does not develop tough pastry. The fat must coat the flour particles so that when the water is added only a small amount of mixing is necessary to blend it into a dough. Cut the shortening into the flour only until the particles are about the size of small peas. Overmixing causes the shortening to clump together, producing a heavy mixture that will not absorb water and so will produce a crumbly pastry that will not hold together.

Be sure to use cold water to prevent the fat particles from melting. Handle dough with hands as little as possible, again to prevent shortening from melting. Add the water a little at a time, sprinkling over one part of the mixture, then pushing moistened portions together and to one side.

Chilling the dough will make it easier to roll out. Be careful not to put too much flour on your pastry board or cloth; this causes tough pastry. Do not stretch dough after rolling when fitting into the pan for then the dough will shrink when baked.

Select pie pans of ovenproof glass or aluminum for a well-baked, browned bottom crust. Shiny metal does not bake the bottom crust as well, because it reflects the heat instead of absorbing it.

When you lift the warm fragrant pie of your family's choice from the oven, you'll be pleased when they say "Mother makes the *best* pies!"

FESTIVE FALL PIES

We selected this collection of pies that are especially good in the fall; try some for the Thanksgiving and Christmas season as a change of pace.

At the peak of the apple crop, you'll want to make several of the Apple Macaroon and Apple/Raisin Pies. Serve with a generous wedge of sharp cheese or a scoop of vanilla ice cream. Raisin Crisscross Pie and Date/Coconut Pie are excellent to carry to church suppers.

After you have finished a meal of baked ham and scalloped potatoes, bring on the Brown Sugar Custard Pie or the Coconut Custard Pie as the grande finale.

APPLE MACAROON PIE

"Our family looks forward to this pie during apple harvest time"

4 c. sliced, pared apples	2 tblsp. butter or regular
1 unbaked 9″ pie shell	margarine
½ c. sugar	1⅓ c. flaked coconut
1 tblsp. flour	½ c. sugar
1 tsp. ground cinnamon	1 egg, well beaten
½ tsp. salt	¼ c. milk
	½ tsp. vanilla

Arrange apples in pie shell.

Combine ½ c. sugar, flour, cinnamon and salt. Sprinkle on top of apples. Dot with butter.

Bake in hot oven (425°) 20 minutes.

Combine coconut, ½ c. sugar, egg, milk and vanilla. Spread on top of filling. Reduce temperature to moderate oven (350°). Bake 30 more minutes or until apples are tender. Cool on rack. Makes 6 to 8 servings.

APPLE / RAISIN PIE

This treasure was found when the old homestead was torn down

2 c. sugar	⅛ tsp. salt
1 c. butter or regular margarine	½ tsp. vanilla
4 eggs	1 c. chopped, unpared apples
1 tblsp. flour	1 c. raisins
¾ tsp. ground cinnamon	1 c. coarsely chopped pecans
¼ tsp. ground nutmeg	1 unbaked 10″ pie shell

Cream together sugar and butter until light and fluffy. Add eggs, one at a time, beating well after each addition. Add flour, cinnamon, nutmeg, salt and vanilla, beating well. Stir in apples, raisins and pecans. Pour into pie shell.

Bake in moderate oven (350°) 45 minutes or until golden brown. Cool on rack. Makes 8 servings.

RAISIN CRISSCROSS PIE

An old-fashioned pie that is still a favorite in many families today

½ c. brown sugar, firmly packed	2 c. raisins
2 tblsp. cornstarch	2 tblsp. butter or regular margarine
½ tsp. ground cinnamon	2 tblsp. lemon juice
¼ tsp. ground nutmeg	Pastry for 2-crust 9″ pie
1½ c. water	

Combine brown sugar, cornstarch, cinnamon, nutmeg, water and raisins in a medium saucepan. Cook over medium heat, stirring constantly, until thickened. Remove from heat. Stir in butter and lemon juice. Cool slightly.

Pour into pastry-lined pie plate. Roll out remaining pastry. Cut into ½″ strips. Lay half of strips over filling about 1″ apart. Repeat with remaining strips, placing them in opposite direction in diamond or square pattern. Trim strips even with pie edge. Turn bottom crust up over rim and ends of strips. Press firmly to seal edge.

Bake in very hot oven (450°) 10 minutes. Reduce temperature to moderate oven (350°). Bake for 20 minutes or until golden brown. Cool on rack. Makes 6 to 8 servings.

DATE / COCONUT PIE

The kind of pie that will appeal to those with a "real sweet tooth"

1 c. sugar	½ c. chopped dates
½ c. butter or regular margarine	½ c. flaked coconut
2 eggs	½ c. chopped walnuts
1 tblsp. vinegar	1 unbaked 9″ pie shell

Cream together sugar and butter until light and fluffy. Add eggs, one at a time, beating well after each addition. Beat in vinegar.

Stir in dates, coconut and walnuts. Pour mixture into pie shell.

Bake in moderate oven (350°) 35 minutes or until filling is set around the edges and top is golden brown. Cool on rack. Makes 6 to 8 servings.

COCONUT CUSTARD PIE

"My three sons practically inhale this pie," a Missouri woman says

3 eggs
1½ c. sugar
½ c. melted butter or regular
   margarine
1 tblsp. lemon juice

2 tsp. vanilla
⅟₁₆ tsp. salt
1⅓ c. flaked coconut
1 unbaked 9″ pie shell

Beat eggs until lemon-colored. Beat in sugar, butter, lemon juice, vanilla and salt. Stir in coconut. Pour into pie shell.

Bake in moderate oven (350°) 40 minutes or until a knife inserted halfway between edge and center of custard comes out clean. (Center will be soft.) Cool on rack. Makes 6 to 8 servings.

GRANDMA'S PUMPKIN CUSTARD PIE

So smooth and velvety, this pie is certain to be a crowd-pleaser

1 (1 lb.) can pumpkin (2 c.)
1½ c. sugar
1 tblsp. cornstarch
1½ tsp. ground cinnamon
1 tsp. salt
1 tsp. ground ginger

½ tsp. ground cloves
½ tsp. ground nutmeg
6 eggs
2 (13½ oz.) cans evaporated
   milk
2 unbaked 9″ pie shells

Combine pumpkin, sugar, cornstarch, cinnamon, salt, ginger, cloves and nutmeg; stir until blended.

Beat eggs until light and lemon-colored. Beat into pumpkin mixture. Gradually add evaporated milk, stirring until smooth. Pour mixture into pie shells.

Bake in moderate oven (350°) 15 minutes. Reduce temperature to slow oven (325°). Bake 30 minutes or until set. Cool on racks.

If you wish, top with puffs of sweetened whipped cream. Makes 12 to 16 servings.

BROWN SUGAR CUSTARD PIE

Family heirloom which is treasured now by the third generation

2 c. brown sugar, firmly packed	$\frac{1}{16}$ tsp. salt
¼ c. butter or regular margarine	3 eggs
	3 c. milk
3 tblsp. flour	½ tsp. vanilla
1 tsp. ground cinnamon	2 unbaked 8″ pie shells
½ tsp. cream of tartar	

Cream together brown sugar and butter until light and fluffy. Add flour, cinnamon, cream of tartar, salt and eggs; beat well. Slowly beat in milk and vanilla. Pour into pie shells.

Bake in moderate oven (375°) 40 minutes or until knife inserted halfway between edge and center of custard comes out clean. (Center will be soft.) Cool on racks. Makes 12 servings.

SPICE CREAM PIE

Sprinkle puffs of soft whipped cream with freshly ground nutmeg

1½ c. sugar	4 eggs, slightly beaten
5 tblsp. flour	3 tblsp. butter or regular margarine
1½ tsp. ground cinnamon	
1 tsp. ground nutmeg	1 tsp. vanilla
1 tsp. ground allspice	1 unbaked 10″ pie shell
⅛ tsp. salt	Sweetened whipped cream
2 c. milk	

Combine sugar, flour, cinnamon, nutmeg, allspice and salt in heavy 2-qt. saucepan. Slowly stir in milk. Cook over medium heat, stirring constantly, until thickened. Stir a small amount of hot mixture into eggs. Stir back into remaining hot mixture. Cook, stirring, for 2 minutes. Remove from heat; stir in butter and vanilla.

Pour into pie shell. Bake in moderate oven (350°) 35 minutes or until set. Cool on rack.

When cool, top with puffs of sweetened whipped cream. Makes 8 servings.

MAPLE-GLAZED APPLE PIE

Gingersnaps joined with maple make this a special pie to serve

6 c. pared, sliced apples	½ tsp. ground cinnamon
Pastry for 2-crust 9″ pie	¼ tsp. salt
½ c. sugar	½ c. chopped walnuts
¼ c. brown sugar, firmly packed	¼ c. melted butter or regular margarine
½ c. crushed gingersnaps	¼ c. maple syrup

Arrange half of the apples in a pastry-lined pie plate. Combine sugar, brown sugar, gingersnaps, cinnamon, salt, walnuts and butter; mix well.

Spread half of sugar mixture over apples. Repeat with remaining apples and sugar mixture.

Roll out remaining pastry. Adjust top crust and flute edges; cut vents. Bake in moderate oven (350°) 35 minutes. Heat maple syrup to boiling; brush over pie and return to oven for 15 minutes longer. Cool on rack. Makes 6 to 8 servings.

MMM! MEN WILL LIKE THESE PIES

Watch your husband's eyes light up when you serve him any one of these pies. Each of them is a husband's favorite which we have received from fine farm cooks. He might even present you with a bouquet of daffodils if you bake him either one of the springtime favorites, Rhubarb Cherry Pie or Rhubarb Surprise Pie.

There's a pie to please the men for every season of the year. When the snow has drifted right up to the window ledge, put on the coffee pot and cut a big wedge of the Oatmeal Pie or crunchy golden Peanut/Coconut Pie.

RHUBARB CHERRY PIE

"My husband often asks for this . . . one of his favorite fruit pies"

3 c. diced rhubarb
2 (1 lb.) cans pitted tart
cherries, drained
1¼ c. sugar

¼ c. quick-cooking tapioca
¼ tsp. almond flavoring
10 drops red food color
Pastry for 2-crust 9″ pie

Combine rhubarb, cherries, sugar, tapioca, almond flavoring and red food color. Let stand for 15 minutes.

Pour into pastry-lined pie plate. Adjust top crust, flute edges and cut steam vents.

Bake in hot oven (400°) 45 minutes or until rhubarb is tender and pie is golden brown. Cool on rack. Makes 6 to 8 servings.

RHUBARB SURPRISE PIE

Serve pie slightly warm with a scoop of creamy vanilla ice cream

1 c. sifted flour
1 tsp. baking powder
½ tsp. salt
2 tblsp. butter or regular
margarine
1 egg, beaten
2 tblsp. milk
3 c. diced fresh rhubarb

1 (3 oz.) pkg. strawberry
flavor gelatin
½ c. unsifted flour
1 c. sugar
½ tsp. ground cinnamon
¼ c. melted butter or regular
margarine

Sift together 1 c. flour, baking powder and salt. Cut in 2 tblsp. butter until mixture is crumbly. Add egg and milk; mix well. Press into greased 9″ pie plate.

Arrange rhubarb in pie shell. Sprinkle with gelatin. Combine ½ c. flour, sugar, cinnamon and ¼ c. butter; mix until crumbly. Sprinkle mixture on top of pie.

Bake in moderate oven (350°) 50 minutes or until rhubarb is tender and top is golden. Cool on rack. Makes 6 to 8 servings.

OATMEAL PIE

"My husband likes this pie topped with a dollop of whipped cream"

3 eggs
1 c. brown sugar, firmly packed
⅔ c. sugar
⅔ c. milk
2 tsp. melted butter or regular margarine

⅛ tsp. salt
1 tsp. vanilla
½ c. quick-cooking rolled oats
⅔ c. flaked coconut
1 unbaked 9″ pie shell

Beat eggs until lemon-colored. Gradually add both sugars, beating well. Blend in milk, butter, salt and vanilla. Stir in oats and coconut. Pour into pie shell.

Bake in moderate oven (375°) 30 minutes or until set around edges. Cool on rack. Makes 6 to 8 servings.

PEANUT / COCONUT PIE

An original recipe that has won several Fair ribbons in New Mexico

4 eggs
1 c. light corn syrup
¾ c. sugar

1 c. chopped salted peanuts
1 c. flaked coconut
1 unbaked 9″ pie shell

Beat eggs until lemon-colored. Gradually add corn syrup and sugar, beating well after each addition. Stir in peanuts and coconut. Pour into pie shell.

Bake in moderate oven (350°) 40 minutes or until filling is set around the edges and center is soft. Cool on rack. Makes 6 to 8 servings.

BLUEBERRY CHESS PIE

A Texas woman is always asked to bring this to community functions

1½ c. sugar
½ c. butter or regular margarine
⅛ tsp. salt
3 eggs
2 tblsp. flour

2 tblsp. cornstarch
1 tblsp. vinegar
1½ tsp. vanilla
1 pt. fresh blueberries
1 unbaked 9″ pie shell

Cream together sugar, butter and salt until light and fluffy. Beat in eggs, one at a time, beating well after each addition. Add flour, cornstarch, vinegar and vanilla; beat until smooth. Stir in blueberries. Pour into pie shell.

Bake in hot oven (400°) 15 minutes. Reduce temperature to slow oven (300°). Bake 35 minutes or until firm in center. Cool on rack. Makes 6 to 8 servings.

AMISH VANILLA PIE

Traditional recipe that is especially good for potlucks and buffets

½ c. brown sugar, firmly packed

1 tblsp. flour

¼ c. dark corn syrup

1½ tsp. vanilla

1 egg, beaten

1 c. water

1 c. unsifted flour

½ c. brown sugar, firmly packed

½ tsp. cream of tartar

½ tsp. baking soda

⅛ tsp. salt

¼ c. butter or regular margarine

1 unbaked 9″ pie shell

Combine ½ c. brown sugar, 1 tblsp. flour, corn syrup, vanilla and egg in 2-qt. saucepan. Slowly stir in water. Cook over medium heat, stirring constantly, until mixture comes to a boil. Let cool.

Combine 1 c. flour, ½ c. brown sugar, cream of tartar, baking soda, salt and butter; mix until crumbly. Pour cooled mixture into pie shell; top with crumbs.

Bake in moderate oven (350°) 40 minutes or until golden brown. Makes 6 to 8 servings.

DEEP FUDGE PIE

Luscious chocolate pie that tastes like brownies baked in a crust

1 unbaked 9″ pie shell

3 (1 oz.) squares unsweetened chocolate

½ c. butter or regular margarine

4 eggs

3 tblsp. light corn syrup

1½ c. sugar

¼ tsp. salt

1 tsp. vanilla

Vanilla ice cream

Prick pie shell with fork. Bake in hot oven (400°) 10 minutes or until golden.

Meanwhile, melt chocolate with butter over hot water. Cool slightly.

Beat eggs until light and fluffy. Slowly beat in corn syrup, sugar, salt and vanilla. Beat in cooled chocolate mixture; blend well. Pour into pie shell.

Bake in moderate oven (350°) 25 to 30 minutes or until top is crusty and filling is set around edges. (Do not overbake.) Cool on rack. Serve topped with scoops of vanilla ice cream. Makes 6 to 8 servings.

LEMON CHESS PIE

Light and lemony, this is a good choice following a heavy meal

4 eggs	1 tsp. cornmeal
2 c. sugar	1 tsp. flour
½ c. lemon juice	⅛ tsp. salt
½ c. melted butter or regular margarine	1 unbaked 9″ pie shell

Beat eggs thoroughly. Gradually beat in sugar. Add lemon juice, butter, cornmeal, flour and salt; beat well. Pour into pie shell.

Bake in moderate oven (350°) 40 minutes or until golden brown. (Do not overbake.) Cool on rack. Makes 6 to 8 servings.

GOLDEN TREASURE PIE

Smooth, creamy cheese cake mixture baked in a golden pie crust

2 (8½ oz.) cans crushed pineapple	¼ c. sifted flour
½ c. sugar	1 c. cream-style cottage cheese
2 tblsp. cornstarch	1 tsp. vanilla
2 tblsp. water	½ tsp. salt
⅔ c. sugar	2 eggs, slightly beaten
1 tblsp. butter or regular margarine	1¼ c. milk
	1 unbaked 10″ pie shell

Combine undrained pineapple, ½ c. sugar, cornstarch and water in small saucepan. Cook over medium heat, stirring constantly, until mixture comes to a boil. Boil for 1 minute. Cool well.

Blend ⅔ c. sugar and butter. Add flour, cottage cheese, vanilla and salt; beat until smooth. Slowly add eggs and milk, beating constantly.

Pour pineapple mixture into crust, spreading evenly. Gently pour custard over pineapple, being careful not to disturb first layer. Bake in very hot oven (450°) 15 minutes, then reduce heat. Bake in moderate oven (325°) 45 minutes longer. Cool on rack. Makes 8 servings.

MARVELOUS MERINGUE PIES

When you think of a meringue pie, it's usually lemon. We have one of those in this group *but* it's a *three*-layer lemon. And in addition we have an exciting list of other pies with a cloud-high golden-tinged meringue. There's a spicy apple, a buttery crunchy peanut butter, meltingly rich pecan and delicate and very different Cantaloupe Meringue Pie.

3-LAYER LEMON MERINGUE PIE

A special-occasion lemon pie that can be made ahead and refrigerated

1⅓ c. sugar	1 tsp. grated lemon rind
½ c. flour	1 tblsp. butter or regular
⅛ tsp. salt	margarine
2 c. water	¼ tsp. cream of tartar
⅓ c. lemon juice	6 tblsp. sugar
3 eggs, separated	1 baked 9″ pie shell
3 drops yellow food color	

Combine 1⅓ c. sugar, flour and salt in a medium saucepan. Gradually stir in water and lemon juice. Cook over medium heat, stirring constantly, until thickened. Stir a small amount of hot mixture into beaten egg yolks. Stir back into remaining hot mixture. Cook, stirring, for 2 minutes. Remove from heat. Stir in yellow food color, lemon rind and butter.

Beat egg whites and cream of tartar until frothy. Gradually add 6 tblsp. sugar, beating until stiff glossy peaks form.

Reserve 1 c. of filling. Pour remaining filling into pie shell. Fold ¾ c. meringue into reserved filling. Spread evenly over filling in pie shell. Top with remaining meringue, sealing edges.

Bake in hot oven (400°) 8 to 10 minutes or until top is golden brown. Cool on rack. Makes 6 to 8 servings.

CANTALOUPE MERINGUE PIE

Use very ripe cantaloupe, so that the delicate melon flavor emerges

1 large very ripe cantaloupe	1 tblsp. lemon juice
⅔ c. sugar	1/16 tsp. salt
2 tblsp. cornstarch	1 baked 9″ pie shell
2 tblsp. water	2 tblsp. sugar
2 eggs, separated	1 tsp. vanilla

Scoop out melon. Cut into 1″ cubes (about 4 cups). Combine melon cubes and ⅔ c. sugar in small saucepan. Cook over low heat, stirring constantly, until mixture is smooth (about 10 minutes).

Combine cornstarch and water. Stir into melon mixture. Slowly stir in egg yolks. Cook over medium heat, stirring constantly, until mixture thickens. Remove from heat. Stir in lemon juice and salt. Cool well.

Pour into pie shell. Beat egg whites until frothy. Gradually add 2 tblsp. sugar; beat until stiff glossy peaks form. Beat in vanilla. Spread meringue over filling, sealing edges.

Bake in moderate oven (375°) 15 minutes or until top is golden brown. Cool on rack. Makes 6 to 8 servings.

CHOCOLATE MERINGUE PIE

"A cherished recipe that is the center of attention at our reunions"

2 oz. unsweetened chocolate	¼ tsp. salt
2 c. milk, scalded	2 eggs, separated
¼ c. sugar	1 tsp. vanilla
¼ c. brown sugar, firmly packed	1 baked 9″ pie shell
¼ c. flour	2 tblsp. sugar
	1 tsp. vanilla

Melt chocolate with milk over low heat in medium saucepan.

Combine ¼ c. sugar, brown sugar, flour and salt. Add to chocolate mixture, stirring well. Cook over medium heat, stirring constantly, until thickened. Stir a small amount of hot mixture into beaten egg yolks. Stir back into remaining hot mixture. Cook, stirring, for 2 minutes. Remove from heat. Add 1 tsp. vanilla. Cool well.

Pour into pie shell.

Beat egg whites until frothy. Gradually add 2 tblsp. sugar, beating until stiff glossy peaks form. Add 1 tsp. vanilla. Spread meringue over filling, sealing edges.

Bake in moderate oven (375°) 12 to 15 minutes or until top is golden brown. Cool on rack. Makes 6 to 8 servings.

APPLE MERINGUE PIE

So good when served slightly warm on a brisk early fall day

5 c. chopped, pared apples	1 c. milk
1 unbaked 9″ pie shell	½ tsp. ground nutmeg
2 eggs, separated	¹⁄₁₆ tsp. salt
½ c. sugar	¼ c. sugar
3 tblsp. butter or regular margarine	1 tsp. vanilla

Arrange apples in pie shell.

Cream together egg yolks and ½ c. sugar until light and fluffy. Add butter, milk and nutmeg; beat until smooth. Pour over apples.

Bake in moderate oven (375°) 40 minutes or until apples are tender.

Beat egg whites and salt until frothy. Gradually add ¼ c. sugar, beating until stiff glossy peaks form. Add vanilla. Spread meringue over filling, sealing edges.

Bake in moderate oven (375°) 10 minutes or until top is golden brown. Cool on rack. Makes 6 to 8 servings.

PEANUT BUTTER CREAM PIE

An energy-rich dessert that becomes the perfect snack with cold milk

⅔ c. confectioners sugar	3 eggs, separated
⅓ c. peanut butter, chunk style	2 tblsp. butter or regular margarine
1 baked 9″ pie shell	½ tsp. vanilla
½ c. sugar	1 tsp. cornstarch
⅓ c. flour	¼ tsp. cream of tartar
⅛ tsp. salt	½ c. sugar
2 c. milk	

Combine confectioners sugar and peanut butter; mix until mealy. Sprinkle ⅔ of mixture in bottom of pie shell.

Combine ½ c. sugar, flour and salt in a medium saucepan. Gradually stir in milk. Cook over medium heat, stirring constantly, until thickened. Stir a small amount of hot mixture into beaten egg yolks. Stir back into remaining hot mixture. Cook, stirring, for 2 minutes. Remove from heat. Stir in butter and vanilla. Cool slightly. Pour into pie shell. Top with remaining peanut butter mixture.

Beat egg whites, cornstarch and cream of tartar until frothy. Gradually add ½ c. sugar, beating until stiff glossy peaks form. Spread meringue over filling, sealing edges.

Bake in hot oven (400°) 5 minutes or until top is golden brown. Cool on rack. Makes 6 to 8 servings.

PECAN MERINGUE PIE

If you fancy pecan pie, try this variation next time you bake

1 c. sugar	2 tsp. vanilla
⅓ c. flour	1½ c. finely chopped pecans
⅛ tsp. salt	4 drops yellow food color
2 c. milk	1 baked 10″ pie shell
4 eggs, separated	⅛ tsp. cream of tartar
1 tblsp. butter or regular	6 tblsp. sugar
margarine	1 tsp. vanilla

Combine 1 c. sugar, flour and salt in a medium saucepan. Slowly stir in milk. Cook over medium heat, stirring constantly, until thickened. Stir a small amount of hot mixture into beaten egg yolks. Stir back into remaining hot mixture. Cook, stirring, for 2 minutes. Remove from heat. Stir in butter, 2 tsp. vanilla, pecans and yellow food color. Cool well.

Pour mixture into pie shell.

Beat egg whites and cream of tartar until frothy. Gradually add 6 tblsp. sugar, beating until stiff glossy peaks form. Beat in 1 tsp. vanilla. Spread meringue over filling, sealing edges.

Bake in hot oven (400°) 5 minutes or until top is golden brown. Cool on rack. Makes 6 to 8 servings.

MAKE-AHEAD-AND-CHILL PIES

Cool and refreshing pies that can be fixed ahead and put in the refrigerator to chill are a big help to the hostess. You'll find a pleasing assortment of flavors to suit everyone's special taste. Many are pretty enough to be show-off desserts at a party.

RASPBERRY PARFAIT PIE

For a change, substitute strawberry gelatin and frozen strawberries

1 (3 oz.) pkg. raspberry flavor
  gelatin
¼ c. sugar
1¼ c. boiling water
1 (10 oz.) pkg. frozen
  raspberries
1 tblsp. lemon juice

1 (3 oz.) pkg. cream cheese
⅓ c. confectioners sugar
¼ tsp. salt
1 tsp. vanilla
1 c. heavy cream, whipped
1 baked 10″ pie shell

Dissolve gelatin and sugar in boiling water. Add raspberries and lemon juice; stir until thawed. Chill until slightly thickened.

Beat together cream cheese, confectioners sugar, salt and vanilla until smooth. Fold in whipped cream.

Spread half of cheese mixture in pie shell. Top with half of raspberry mixture. Repeat layers. Chill well. Makes 8 servings.

STRAWBERRY ICE CREAM PIE

Spoon fresh, sliced strawberries over pie wedges before serving

4 egg whites
1 c. sugar
1 tsp. vanilla
½ c. graham cracker crumbs

½ c. flaked coconut
½ c. chopped walnuts
Strawberry ice cream

Beat egg whites until frothy. Gradually add sugar, beating until stiff glossy peaks form. Add vanilla. Fold in graham cracker crumbs, coconut and walnuts. Spread mixture in greased 9″ pie plate.

Bake in slow oven (275°) 1 hour or until pale brown. Cool on rack away from drafts.

Fill with small scoops of strawberry ice cream. Freeze until serving time. Makes 6 to 8 servings.

TROPICAL DELIGHT PIE

Refreshing dessert developed by an Idaho woman for hot days

1 (11 oz.) can mandarin oranges
1 (8½ oz.) can crushed pineapple
1 (3 oz.) pkg. lemon flavor gelatin

1 pint vanilla ice cream
2 bananas, diced
1 c. flaked coconut
12 maraschino cherries, cut up
1 baked 9" graham cracker shell

Drain mandarin oranges and pineapple, reserving juice. Add enough water, if necessary, to make 1 c. Heat juice to boiling point.

Combine gelatin and fruit juice, stirring until dissolved. Add ice cream; stir until melted. Chill until mixture is slightly thickened (about 20 minutes).

Fold in mandarin oranges, pineapple, bananas, coconut and maraschino cherries. Pour into graham cracker shell. Chill for about 1 hour. Makes 6 to 8 servings.

LEMON VELVET PIE

Capture the attention at your next dessert buffet with this beauty

1⅓ c. sugar
6 tblsp. cornstarch
½ tsp. salt
1½ c. cold water
2 egg yolks, slightly beaten
2 tblsp. butter or regular margarine
⅓ c. lemon juice

1 tsp. grated lemon rind
1 tsp. vanilla
1 envelope unflavored gelatin
¼ c. cold water
1 c. light cream
2 egg whites, stiffly beaten
1 baked 9" pie shell
1 c. heavy cream, whipped

Combine sugar, cornstarch and salt in 2-qt. saucepan. Gradually stir in 1½ c. water. Cook over medium heat, stirring constantly, until mixture is smooth and thick enough to mound when dropped from a spoon. Stir some of the hot mixture into the egg yolks. Slowly stir yolks and butter into remaining hot mixture; cook for 2 minutes.

Remove from heat and stir in lemon juice, lemon rind and vanilla. Remove 1 c. filling and set aside to cool.

Soften gelatin in ¼ c. water. Add to remaining hot filling and stir until dissolved. Gradually stir in light cream. Chill until mixture begins to thicken.

Fold in egg whites. Pour into pie shell. Chill 15 minutes. Spread with reserved 1 c. filling. Chill until set. Decorate with puffs of whipped cream. Makes 6 to 8 servings.

LEMON / ORANGE PIE

Cool summer evenings demand light and tangy pies like this one

1 envelope unflavored gelatin	¼ c. lemon juice
¾ c. cold milk	1 tsp. grated orange rind
1 c. sugar	½ tsp. grated lemon rind
¼ tsp. salt	1 c. heavy cream, whipped
3 egg yolks, beaten	1 baked 9″ pie shell
¾ c. orange juice	

Soften gelatin in milk. Combine gelatin mixture, sugar, salt and egg yolks in small saucepan. Heat, stirring constantly, until gelatin dissolves. Stir in orange juice, lemon juice, orange rind and lemon rind. Chill mixture until slightly thickened.

Fold whipped cream into gelatin mixture. Turn into pie shell. Chill several hours or until set. Makes 6 to 8 servings.

PEACH CHEESE PIE

Smooth and creamy-rich, this lovely pie is an enticing dessert

1 (8 oz.) pkg. cream cheese	1 (29 oz.) can sliced peaches
2 eggs	1 tblsp. cornstarch
½ c. sugar	¼ c. sugar
2 tblsp. milk	1 tsp. lemon juice
1 tsp. vanilla	¼ tsp. almond extract
1 unbaked 9″ pie shell	1 maraschino cherry

Soften cream cheese. Add eggs, ½ c. sugar, milk and vanilla; blend well. Pour into pie shell.

Bake in moderate oven (375°) 30 minutes. Cool well.

Drain peaches; reserve 1 c. juice. Combine cornstarch and ¼ c. sugar in small saucepan. Stir in reserved peach juice, lemon juice and almond extract. Cook over medium heat, stirring constantly, until thickened. Arrange peaches petal fashion on cheese filling. Garnish with a maraschino cherry in the center. Spoon glaze over fruit. Chill for 1 hour. Makes 6 to 8 servings.

DATE CHIFFON PIE

For a special treat, add 2 tblsp. sesame seeds to the pastry

1 envelope unflavored gelatin	1 tsp. vanilla
¼ c. cold water	⅛ tsp. ground nutmeg
¼ c. sugar	1 c. finely chopped dates
¼ tsp. salt	¾ c. heavy cream, whipped
2 eggs, separated	2 tblsp. sugar
1 c. milk	1 baked 9″ pie shell
1 tblsp. lemon juice	

Soften gelatin in water.

Combine ¼ c. sugar, salt, beaten egg yolks and milk in medium saucepan. Cook over medium heat, stirring constantly, until mixture coats a spoon. Add softened gelatin, lemon juice, vanilla and nutmeg, stirring until gelatin is dissolved. Chill until partially thickened.

Fold in dates and whipped cream.

Beat egg whites until frothy. Gradually add 2 tblsp. sugar, beating until stiff and glossy. Fold into date mixture. Turn into pie shell. Chill until set. Makes 6 to 8 servings.

Chapter 9

ALL KINDS OF COOKIES...
Every One a Favorite

We have dipped into the cookie jars of country kitchens for the cookies found there most often—by family request—so that we could fill this chapter with some of the best cookies you've ever tasted. Crisp, tender sugar cookie circles . . . chewy, fruit-studded drop cookies . . . all kinds of bake-and-cut bars and squares that taste so good with a cold glass of milk . . . fudgy brownies . . . crisp molasses wafers . . . tart lemon strips . . . fancy cookies for special parties—there's a cookie for every occasion. Some of these have captured Blue Ribbons at fairs. Many have been treasured and carefully handed down through several generations of family favoritism.

Tips for turning out perfect batches of cookies every time are included throughout this chapter. (Did you know that you bake cookies on a *shiny* baking sheet for best results?)

When it's time to store your cooled cookies, you can "lock in" the homemade flavor by putting soft cookies—bars and squares—in a tightly covered container; or keep in the baking pan, but covered with aluminum foil. Crisp cookies should be stored in a container with a loose-fitting cover. If crisp cookies do begin to soften, place them in a 300° oven for about 5 minutes before serving. Never store soft and crisp cookies together.

Treasured recipes you especially won't want to miss are lunch box brighteners such as Chocolate/Raisin Bars, Peanut Butter Fingers, Date-Filled Oatmeal Cookies and Date and Apricot Bars. They're filled with nutrition as well as good flavor. And if you're involved with bake sales or bazaars, we have cookies with money-making reputations.

Enjoy them all, right down to the very last tender crumb!

BAKE SALES AND BAZAARS

These cookies will be snapped up almost as fast as you can un-pack them. You'll find a grand assortment to appeal to all tastes . . . crisp molasses, chewy oatmeal, spicy pumpkin and crunchy nut-studded cookies.

PRIDE OF IOWA COOKIES

You'll be asked again and again for this all-time cookie favorite

1 c. shortening	1 tsp. baking powder
1 c. sugar	1 tsp. baking soda
1 c. brown sugar, firmly packed	½ tsp. salt
2 eggs	3 c. quick-cooking rolled oats
2 tsp. vanilla	1 c. flaked coconut
2 c. sifted flour	½ c. chopped walnuts

Cream together shortening and sugars until light and fluffy. Beat in eggs, one at a time, beating well after each addition. Beat in vanilla.

Sift together flour, baking powder, baking soda and salt. Gradually stir into creamed mixture. Stir in oats, coconut and walnuts. Drop by teaspoonfuls 2″ apart on greased baking sheet. Flatten with floured fork or bottom of drinking glass.

Bake in moderate oven (350°) 8 to 10 minutes or until golden. Remove from pan. Cool on racks. Makes about 8 dozen.

MOLASSES / GINGER COOKIES

This spicy cookie was a two-time Blue Ribbon winner in Minnesota

½ c. shortening	3 c. sifted flour
½ c. sugar	½ tsp. baking soda
½ c. light molasses	½ tsp. ground cinnamon
½ tblsp. vinegar	½ tsp. ground ginger
1 egg, beaten	¼ tsp. salt

Combine shortening, sugar, molasses and vinegar in small saucepan. Bring mixture to a boil and remove from heat. Cool well and beat in egg.

Sift together flour, baking soda, cinnamon, ginger and salt. Gradually stir into molasses mixture. Chill for 1 hour.

Divide dough in half. Roll on floured surface 1/8" thick. Cut into desired shapes with floured cookie cutters. Place 1" apart on greased baking sheet.

Bake in moderate oven (375°) 10 minutes or until done. Remove from pans. Cool on racks. Makes about 2½ dozen.

OATMEAL REFRIGERATOR COOKIES

Dough keeps well in refrigerator; just slice and bake when needed

1 c. butter or regular margarine	½ tsp. salt
1 c. sifted confectioners sugar	1 c. quick-cooking rolled oats
2 tsp. vanilla	⅓ c. chocolate jimmies
1¼ c. sifted flour	

Cream together butter and confectioners sugar until light and fluffy. Beat in vanilla.

Sift together flour and salt. Gradually stir into creamed mixture. Stir in oats. Shape dough into roll, about 2" in diameter. Roll in chocolate jimmies. Chill for 1 hour.

Cut roll into ¼" thick slices. Place 2" apart on greased baking sheet.

Bake in slow oven (325°) 15 minutes or until golden. Remove from pans. Cool on racks. Makes about 3 dozen.

SPICY PUMPKIN BARS

Serve with steaming mugs of apple cider after a brisk autumn hike

½ c. shortening	1¼ tsp. ground cinnamon
1 c. brown sugar, firmly packed	1 tsp. ground nutmeg
¼ c. sugar	1 tsp. ground ginger
4 eggs	½ tsp. salt
2 c. canned pumpkin	Cream Cheese Icing (recipe
2 c. sifted flour	follows)
4 tsp. baking powder	

Cream together shortening and sugars until light and fluffy. Add eggs, one at a time, beating well after each addition. Beat in pumpkin.

Sift together flour, baking powder, cinnamon, nutmeg, ginger and salt. Gradually stir in dry ingredients. Spread mixture in greased 15½ × 10½ × 1″ jelly roll pan.

Bake in moderate oven (350°) 30 minutes or until it tests done. Cool in pan on rack. Spread with Cream Cheese Icing. If you wish, sprinkle with chopped walnuts. Cut into 3½ × 1¼″ bars. Makes 32.

Cream Cheese Icing: Combine 1 (3 oz.) pkg. softened cream cheese, 1 tblsp. butter or regular margarine, 2½ c. sifted confectioners sugar, 1 tsp. grated lemon peel, pinch salt and 1 tblsp. milk. Stir until smooth.

SIX-IN-ONE REFRIGERATOR COOKIES

So easy to make—an excellent choice for bazaars or bake sales

2 c. butter or regular margarine
1 c. sugar
1 c. light brown sugar, firmly packed
2 eggs, beaten
1 tsp. vanilla
4 c. unsifted flour
1 tsp. baking soda
½ tsp. salt

½ c. shredded coconut
½ c. finely chopped pecans
½ tsp. ground nutmeg
1 tsp. ground cinnamon
1 (1 oz.) square unsweetened chocolate, melted
¼ c. finely chopped candied cherries

Cream butter. Gradually add sugars; beat until light and fluffy.
Add eggs and vanilla; mix well.

Sift together flour, baking soda and salt. Gradually add to creamed mixture.

Divide dough in 6 (1 cup) portions. Add coconut to one part; pecans to second; nutmeg and cinnamon to third; melted chocolate to fourth; and candied cherries to fifth. Leave the last portion plain. Chill for 30 minutes or longer.

Shape dough into 6 rolls about 1¾″ in diameter. Wrap tightly in plastic wrap or waxed paper and refrigerate overnight.

When ready to use, slice with sharp knife in ⅛″ slices. Place on lightly greased baking sheet.

Bake in moderate oven (375°) 10 to 12 minutes. Remove from pans. Cool on racks. Makes 18 dozen.

CORNMEAL COOKIES

Crisp, golden cookies that are perfect for picnics and camping

1 c. shortening	1 c. yellow cornmeal
1½ c. sugar	1½ tsp. baking powder
3 eggs	1 tsp. ground nutmeg
1 tsp. lemon extract	½ tsp. salt
½ tsp. vanilla	½ c. raisins
3 c. sifted flour	Sugar

Cream together shortening and 1½ c. sugar. Add eggs, one at a time, beating until light and fluffy. Add lemon and vanilla extracts.

Sift together flour, cornmeal, baking powder, nutmeg and salt. Add to creamed mixture. Add raisins.

Roll dough ⅛″ thick on floured surface. Cut cookies with 2½″ cutter. Place on greased baking sheet. Sprinkle with sugar.

Bake in hot oven (400°) 10 minutes or until golden brown. Remove from pans. Cool on racks. Makes 80.

COCONUT SQUARES

Makes a yummy snack served with frothy mugs of piping hot cocoa

1¼ c. sifted flour	2 eggs
½ tsp. baking powder	1 tsp. vanilla
¼ tsp. salt	½ tsp. almond extract
1 c. brown sugar, firmly packed	1 c. flaked coconut
¼ c. butter or regular margarine	½ c. chopped walnuts
	Lemon Glaze (recipe follows)

Sift together flour, baking powder and salt.

Cream together brown sugar and butter until light and fluffy. Add eggs, one at a time, beating well after each addition. Beat in vanilla and almond extract.

Gradually add flour, beating well after each addition. Stir in coconut and walnuts. Spread mixture in greased 9″ square pan.

Bake in slow oven (325°) 30 minutes or until golden brown. Spread with Lemon Glaze while warm. Cool in pan on rack. Cut in 1½″ squares. Makes 1½ dozen.

Lemon Glaze: Combine 1 c. sifted confectioners sugar, ½ tsp. grated lemon rind and 1 tblsp. hot milk. Blend until smooth.

LUNCH BOX SURPRISES

When you're packing a lunch for a school child or for men in the field, it's fun to add a little surprise for dessert. Chocolate/Cream Cheese Cookies and Chocolate/Raisin Cookies will please the chocolate lovers. We also have peanut butter, date, oatmeal and sugar-topped spice cookies—a sweet nibble to cater to every taste.

CHOCOLATE / CREAM CHEESE COOKIES

Avid chocolate fans will love these cookies with hot fudge sundaes

1 c. butter or regular margarine	2 (1 oz.) squares unsweetened
1 (3 oz.) pkg. cream cheese	chocolate, melted
1½ c. sugar	2¼ c. sifted flour
1 egg	1½ tsp. baking soda
1 tsp. vanilla	½ tsp. salt
2 tblsp. milk	½ c. chopped walnuts

Cream together butter, cream cheese and sugar until light and fluffy. Add egg, vanilla, milk and chocolate; beat well.

Sift together flour, baking soda and salt. Gradually stir into creamed mixture. Stir in walnuts. Drop by teaspoonfuls 2″ apart on greased baking sheet.

Bake in moderate oven (350°) 10 minutes. Remove from pans. Cool on racks. Makes 6 dozen.

CHOCOLATE / RAISIN BARS

A family favorite that won first prize in a local baking contest

1 (15 oz.) can sweetened condensed milk

2 (1 oz.) squares unsweetened chocolate

2 c. raisins

1 c. butter or regular margarine

1⅓ c. brown sugar, firmly packed

½ tsp. vanilla

1¾ c. sifted flour

¾ tsp. salt

½ tsp. baking powder

2 c. quick-cooking rolled oats

Combine sweetened condensed milk and chocolate. Heat over hot water until chocolate melts. Stir in raisins; cool slightly.

Cream together butter and brown sugar until light and fluffy. Add vanilla; beat well.

Sift together flour, salt and baking powder. Gradually stir into creamed mixture. Add oats; mix until crumbly.

Press half of crumb mixture in greased 13 × 9 × 2″ pan. Spread with chocolate mixture. Sprinkle with remaining crumbs.

Bake in moderate oven (350°) 30 to 35 minutes. Cool in pan on rack. Cut in 3 × 1″ bars. Makes 3 dozen.

DATE AND APRICOT BARS

"I'm always asked for this recipe," an Oklahoma farm woman says

1½ c. dried apricots

2 c. water

1 c. cut-up dates

½ c. sugar

1 tsp. grated lemon rind

½ c. chopped pecans

1/16 tsp. salt

2 c. sifted flour

2 c. quick-cooking rolled oats

1 c. brown sugar, firmly packed

¾ c. melted butter or regular margarine

1 tsp. baking soda

1 tsp. vanilla

Cook apricots in water until tender. Drain and reserve 3 tblsp. cooking liquid. Combine cooked apricots, dates, sugar and reserved liquid in saucepan. Simmer for 3 minutes. Stir in lemon rind, pecans and salt. Cool well.

Combine flour, oats, brown sugar, butter, baking soda and vanilla;

mix well. Press half of mixture in greased 13 × 9 × 2″ pan. Spread with cooled filling. Top with remaining crumb mixture.

Bake in moderate oven (375°) 35 minutes. Cool in pan on rack. Cut in 3 × 1″ bars. Makes about 3 dozen.

PEANUT BUTTER FINGERS

A first prize winner in a local baking contest for a Montana woman

½ c. butter or regular	½ tsp. baking soda
margarine	¼ tsp. salt
½ c. sugar	1 c. quick-cooking rolled oats
½ c. brown sugar, firmly packed	1 (6 oz.) pkg. semi-sweet
1 egg	chocolate pieces
⅓ c. peanut butter	½ c. confectioners sugar
½ tsp. vanilla	¼ c. peanut butter
1 c. sifted flour	2 to 4 tblsp. milk

Cream together butter and sugars until light and fluffy. Add egg; beat well. Beat in ⅓ c. peanut butter and vanilla.

Sift together flour, baking soda and salt. Stir dry ingredients and oats gradually into creamed mixture. Spread mixture in greased 13 × 9 × 2″ pan.

Bake in moderate oven (350°) 20 to 25 minutes. Sprinkle top with chocolate pieces. Let stand for 5 minutes. Spread melted chocolate over top of bars. Combine confectioners sugar, ¼ c. peanut butter and enough milk to make a thin icing. Drizzle over melted chocolate. Cool in pan on rack. Cut into 3 × 1″ bars. Makes about 3 dozen.

SUGAR AND SPICE COOKIES

Try to keep your cookie jar filled with these mouth-watering gems

¾ c. shortening	1 tsp. ground cinnamon
1 c. sugar	¾ tsp. ground ginger
1 egg	½ tsp. ground cloves
¼ c. molasses	¼ tsp. salt
2 c. sifted flour	2 tsp. sugar
2 tsp. baking soda	1 tsp. ground cinnamon

Cream together shortening and 1 c. sugar until fluffy. Add egg and molasses, blending well.

Sift together flour, baking soda, 1 tsp. cinnamon, ginger, cloves and salt. Stir into creamed mixture. Form into balls using 1 tsp. dough. Roll in a mixture of 2 tsp. sugar and 1 tsp. cinnamon.

Place about 2″ apart on a greased baking sheet. Bake in moderate oven (375°) 10 minutes or until golden brown. Remove from pan. Cool on racks. Makes about 3 dozen.

CINNAMON JUMBLES

"My son says I ought to sell these cookies and make a lot of money"

1 c. butter or regular margarine	1 tsp. baking soda
2 c. sugar	1 tsp. salt
2 eggs	1½ c. buttermilk
2 tsp. vanilla	½ c. sugar
4 c. sifted flour	2 tsp. ground cinnamon

Cream together butter and 2 c. sugar until light and fluffy. Add eggs, one at a time, beating well after each addition. Beat in vanilla.

Sift together flour, baking soda and salt. Add dry ingredients alternately with buttermilk to creamed mixture, beating well after each addition. Chill dough overnight.

Drop by rounded teaspoonfuls 2″ apart on greased baking sheet. Combine ½ c. sugar and cinnamon; sprinkle mixture on each cookie.

Bake in hot oven (400°) 8 to 10 minutes or until golden. Remove from pan. Cool on racks. Makes about 5 dozen.

CHOCOLATE NUT COOKIES

These refrigerator cookies are a first prize winner at an Arizona fair

⅔ c. butter or regular margarine	½ c. cocoa
	½ tsp. baking soda
1 c. sugar	½ tsp. salt
1 egg	2 tblsp. milk
1 tsp. vanilla	1 c. chopped walnuts
1½ c. sifted flour	

Cream together butter and sugar until light and fluffy. Add egg and vanilla; beat well.

Sift together flour, cocoa, baking soda and salt. Add dry ingredients alternately with milk to creamed mixture, mixing well after each addition. Stir in walnuts. Chill dough.

Shape dough into 2 (7″) rolls. Chill well. Cut in ¼″ slices. Place about 2″ apart on greased baking sheet.

Bake in moderate oven (375°) 8 minutes. Remove from pan. Cool on rack. Makes 6 dozen.

DOUBLE TREAT COOKIES

Always a winner . . . tuck in packed lunches with thermos of cocoa

2 c. sifted flour	2 eggs
2 tsp. baking soda	1 tsp. vanilla
½ tsp. salt	1 c. peanut butter
1 c. shortening	1 c. chopped, salted peanuts
1 c. sugar	1 (6 oz.) pkg. semi-sweet
1 c. brown sugar, firmly packed	chocolate pieces

Sift together flour, baking soda and salt.

Cream together shortening and sugars until light and fluffy. Add eggs, one at a time, beating well after each addition. Beat in vanilla. Blend in peanut butter. Add dry ingredients. Stir in peanuts and chocolate pieces.

Shape into small balls; place on ungreased baking sheet. Flatten with bottom of a glass dipped in sugar.

Bake in moderate oven (350°) 8 minutes or until brown. Remove from pan. Cool on racks. Makes 7 dozen.

DATE-FILLED OATMEAL COOKIES

These cookies, a family heirloom, are from a North Dakota cook

1 (8 oz.) pkg. dates, cut up	2 eggs
1 c. sugar	1 tsp. vanilla
1 c. water	2½ c. sifted flour
⅛ tsp. salt	1½ tsp. cream of tartar
1 c. shortening	1 tsp. baking soda
1½ c. brown sugar, firmly packed	1 tsp. hot water
	1½ c. quick-cooking rolled oats

Cook dates, sugar, water and salt in small saucepan until dates are tender. Set aside to cool.

Cream together shortening and brown sugar until light and fluffy. Add eggs and vanilla; beat well.

Sift together flour and cream of tartar. Gradually stir into creamed mixture. Dissolve baking soda in hot water. Stir soda mixture and oats into creamed mixture.

Roll dough on floured surface ⅜" thick. Cut in 2½" rounds. Place 2" apart on greased baking sheet and spoon date filling on each. Top with another round and press edges together to seal.

Bake in moderate oven (350°) 10 to 12 minutes or until golden brown. Remove from pans. Cool on racks. Makes about 3½ dozen.

BAKE FOR THE HOLIDAYS

In November farm cooks start to plan their Christmas cookie baking. By early December, some of the fruit-studded varieties are baked and frozen—all ready for Christmas feasting. Treat the family to the Mincemeat Pie-Bars and the Pumpkin Pie Squares for a Thanksgiving dessert. We predict they will request them again for the Christmas season!

MINCEMEAT PIE-BARS

Serve topped with ice cream for a special Thanksgiving dessert

2½ c. sifted flour	5 to 6 tblsp. water
1 tsp. salt	2 c. prepared mincemeat
1 c. shortening	2 tblsp. sugar

Combine flour and salt; cut in shortening until crumbly. Add enough water to make dough moist enough to hold together.

Divide dough in half. Roll one part on floured surface to make a 14 × 9" rectangle. Place on ungreased baking sheet. Spread mincemeat to within ½" of edges.

Roll remaining half of dough to 14 × 9" rectangle. Place on mincemeat; seal edges with fork. Prick top with fork. Sprinkle with sugar.

Bake in hot oven (400°) 30 minutes or until golden. Serve warm or cold, cut in 2" squares. Makes 28.

Time is running out for the KQED Capital Fund. Failure to raise additional funds soon will mean cuts in the programming budget -- cuts that may change what you actually see on your television screen. Your one-time contribution to the KQED Capital Fund can help prevent these programming cuts.

Remember, giving to KQED at year-end is tax-deductible. After taking a look at your estimated tax bill, you might be surprised at how much you can actually afford to donate.

The entire staff of KQED is working hard to improve the scope and quali-ty of programs that you see on public television. I personally urge you to help by donating now to the KQED Capital Fund.

Sincerely,

Philip D. Armour III

PUMPKIN PIE SQUARES

Top with a swirl of soft whipped cream and toasted pecan halves

1 c. sifted flour
½ c. quick-cooking rolled oats
½ c. brown sugar, firmly packed
½ c. butter or regular
  margarine
1 (1 lb.) can pumpkin (2 c.)
1 (13½ oz.) can evaporated
  milk
2 eggs

¾ c. sugar
½ tsp. salt
1 tsp. ground cinnamon
½ tsp. ground ginger
¼ tsp. ground cloves
½ c. chopped pecans
½ c. brown sugar, firmly packed
2 tblsp. butter or regular
  margarine

Combine flour, rolled oats, ½ c. brown sugar and ½ c. butter in mixing bowl. Mix until crumbly, using electric mixer on low speed. Press into ungreased 13 × 9 × 2″ pan. Bake in moderate oven (350°) 15 minutes.

Combine pumpkin, evaporated milk, eggs, sugar, salt, cinnamon, ginger and cloves in mixing bowl; beat well. Pour into crust.

Bake in moderate oven (350°) 20 minutes.

Combine pecans, ½ c. brown sugar and 2 tblsp. butter; sprinkle over pumpkin filling. Return to oven and bake 15 to 20 minutes or until filling is set. Cool in pan on rack. Cut in 2″ squares. Makes 2 dozen.

CHRISTMAS CHERRY BELLS

You don't need a bell-shaped cookie cutter for these spicy treats

1 c. butter or regular margarine
1¼ c. brown sugar, firmly
  packed
¼ c. dark corn syrup
1 egg
1 tblsp. light cream
3 c. sifted flour
½ tsp. baking soda
½ tsp. salt

½ tsp. ground ginger
½ tsp. ground cinnamon
1½ c. finely chopped pecans
⅓ c. brown sugar, firmly
  packed
3 tblsp. maraschino cherry juice
1 tblsp. butter
Maraschino cherries

Cream together 1 c. butter and 1¼ c. brown sugar until light and fluffy. Add syrup, egg and light cream; beat well.

Sift together flour, baking soda, salt, ginger and cinnamon. Gradually stir into creamed mixture. Chill for 1 hour.

Divide dough into 3 parts. Roll dough on floured surface ⅛″ thick. Cut into 2½″ rounds and place 2″ apart on ungreased baking sheet.

Combine pecans, ⅓ c. brown sugar, cherry juice and 1 tblsp. butter. Place ½ tsp. pecan filling in center of each round. Shape into bell by folding sides to center over filling, overlapping slightly. Fold edges so that top is narrower than bottom. Place a piece of maraschino cherry at bottom of bell for clapper.

Bake in slow oven (325°) 12 to 15 minutes or until golden brown. Remove from pan. Cool on racks. Makes about 6 dozen.

LEMON BUTTER COOKIES

These butter cookies are also attractive sprinkled with colored sugars

1½ c. butter or regular margarine	1 tsp. grated lemon rind
	4½ c. sifted flour
1 c. sugar	¼ tsp. salt
2 eggs	

Cream together butter and sugar. Add eggs and rind, beat well. Sift together flour and salt; add gradually to creamed mixture. Chill dough for 3 to 4 hours.

Roll out on lightly floured surface ⅛″ thick and cut in desired shapes. Place on greased baking sheet.

Bake in hot oven (400°) 6 to 8 minutes or until golden. Remove cookies from oven. Using a toothpick, twist a small hole in the top of each cookie. Cool slightly. Remove cookies from baking sheet. Cool on racks. Makes 6 dozen.

To decorate the cookies, pour food coloring in small saucers. Add a few drops of water. You can make many beautiful colors by mixing the basic colors. Use narrow brushes for fine lines and wider brushes for large areas. Rinse brush out in water when you change colors so that your colors will be clear and not murky. With colors of your choice, paint your own original designs on the cookies.

To hang cookies on the tree, draw narrow colored cord through the hole in each cookie.

CHRISTMAS JEWEL COOKIES

Attractive jelly-filled rounds that are deliciously mouth-watering

1 c. butter	1 tsp. vanilla
½ c. sugar	2 c. sifted flour
3 hard-cooked egg yolks	Strawberry or currant jelly

Cream together butter and sugar until light and fluffy. Break up egg yolks and beat into creamed mixture; blend well. Add vanilla.

Gradually stir in flour. Chill for 1 hour. Shape dough into 1" balls and place 1" apart on ungreased baking sheet. Make a small dent in top of each cookie with finger.

Bake in moderate oven (375°) 10 minutes. Remove from oven and fill dents with jelly. Return to oven and bake 1 to 2 more minutes to set jelly. If you wish, top with your favorite glaze while still warm. Remove from pan. Cool on racks. Makes 5 dozen.

HOLIDAY FRUIT COOKIES

Chewy cookies that will add color to your holiday cookie plate

½ c. shortening	1 c. chopped dates
1 c. sugar	1 c. chopped candied cherries
1 egg	¾ c. chopped walnuts
1¾ c. sifted flour	½ c. mixed candied fruit
½ tsp. baking soda	⅓ c. buttermilk
½ tsp. salt	

Cream together shortening and sugar until light and fluffy. Add egg; beat well.

Sift together flour, baking soda and salt. Reserve ¼ c. flour mixture; mix with dates, candied cherries, walnuts and mixed candied fruit. Gradually add remaining dry ingredients alternately with buttermilk to creamed mixture, beating well after each addition. Stir in fruit/nut mixture. Drop by heaping teaspoonfuls about 2" apart on greased baking sheet.

Bake in hot oven (400°) 10 to 13 minutes or until golden. Remove from pan. Cool on racks. Makes 3½ dozen.

DANISH SUGAR COOKIES

"An ideal recipe for beginning cooks," says a Minnesota farm woman

½ c. butter	2 c. sifted flour
½ c. shortening	½ tsp. baking soda
1 c. sugar	½ tsp. cream of tartar
1 egg	⅛ tsp. salt
½ tsp. vanilla	Sugar
½ tsp. lemon extract	

Cream together butter, shortening and sugar until light and fluffy. Add egg, vanilla and lemon extract; beat well.

Sift together flour, baking soda, cream of tartar and salt. Stir gradually into creamed mixture. Chill well.

Shape dough into 1″ balls and roll in sugar. Place 1″ apart on greased baking sheet. Flatten by pressing with bottom of drinking glass.

Bake in moderate oven (350°) 8 minutes or until golden. Remove from pans. Cool on racks. Makes about 5 dozen.

SPICY DATE BARS

The ideal snack with cups of hot coffee after a winter football game

⅔ c. butter or regular margarine	½ tsp. salt
	1 tsp. ground cinnamon
1 c. brown sugar, firmly packed	½ tsp. ground ginger
2 eggs	½ tsp. ground nutmeg
½ c. light molasses	1 c. finely chopped dates
1 tsp. vanilla	1 c. finely chopped walnuts
2 c. sifted flour	Creamy Vanilla Frosting (recipe
½ tsp. baking soda	follows)

Cream together butter and brown sugar until light and fluffy. Add eggs, one at a time, beating well after each addition. Beat in molasses and vanilla.

Sift together flour, baking soda, salt, cinnamon, ginger and nutmeg. Reserve ¼ c. flour mixture and mix with dates and walnuts. Gradually stir dry ingredients into creamed mixture. Stir in date-nut mixture. Spread in greased 15½ × 10½ × 1″ jelly roll pan.

Bake in moderate oven (375°) 20 to 25 minutes. While warm, spread with Creamy Vanilla Frosting. Cool in pan on rack. Cut into 2½ × 1½" bars. Makes 48 bars.

Cream Vanilla Frosting: Combine 1¼ c. sifted confectioners sugar, 1 tblsp. soft butter or regular margarine, ½ tsp. vanilla, ⅛ tsp. almond extract and 1½ tsp. milk. Beat until smooth.

APRICOT SNOWDRIFTS

Attractive holiday bars with a tangy and chewy apricot layer

⅔ c. dried apricots	¼ tsp. salt
1 c. sifted flour	2 eggs
¼ c. sugar	1 c. brown sugar, firmly packed
½ c. butter or regular margarine	½ c. chopped walnuts
⅓ c. sifted flour	½ tsp. vanilla
½ tsp. baking powder	Confectioners sugar
	Candied cherries

Cook apricots in boiling water for 10 minutes; drain. Cool and cut up. Set aside.

Combine 1 c. flour, sugar and butter; mix until crumbly. Press into greased 9" square pan. Bake in moderate oven (350°) 18 minutes.

Sift together ⅓ c. flour, baking powder and salt.

Beat eggs well. Slowly beat in brown sugar, blending well. Add flour mixture; stir well. Add apricots, nuts and vanilla. Spread over baked layer.

Bake in moderate oven (350°) 25 minutes or until golden brown. Cool in pan on rack. Cut into bars with a wet knife. Roll in confectioners sugar. Decorate each bar with candied cherry half. Makes 32 (2 × 1") bars.

MAIL A BOX OF COOKIES

A package of cookies from home is just about the nicest surprise that a far-away friend or relative can receive. Any one of these cookies travels well and will arrive in mint condition if carefully packed. In fact, they will taste even better than the day they were baked. They mellow to a perfect flavor on the way to their destination.

TUTTI-FRUTTI SQUARES

Ideal cookies for long-distance mailing because they mellow with age

2 eggs	1 c. chopped walnuts
1 c. sifted confectioners sugar	¼ c. chopped candied orange
3 tblsp. melted shortening	peel
¾ c. sifted flour	¼ c. chopped candied lemon
1½ tsp. baking powder	peel
½ tsp. salt	¼ c. chopped candied pineapple
1 c. chopped dates	Confectioners sugar

Beat eggs until light and lemon-colored. Gradually beat in 1 c. confectioners sugar and shortening.

Sift together flour, baking powder and salt. Gradually stir into creamed mixture. Stir in dates, walnuts, orange peel, lemon peel and pineapple. Spread mixture in greased 8" square pan.

Bake in moderate oven (350°) 35 to 40 minutes. Let cool for 10 minutes and cut into 2" squares. Cool completely, roll cookies in confectioners sugar. Makes 16.

PINEAPPLE NUT COOKIES

Moist drop cookies that will make a big hit at the Christmas bazaar

1 c. butter or regular margarine	1 tsp. baking soda
1 c. sugar	1 (8½ oz.) can crushed
1 c. brown sugar, firmly packed	pineapple
2 eggs	1 c. chopped walnuts
1 tsp. vanilla	¼ c. chopped maraschino
4¼ c. sifted flour	cherries

Cream together butter and sugars until light and fluffy. Add eggs, one at a time; beat well. Beat in vanilla.

Sift together flour and baking soda. Drain pineapple, reserving juice. Add dry ingredients alternately with pineapple juice to creamed mixture, beating well after each addition. Stir in pineapple, walnuts and maraschino cherries. Drop by teaspoonfuls about 2" apart on greased baking sheet.

Bake in moderate oven (350°) 8 to 10 minutes or until golden brown. Remove from pan. Cool on racks. Makes 9 dozen.

PUMPKIN DROP COOKIES

Tuck these spicy treats and a crisp red apple into lunch buckets

⅓ c. shortening
1 c. sugar
1 c. canned pumpkin
2 eggs
1 tsp. lemon juice
1 tsp. vanilla
2¼ c. unsifted flour
2 tsp. baking powder

1 tsp. ground cinnamon
1 tsp. ground allspice
½ tsp. salt
¼ tsp. ground ginger
1 c. raisins
½ c. flaked coconut
½ c. chopped walnuts

Cream together shortening and sugar until light and fluffy. Beat in pumpkin, eggs, lemon juice and vanilla; blend well.

Sift together flour, baking powder, cinnamon, allspice, salt and ginger. Gradually stir into creamed mixture. Stir in raisins, coconut and walnuts. Drop by heaping teaspoonfuls 2″ apart on greased baking sheet.

Bake in moderate oven (350°) 10 to 12 minutes. Remove from pan. Cool on racks. Makes about 4 dozen.

SPICY NUT AND FRUIT SQUARES

Serve frosty dishes of lemon sherbet with these unusual cookies

½ c. butter or regular
  margarine
1 c. dark brown sugar, firmly
  packed
1 egg, separated
1 tsp. vanilla
1¾ c. sifted flour
¼ tsp. baking soda

¼ tsp. salt
3 tblsp. sugar
1 tsp. ground cinnamon
1 tsp. ground nutmeg
¼ tsp. ground cloves
1 c. chopped mixed candied
  fruit
1 c. chopped walnuts

Cream together butter and brown sugar until light and fluffy. Add egg yolk and vanilla; beat well.

Sift together flour, baking soda and salt. Gradually stir into creamed mixture, mixing well. (Dough will be very crumbly.) Press dough into ungreased 13 × 9 × 2″ pan.

Beat egg white slightly. Add sugar, cinnamon, nutmeg, cloves, candied fruit and walnuts; mix well. Spread evenly over dough.

Bake in moderate oven (350°) 20 to 25 minutes or until golden. Cool in pan on rack. Cut in 2″ squares. Makes 2 dozen.

SOFT MOLASSES DROPS

These chewy cookies keep well and are perfect for mailing overseas

¾ c. butter or regular margarine	1 tsp. vanilla
1½ c. brown sugar, firmly packed	2 tblsp. molasses
	1 tsp. baking soda
3 eggs	3 c. sifted flour
	1 c. raisins

Cream butter and sugar until light and fluffy. Add eggs, one at a time, beating well after each addition. Beat in vanilla.

Combine molasses and baking soda. Add to creamed mixture. Gradually stir in flour. Add raisins. Drop by teaspoonfuls onto greased baking sheet.

Bake in moderate oven (350°) 8 minutes or until brown. Remove from pan. Cool on racks. Makes about 6 dozen.

THE VERY BEST BROWNIES

Everyone loves brownies and we have three that are just a bit different but good down to the very last fudgy crumb! Rich and creamy Cottage Cheese Brownies, nutty Whole Wheat Brownies and chocolate frosted Orange and Fudge Brownies . . . the recipes are here.

WHOLE WHEAT BROWNIES

Energy-packed brownies are perfect for school lunch boxes

½ c. butter or regular margarine	¼ tsp. salt
1 c. brown sugar, firmly packed	6 tblsp. cocoa
2 eggs	2 tblsp. melted butter or regular margarine
½ tsp. vanilla	1 c. chopped walnuts
½ c. whole wheat flour	

Cream together ½ c. butter and brown sugar until light and fluffy. Add eggs, one at a time, beating well after each addition. Beat in vanilla.

Gradually stir in whole wheat flour and salt. Combine cocoa and 2 tblsp. butter. Add cocoa mixture and walnuts; mix well. Spread mixture in greased 9" square pan.

Bake in slow oven (325°) 45 minutes or until done. Cool in pan on rack. Cut into 3 × 1" bars. Makes about 2 dozen.

COTTAGE CHEESE BROWNIES

"These are real winners in my family," an Ohio farm woman confides

1 c. cream-style cottage cheese, sieved	⅔ c. sugar
	½ c. cocoa
¼ c. sugar	¾ tsp. baking powder
1 egg, well beaten	¼ tsp. salt
1 tblsp. cornstarch	¼ c. melted butter or regular
¼ tsp. salt	margarine
1 tsp. vanilla	2 eggs
½ tsp. ground cinnamon	¼ c. milk
1 c. sifted flour	1 tsp. vanilla

Blend together cottage cheese, ¼ c. sugar, 1 egg, cornstarch, ¼ tsp. salt, 1 tsp. vanilla and cinnamon; set aside.

Sift together flour, ⅔ c. sugar, cocoa, baking powder and ¼ tsp. salt into large bowl. Combine butter, 2 eggs, milk and 1 tsp. vanilla. Add to dry ingredients and beat at medium speed for 2 to 3 minutes. Spread half of batter in greased 8" square pan. Top with cottage cheese mixture. Spread with remaining batter.

Bake in moderate oven (350°) 40 minutes or until it tests done. Cool in pan on rack. Cut into 3 × 1" bars. Makes 2 dozen.

ORANGE AND FUDGE BROWNIES

This unusual brownie recipe is shared by a Rhode Island farm woman

1 c. butter or regular margarine	1 c. sugar
2 c. sugar	¾ c. sifted flour
4 eggs	1 tsp. grated orange rind
2 tsp. vanilla	½ tsp. almond extract
1½ c. sifted flour	1 egg
6 tblsp. cocoa	2 tblsp. orange juice
¼ tsp. salt	Fudge Frosting (recipe follows)

Cream together butter and 2 c. sugar until light and fluffy. Add 4 eggs, one at a time, beating well after each addition. Add vanilla.

Sift together 1½ c. sifted flour, cocoa and salt. Gradually stir into creamed mixture. Set aside.

Combine 1 c. sugar and ¾ c. flour in a bowl. Add orange rind, almond extract, 1 egg and orange juice; blend well.

Spread half of fudge batter in greased 13 × 9 × 2″ pan. Top with orange batter. Spread remaining fudge batter over all.

Bake in moderate oven (350°) 30 minutes or until done. Cool in pan on rack. Frost with Fudge Frosting. Cut into 3 × 1″ bars. Makes 3 dozen.

Fudge Frosting: Combine 1½ c. sifted confectioners sugar, 3 tblsp. soft butter or regular margarine, 3 tblsp. cocoa, 3 tblsp. milk and ½ tsp. vanilla. Beat until smooth.

HEIRLOOM TREASURES

Everyone remembers "cookies Mother used to make." We have some delicious cookie recipes that have been passed down through generations. There are sturdy oatmeal, delicate lemon wafers and sugar-dusted Norwegian cookies, just to name a few.

COFFEE / OATMEAL COOKIES

A homemaker has baked these for her appreciative family for 20 years

½ c. shortening	¼ tsp. ground nutmeg
1 c. brown sugar, firmly packed	⅓ c. cold coffee
2 eggs	¼ c. light cream
2 c. sifted flour	1 c. quick-cooking rolled oats
1 tsp. baking soda	1 c. raisins
1 tsp. ground cinnamon	½ c. chopped walnuts
½ tsp. ground cloves	

Cream together shortening and brown sugar until light and fluffy. Add eggs and beat well.

Sift together flour, baking soda, cinnamon, cloves and nutmeg. Add dry ingredients alternately with coffee and cream to creamed mixture, beating well after each addition. Stir in oats, raisins and walnuts. Drop by rounded teaspoonfuls 2″ apart on greased baking sheet. Flatten with floured bottom of drinking glass.

Bake in moderate oven (350°) 8 to 10 minutes or until light brown. Remove from pan. Cool on racks. Makes 6 dozen.

LEMON SLICES

Rich and lemony—these bars will become a "regular" with your family

2 c. sifted flour
½ c. sifted confectioners sugar
1 c. butter or regular margarine
4 eggs
2 c. sugar
½ tsp. salt

⅓ c. lemon juice
1 tsp. grated lemon rind
¼ c. unsifted flour
2 tsp. confectioners sugar
Confectioners sugar

Combine 2 c. flour and ½ c. confectioners sugar in a bowl. Cut in butter until mixture is crumbly. Press mixture into ungreased 13 × 9 × 2″ pan.

Bake in moderate oven (350°) 25 minutes or until golden.

Beat eggs until thick and lemon-colored. Slowly beat in sugar, salt, lemon juice and lemon rind. Combine ¼ c. flour and 2 tsp. confectioners sugar. Stir into egg mixture. Pour over baked crust and return to oven and bake 25 minutes or until brown.

Cool in pan on rack. Cut into 2 × 1″ bars. Roll bars in confectioners sugar. Makes about 4 dozen.

FATTIGMAN

A traditional crisp cookie—popular during the Christmas season

6 egg yolks
½ tsp. salt
⅓ c. light cream
⅓ c. sugar
1 tblsp. melted butter or regular margarine

2¼ c. sifted flour
¼ tsp. ground nutmeg
1 tblsp. grated lemon rind
Confectioners sugar

Beat together egg yolks and salt until thick and light. Beat in light cream, sugar and butter.

Sift together flour and nutmeg. Add to egg yolk mixture with lemon rind, mixing well. Chill for 1 hour.

Roll out ¼ of dough at a time, keeping remaining dough chilled. Roll ¹⁄₁₆″ thick and cut in strips about 1½″ wide with sharp knife. Cut diagonally at 4″ intervals. Make 1″ slits lengthwise in center of each piece. Slip one end through slit. Fry a few at a time in deep hot fat at 350° for 1 to 2 minutes or until golden. Remove from fat with slotted spoon. Drain on paper towels and sprinkle with sifted confectioners sugar. Store in an airtight container. Makes 6 dozen.

FOR THAT EXTRA SPECIAL OCCASION

We often receive requests for a cookie recipe that must be perfect for a shower, wedding or anniversary party. Usually these recipes take a little extra time and effort but when you have lifted the last tasty beauty from the cookie sheet, you know that it is time well spent. You'll be proud to arrange a batch of any one of these dress-up cookies on your prettiest platter or tray.

KRINGLA

An Iowa woman used to sell these in a grocery every Saturday

½ c. butter or regular margarine
1 c. sugar
1 egg
1 tsp. vanilla
3¼ c. sifted flour

2½ tsp. baking powder
1 tsp. baking soda
½ tsp. salt
1 c. buttermilk
Vanilla Glaze (recipe follows)

Cream together butter and sugar until light and fluffy. Add egg and vanilla; beat well.

Sift together flour, baking powder, baking soda and salt. Add dry ingredients alternately with buttermilk to creamed mixture, beating well after each addition. Chill several hours or overnight.

Roll 1 tablespoon of dough on a floured surface, making a 5″ stick. Place on greased baking sheet. Shape each stick into a ring and join ends. Repeat with remaining dough.

Bake in moderate oven (350°) 12 minutes or until golden. Remove from pan. Cool on racks. When cool, spread with Vanilla Glaze. Makes about 5½ dozen.

Vanilla Glaze: Combine 1½ c. sifted confectioners sugar, 1½ tblsp. water and 1 tsp. vanilla. Beat until smooth. If necessary, add more water to make a thin glaze.

ALMOND / RASPBERRY BARS

Rich, buttery bars that won a Blue Ribbon at the New York Fair

1½ c. sifted flour	½ c. ground blanched almonds
½ c. sugar	1 egg
½ tsp. baking powder	½ tsp. almond extract
½ tsp. ground cinnamon	¾ c. raspberry jam
½ c. butter or regular margarine	Vanilla Icing (recipe follows)

Sift together flour, sugar, baking powder and cinnamon into a bowl. Cut in butter until mixture is crumbly. Add almonds, egg and almond extract; mix well. Spread ½ of dough in an 8″ square on waxed paper. Chill. Meanwhile, press remaining dough in ungreased 8″ square pan. Spread with jam. Top with chilled dough.

Bake in moderate oven (350°) 35 to 40 minutes or until golden brown. Cool in pan on rack. When cool, drizzle with Vanilla Icing. Cut into 2½ × ¾″ bars. Makes about 2 dozen.

Vanilla Icing: Combine ½ c. sifted confectioners sugar, 2 tsp. milk and ¼ tsp. almond extract. Beat until smooth.

PARTY WHIRLS

These delightful swirls are lovely for teas or wedding receptions

1 c. butter or regular margarine	½ tsp. salt
1 c. sugar	½ tsp. ground cinnamon
2 eggs	3 drops red food color
½ tsp. vanilla	½ oz. square semi-sweet
3 c. sifted flour	chocolate, melted

Beat together butter and sugar until light and fluffy. Beat in eggs and vanilla; blend well.

Sift together flour, salt and cinnamon; add to creamed mixture. Divide dough into thirds. Tint one-third pink with red food color; add chocolate to the second, and leave the last third untinted.

Roll each third of dough separately on lightly floured waxed paper into a 13 × 10″ rectangle. Cover baking sheet with waxed paper. Invert untinted dough on baking sheet; remove paper. Repeat with pink and chocolate dough. Cut edges with knife to straighten if necessary. Chill until firm.

Roll up dough tightly as for jelly roll, using waxed paper to help shape log. Wrap tightly in waxed paper and chill.

To bake, cut dough in ⅛″ to ¼″ slices with sharp knife. Place ½″ apart on ungreased baking sheet.

Bake in hot oven (400°) about 8 minutes. Remove from pan. Cool on racks. Makes about 7 dozen.

PECAN LACE ROLL-UPS

Complement ice cream sundaes with these crisp wafer cookie rolls

2 eggs	¼ c. melted butter or regular
⅔ c. brown sugar, firmly	margarine
packed	¼ c. sifted flour
1 tsp. vanilla	⅔ c. finely chopped pecans

Beat eggs until thick. Add brown sugar, 1 tblsp. at a time, beating constantly. Beat in vanilla. Slowly add butter. Fold in flour and pecans.

Place a tablespoonful of batter on well-greased baking sheet, spreading it to make a 4″ circle. Cookies should be 2″ apart and no more than 4 on one baking sheet.

Bake in moderate oven (375°) 5 to 6 minutes, or until browned. Loosen cookies with a wide spatula. Place the handle of a wooden spoon on one end of cookie and quickly roll up loosely to make a cylinder. Place on rack to cool. Repeat with other baked cookies. Makes 15.

CINNAMON CRESCENTS

Pass a plate of these buttery-rich cookies for a midmorning break

1 c. butter or regular margarine	¾ c. finely chopped walnuts
2 c. sifted flour	1 tsp. ground cinnamon
1 egg yolk	1 egg white, slightly beaten
¾ c. dairy sour cream	1 tblsp. water
¾ c. sugar	

Cut butter into flour until mixture resembles coarse crumbs. Stir in egg yolk and sour cream. Mix with fork until dough forms a ball. Wrap in plastic wrap. Chill 2 hours.

Combine sugar, walnuts and cinnamon.

Divide dough into fourths. Roll each portion in 11″ circle. Sprinkle with ¼ sugar mixture. Cut into 16 wedges. Roll up wedges, starting at widest end. Place rolls on ungreased baking sheet. Brush with combined egg white and water.

Bake in moderate oven (350°) 20 minutes or until golden brown. Remove from pan. Cool on racks. Makes 64.

GIVE A SWEET THOUGHT

An attractive box filled with picture-pretty homemade cookies is a delightful gift to give a friend or neighbor at any time of the year. We have selected some of our cookies that will bring gasps of delight when they are presented. Scallop-edged cookies filled with assorted fruit fillings, lemon-iced bars, chewy fruit strips and other thoughtful treats. Some of the recipes are excellent to freeze now and frost at the last minute . . . good gifts to have on hand.

GOLDEN FRUIT COOKIES

Fill foil-wrapped coffee cans with these moist cookies for gifts

1 c. shortening	1 tsp. ground cinnamon
½ c. sugar	1 tsp. baking soda
3 eggs	½ tsp. salt
2 tblsp. molasses	1 c. stewed mixed dried fruit
1 tsp. vanilla	1 c. raisins
3½ c. sifted flour	1½ c. chopped walnuts
1 tsp. ground cloves	2 tsp. grated lemon rind

Cream together shortening and sugar until light and fluffy. Add eggs, one at a time, beating well after each addition. Beat in molasses and vanilla.

Sift together flour, cloves, cinnamon, baking soda and salt. Drain stewed dried fruit and reserve ¼ c. liquid. Add dry ingredients alternately with reserved liquid, beating well after each addition. Stir in drained stewed fruit, raisins, walnuts and lemon rind. Drop by teaspoonfuls about 2" apart on greased baking sheet.

Bake in moderate oven (350°) 10 to 12 minutes or until golden brown. Remove from pan. Cool on racks. Makes about 6 dozen.

CANDIED FRUIT BARS

These bars have become a Christmas specialty in a Minnesota family

4 eggs, beaten	1 tsp. baking powder
½ c. melted shortening	½ tsp. salt
½ tsp. vanilla	1½ c. candied mixed fruit
1½ c. sifted flour	Orange Frosting (recipe follows)
1¾ c. sugar	

Combine eggs, shortening and vanilla; beat until thick and lemon-colored.

Sift together flour, sugar, baking powder and salt. Reserve ¼ c. flour mixture; mix with candied fruit. Gradually stir remaining dry ingredients into eggs; mix well. Add floured candied fruit. Spread mixture in greased 13 × 9 × 2" pan.

Bake in moderate oven (350°) 30 minutes. While warm, frost with Orange Frosting. Cool in pan on rack. Cut into 3 × 1" bars. Makes about 3 dozen.

Orange Frosting: Combine 1 c. sifted confectioners sugar, 1½ tblsp. orange juice and ½ tsp. grated orange peel. Beat until smooth.

LEMON / COCONUT SQUARES

Team with refreshing lime sherbet for a delightful summer dessert

¼ c. butter or regular margarine	1 tsp. vanilla
	¾ c. flaked coconut
1 c. sifted flour	½ c. chopped pecans
2 eggs	⅛ tsp. baking powder
1 c. brown sugar, firmly packed	Lemon Icing (recipe follows)

Cut butter into flour forming fine crumbs. Press mixture into ungreased 11 × 7 × 1½″ baking pan.

Bake in moderate oven (350°) 12 to 15 minutes or until lightly browned.

Beat eggs until light and lemon-colored. Gradually beat in brown sugar and vanilla. Stir in coconut, pecans and baking powder. Spread over baked crust.

Bake in moderate oven (350°) 20 more minutes. Spread with Lemon Icing while still warm. Cool in pan on rack. Cut into 2″ squares. Makes 15.

Lemon Icing: Combine 1 c. sifted confectioners sugar, 2 tblsp. lemon juice and 1 tsp. grated lemon rind. Stir until smooth.

FRENCH BARS

Decorate with candied fruit or walnut halves for the holidays

2¼ c. brown sugar, firmly
    packed
4 eggs, well beaten
1½ c. soured evaporated milk
    (see Note)
2¼ c. unsifted flour
1½ tsp. baking soda

1 tsp. ground cinnamon
½ tsp. salt
1½ c. chopped walnuts
1½ c. cut-up dates
1 c. toasted flaked coconut
Orange Butter Frosting (recipe
    follows)

Add sugar to eggs; beat until thick. Stir in soured evaporated milk. Blend in flour, baking soda, cinnamon and salt. Stir in nuts, dates and coconut. Do not overmix batter. Spread dough evenly in 2 lightly greased 15½ × 10½ × 1″ jelly roll pans.

Bake in moderate oven (350°) about 20 minutes. Cool in pan on rack. Frost and cut in 2½ × 1″ bars. Makes 80.

Note: To sour evaporated milk, pour 1½ tblsp. vinegar into 2-cup measure. Add evaporated milk until measurement is 1½ c. Stir.

Orange Butter Frosting: Combine 1 lb. confectioners sugar, sifted, with ¼ c. butter or regular margarine, ¼ c. orange juice, ½ tsp. salt and 1 tsp. grated orange rind. Beat until creamy. Spread on cooled bars.

FRUIT BLOSSOM COOKIES

Soft, fruit-filled cookies—reminiscent of old-fashioned holidays

⅔ c. shortening	1½ tsp. baking powder
¾ c. sugar	¼ tsp. salt
1 egg	2 tblsp. milk
½ tsp. vanilla	Fillings (recipes follow)
2 c. sifted flour	

Cream together shortening and sugar. Add egg; beat until light and fluffy. Add vanilla.

Sift together flour, baking powder and salt. Add to creamed mixture along with milk. Divide dough in half. Chill for 1 hour.

Roll dough ¹⁄₁₆ to ⅛" thick. Cut with 3" scalloped cookie cutter. Place about ½ tsp. filling in centers of half the cookies. Place 1½" apart on greased baking sheet. Cut out centers of remaining half of cookies with 1" round cutter; place on filled bottoms and press edges with fork to seal.

Bake in moderate oven (350°) 10 to 12 minutes. Remove from pan. Cool on racks. Makes about 2 dozen.

Apricot Filling: Combine ¼ c. chopped dried apricots, 1½ tsp. orange juice, ¼ tsp. lemon juice, 3 tblsp. water and 1 tsp. flour in a saucepan. Bring to a boil, stirring constantly. Cook for about 5 minutes. Cool.

Pineapple Filling: Combine in saucepan ¾ tsp. cornstarch and ¼ c. crushed pineapple, undrained. Cook until clear, stirring constantly. Cool.

Cherry Filling: Mash ¼ c. cherry pie filling. Add a few drops almond extract, if desired.

Chapter 10

FAMILY DESSERTS...
Make It Again, Mom

How often do you hear "What's for dessert, Mom?" Farm women are old hands at turning out desserts that are easy to prepare, require only staple ingredients and yet have a certain twist that makes them special. And for those party or holiday occasions they turn to their recipe files and pull out heirlooms that have been passed down through the generations or recipes that have become a part of their traditional holiday feasting.

There are specialties that go to every family reunion or to a church supper or bazaar. And of course every farm woman has a freezer stand-by that goes with a cup of coffee when neighbors drop in unexpectedly.

Raspberry/Vanilla Cloud is one farm woman's favorite for a make-ahead dessert—a square of delicate white gelatin-based goodness covered with a sauce of tart thickened raspberries. Baked Fruit Dessert has stood the test of three generations in Missouri—cheese and bread crumbs laced with golden pineapple. From a New York state farm cook, we share a regal Walnut Torte, her birthday special—layers of crunchy nut-filled meringue filled with whipped cream—rich, but oh so good!

"My Brownie Ice Cream Slices are always requested when we are having a church supper," says a Minnesota farm woman. The nutritious tart and tangy Lemon Fluff has been family-tested for years . . . it bakes with a golden brown crown and looks quite elegant when it's brought hot and quivering to the table.

Do try the Tart Cranapple Squares on a cool fall day—the family will praise your efforts. Make up the rich spicy Suet Pudding for the Christmas holidays. The Iowa farm woman who contributed Old-Fashioned Apple Pudding says "My family eats this big recipe at one sitting."

Many of these desserts are rich in protein, vitamins and minerals as they are made with eggs, dairy products and a good variety of fresh fruit. Some are rich and creamy, some are light and luscious; some old-fashioned, others quick-and-easy modern style. But every one is downright delicious!

TASTES OF SPRING

Rhubarb and strawberries are special to the spring season. We have some family favorites that appear as soon as these ingredients arrive in gardens. Some for family, some for church suppers and others for company dinners . . . they all taste special in spring.

BANANA-STRAWBERRY PUDDING

Guests can serve themselves this attractive dessert-in-a-bowl

1 c. sugar	1 (3 oz.) pkg. lady fingers, cut in thirds (12)
¼ c. flour	
2½ c. milk	1 pt. fresh strawberries, sliced
3 eggs, beaten	3 bananas, sliced
2 tblsp. butter or regular margarine	1 envelope whipped topping mix
1 tsp. vanilla	⅓ c. toasted flaked coconut

Combine sugar and flour in 2-qt. saucepan. Slowly stir in milk. Add eggs slowly to mixture. Cook over medium heat, stirring, until thick. (Do not boil.) Remove from heat; add butter and vanilla. Cool.

Layer cooled custard, lady fingers, strawberries and bananas in 2-qt. glass bowl. Chill well. Prepare whipped topping mix according to package directions. Spread topping on pudding; sprinkle with coconut. Makes 8 servings.

Bubbling *Bacon Cheddar Fondue* (page 254) is a perfect choice to serve to last-minute guests. Invite each one to dip chunks of crusty French bread in this variation of the classic Swiss fondue. Nourishing and delicious!

Brighten the breakfast routine by serving *Golden Crispies* (page 260), a home-made cereal full of protein, vitamins and minerals. Top with sliced fruit and country-fresh milk. Everyone will love this energy-packed cereal.

The men in your family will say "Let's have this again!" when you dish up *Pork Chop Skillet Dinner* (page 12). This main dish meal is especially good on a frosty winter night—it's chock-full of meat, potatoes and rich gravy.

These five beauties won a blue satin ribbon at a fair: creamy *Peach Cheese Pie* (page 184), *Sugar and Spice Cookies* (page 193), *Cocoa Chiffon Cake* (page 150), *Pear Relish* (page 246) and golden *Chicken-Rice Pyramids* (page 38).

STRAWBERRY SWIRL

A velvety light dessert that will delight your card club members

1 c. graham cracker crumbs	1 c. boiling water
1 tblsp. sugar	1 c. cold water
¼ c. melted butter or regular margarine	1 c. chopped fresh strawberries
	½ lb. marshmallows (about 38)
1 (3 oz.) pkg. strawberry flavor gelatin	½ c. milk
	1 c. heavy cream, whipped

Mix together graham cracker crumbs, sugar and butter. Press mixture into 8″ square pan. Chill.

Dissolve gelatin in boiling water. Add cold water and chill until thick and syrupy. Add strawberries.

Meanwhile, heat marshmallows in milk over medium heat until melted. Cool well. Fold cooled mixture into whipped cream.

Spread half of marshmallow mixture over crumbs. Spoon gelatin mixture on top. Top with remaining marshmallow mixture. Use a spatula to swirl layers to give marbled effect. Chill until set. Makes 9 servings.

RHUBARB CUSTARD KUCHEN

"My husband likes this for breakfast too," a Wisconsin woman says

1¾ c. sifted flour	1½ c. sugar
½ tsp. baking powder	2 tblsp. flour
⅛ tsp. salt	1 tsp. ground cinnamon
¾ c. shortening	1 egg, beaten
1 egg, beaten	¾ c. milk
1 tblsp. milk	1 tsp. vanilla
4 c. diced fresh rhubarb	

Sift together 1¾ c. flour, baking powder and salt into a mixing bowl. Cut in shortening until mixture resembles coarse crumbs.

Combine 1 egg and 1 tblsp. milk; stir into crumb mixture. Mix well. Pat mixture into the bottom and sides of ungreased 13 × 9 × 2″ cake pan.

Fill crust with rhubarb. Combine sugar, 2 tblsp. flour and cinnamon; sprinkle over top of rhubarb. Mix together 1 egg, ¾ c. milk and vanilla; pour over all.

Bake in hot oven (425°) 20 minutes. Reduce heat to 375° and bake 15 minutes more or until rhubarb is tender. Makes 12 servings.

RHUBARB / CHERRY CRUNCH

A dollop of whipped cream makes this dessert even more enticing

4 c. diced fresh rhubarb	¾ c. quick-cooking rolled oats
½ c. sugar	¾ c. brown sugar, firmly packed
2 tblsp. cornstarch	¾ c. sifted flour
1 c. water	¹⁄₁₆ tsp. salt
1 (1 lb. 8 oz.) jar prepared cherry pie filling	⅓ c. butter or regular margarine
5 drops red food color	½ c. chopped walnuts
1 tsp. almond extract	

Place rhubarb in 11 × 7 × 1½" baking dish. Combine sugar and cornstarch in small saucepan. Gradually stir in water. Cook, stirring constantly, over medium heat until thick. Stir in pie filling, food color and almond extract. Pour over rhubarb.

Combine oats, brown sugar, flour, salt and butter; mix until crumbly. Add walnuts. Sprinkle over fruit mixture.

Bake in moderate oven (350°) 45 minutes or until golden brown and rhubarb is tender. Makes 6 to 8 servings.

RHUBARB MERINGUE SQUARES

This creamy rhubarb dessert is certain to delight your family

1 c. sifted flour	4½ tblsp. flour
2 tblsp. sugar	¾ c. light cream
½ c. butter or regular margarine	4 c. diced fresh rhubarb
3 eggs, separated	¼ c. sugar
1¾ c. sugar	¼ tsp. vanilla

Combine 1 c. flour and 2 tblsp. sugar in a bowl. Cut in butter until mixture is crumbly. Press mixture into 11 × 7 × 1½" baking pan. Bake in moderate oven (325°) 20 minutes.

Meanwhile, beat egg yolks well. Slowly beat in 1¾ c. sugar, 4½ tblsp. flour and light cream.

Place rhubarb on baked crust. Pour egg mixture over all. Bake in moderate oven (325°) 45 minutes or until rhubarb is tender.

Beat egg whites until stiff. Gradually beat in ¼ c. sugar and vanilla; beat until soft peaks form. Spread over rhubarb. Return to oven; bake for an additional 10 minutes or until top is golden brown. Serve slightly warm. Makes 6 to 8 servings.

COMPANY DAZZLERS

For that very special occasion when you want to serve a very special dessert, we have a sampling of recipes that have received rave reviews. Try the Elegant Strawberry Torte or light airy Walnut Torte with three whipped cream filled layers. These are not non-caloric finales, but they are so good!

ELEGANT STRAWBERRY TORTE

Dazzle your guests with this easy but elegant strawberry torte

3 c. sifted cake flour

2 c. brown sugar, firmly packed

½ tsp. salt

1 c. butter or regular margarine

1 egg, slightly beaten

1 c. sour milk

1 tsp. baking soda

½ c. chopped nuts

1 pt. heavy cream, whipped and sweetened

1 pt. fresh strawberries, sliced

Mix together flour, brown sugar, salt and butter until crumbly. Reserve 1 c. crumb mixture; set aside.

Combine egg, milk and baking soda. Add to remaining crumb mixture; stir well. Pour into 2 greased, paper-lined 9″ layer pans. Sprinkle with reserved crumb mixture; then nuts.

Bake in moderate oven (375°) 25 to 30 minutes or until cake tests done. Cool.

Place one layer, nut side up on serving plate. Spread with half of the whipped cream. Top with sliced strawberries. Place other layer on top. Spoon remaining whipped cream into puffs around cake. Garnish with sliced strawberries. Serve immediately. Makes 12 servings.

WALNUT TORTE

Chopped pecans can be substituted for the walnuts in this dessert

8 eggs, separated	16 saltine crackers, crushed
2 c. sugar	2 tsp. baking powder
4 tsp. vanilla	3 c. heavy cream
1 tsp. almond extract	3 tblsp. sugar
2 c. finely chopped walnuts	1 tsp. vanilla

Beat egg yolks until thick and lemon-colored. Gradually beat in 2 c. sugar. Add 4 tsp. vanilla and almond extract; beat well. Stir in walnuts, crushed saltine crackers and baking powder.

Beat egg whites until stiff. Fold into yolk mixture. Spread mixture in 3 waxed-paper-lined 9" round cake pans.

Bake in slow oven (325°) 30 minutes. Remove from pans immediately. Cool on racks.

Whip heavy cream with 3 tblsp. sugar and 1 tsp. vanilla. Put layers together with whipped cream. Spread top layer with cream. Decorate with walnuts and maraschino cherries, if you wish. Refrigerate until serving time. Makes 12 servings.

BROWNIE / ICE CREAM SLICES

Keep plenty of these yummy treats frozen for after-school snacks

½ c. butter or regular margarine	1 tsp. vanilla
	1½ c. sifted flour
1 c. sugar	1 tsp. baking powder
4 eggs	¼ tsp. salt
1 (1 lb.) can chocolate flavored syrup	1 c. chopped walnuts
	1 qt. vanilla ice cream, softened

Cream together butter and sugar until light and fluffy. Add eggs, one at a time, beating well after each addition. Beat in chocolate syrup and vanilla.

Sift together flour, baking powder and salt. Gradually stir into creamed mixture. Stir in walnuts. Pour mixture in greased 15½ × 10½ × 1" jelly roll pan.

Bake in moderate oven (350°) 30 minutes or until it tests done. Cool well.

Remove cake from pan and cut in half, making two 7½ × 5"

pieces. Spread ice cream over one layer and top with other layer. Wrap tightly in aluminum foil and freeze.

Before serving, cut into 3 sections. Cut each section into 8 slices. Makes 24 slices.

LEMON FLUFF

Place in oven just before dinner so it will be ready for dessert

1 c. sugar	2 tblsp. melted butter or regular
¼ c. flour	margarine
3 eggs, separated	1 tsp. grated lemon rind
3 tblsp. lemon juice	1 c. milk

Combine sugar and flour in a bowl. Beat together egg yolks, lemon juice, butter, lemon rind and milk. Add to dry ingredients; beat well. Beat egg whites until stiff. Fold into egg yolk mixture. Pour mixture into greased 1½-qt. casserole and set in a pan of hot water.

Bake in moderate oven (350°) 40 minutes or until golden brown. Makes 4 servings.

RASPBERRY / VANILLA CLOUD

Make ahead and serve guests at a bridal shower, reception or tea

1⅔ c. graham cracker crumbs	1¾ c. milk
¼ c. sugar	3 egg whites
1 tsp. ground cinnamon	¼ tsp. cream of tartar
⅓ c. melted butter or regular	½ c. sugar
margarine	1 tsp. vanilla
½ c. sugar	½ c. heavy cream, whipped
¼ c. flour	Raspberry Sauce (recipe
1 pkg. unflavored gelatin	follows)
½ tsp. salt	

Mix together graham crumbs, ¼ c. sugar, cinnamon and butter. Press in 9″ square pan. Bake in moderate oven (375°) 4 minutes. Cool.

Combine ½ c. sugar, flour, gelatin and salt in 2-qt. saucepan. Slowly stir in milk. Bring to a boil, stirring constantly. Boil for 1 minute. Cool thoroughly.

Beat egg whites with cream of tartar until stiff. Gradually beat in ½ c. sugar. Add vanilla.

Fold egg whites and whipped cream into cooled mixture. Turn into crust. Chill well. Cut in squares and serve topped with Raspberry Sauce. Makes 9 servings.

Raspberry Sauce: Drain 2 (10 oz.) pkgs. frozen raspberries, thawed. Add water to juice to make 1½ c. Combine juice, ¼ c. sugar, 2 tblsp. cornstarch and 1 tblsp. lemon juice. Cook, stirring, until mixture boils for 1 minute. Add raspberries and cool thoroughly.

FAMILY-STYLE FAVORITES

These are the old familiars that every family loves, such as creamy Easy Rice Pudding studded with raisins, light fluffy Dessert Dumplings with a choice of three sauces, and Old-Fashioned Apple Pudding. Even though they are daily fare, they are all delicious to serve to guests.

EASY RICE PUDDING

"One of my husband's favorites," an Indiana farm woman told us

2 eggs, slightly beaten	1 tsp. vanilla
2¼ c. milk, scalded	½ tsp. grated lemon rind
⅓ c. sugar	¼ tsp. salt
¾ c. cooked regular rice	½ tsp. ground cinnamon
¼ c. raisins	

Beat together eggs and milk. Stir in sugar, rice, raisins, vanilla, lemon rind and salt. Pour into greased 1½-qt. casserole. Sprinkle with cinnamon. Set casserole in pan of hot water (½″ deep).

Bake in moderate oven (350°) 45 minutes or until set around the edges. Makes 6 servings.

DESSERT DUMPLINGS

For a special treat, top servings with whipped cream or ice cream

Dessert Sauce (recipes follow)	1 tblsp. butter or regular
⅔ c. sifted flour	margarine
2 tblsp. sugar	1 egg, beaten
¾ tsp. baking powder	1 tblsp. milk
⅛ tsp. salt	¼ tsp. vanilla

Prepare one of the following dessert sauces.

Sift together flour, sugar, baking powder and salt into a bowl. Cut in butter. Add egg, milk and vanilla; mix until moistened.

Bring prepared Dessert Sauce to a boil. Drop dumpling mixture by spoonfuls into boiling sauce, making 8 dumplings. Cover; reduce heat to low; cook for 20 minutes. Do not remove cover during cooking period. Makes 4 servings.

Maraschino Cherry Sauce: Drain 1 (8 oz.) jar maraschino cherries, reserving ½ c. juice. Chop cherries; set aside. Combine ½ c. sugar, 3 tblsp. cornstarch and ¼ tsp. salt in 10″ skillet. Gradually stir in ½ c. cherry juice and 1½ c. water. Add cherries, ¼ c. butter, 1 tblsp. lemon juice, ½ tsp. almond extract, ½ tsp. grated lemon rind and 3 drops red food color. Bring to a boil, stirring constantly. Reduce heat; simmer for 1 minute. Set aside; prepare Dumplings.

Orange Sauce: Combine ¼ c. sugar, 4 tsp. cornstarch and dash salt in 10″ skillet. Stir in 1¼ c. reconstituted frozen orange juice, ½ c. water, 1 tblsp. butter and ½ tsp. grated orange rind. Bring to a boil, stirring constantly. Reduce heat; simmer for 2 minutes. Set aside; prepare Dumplings.

Chocolate Sauce: Melt 1 (1 oz.) square unsweetened chocolate with 1½ c. water and 1 tblsp. butter or regular margarine in 10″ skillet; bring to a boil. Combine 1 c. sugar, 1 tsp. cornstarch and ⅛ tsp. salt. Gradually stir into boiling chocolate mixture; add ¼ tsp. vanilla. Reduce heat; simmer for 2 minutes. Set aside; prepare Dumplings.

OLD-FASHIONED APPLE PUDDING

An Iowa farm woman told us "This can be stirred up in a hurry."

¼ c. butter or regular margarine	1 tsp. ground cinnamon
1 c. sugar	½ tsp. ground nutmeg
1 egg	¼ tsp. salt
1 c. sifted flour	2 c. shredded, pared apples
1 tsp. baking soda	½ c. chopped walnuts
	Pudding Sauce (recipe follows)

Cream together butter and sugar until light and fluffy. Add egg; beat well.

Sift together flour, baking soda, cinnamon, nutmeg and salt. Gradually stir dry ingredients into creamed mixture. Stir in apples and walnuts. Spread batter in greased 8″ square pan.

Bake in moderate oven (350°) 40 to 45 minutes or until cake tests done. Cut into squares. Serve warm with Pudding Sauce. Makes 6 to 9 servings.

Pudding Sauce: Combine ½ c. butter or regular margarine, 1 c. sugar and ½ c. light cream in small saucepan. Cook, stirring occasionally, over low heat until slightly thickened (about 15 minutes). Add 1½ tsp. vanilla and ¹⁄₁₆ tsp. ground nutmeg. Serve warm.

APPLE OATMEAL SQUARES

An easy-to-tote dessert for your next family reunion or picnic

2 c. quick-cooking rolled oats	1 tsp. vanilla
2 c. sifted flour	½ tsp. salt
1½ c. brown sugar, firmly packed	8 c. sliced, pared apples
1 c. melted butter or regular margarine	¼ c. sugar
	4 tsp. ground cinnamon

Combine oats, flour, brown sugar, butter, vanilla and salt. Mix until crumbly. Press half of mixture in greased 13 × 9 × 2″ pan. Top with apples. Combine sugar and cinnamon; sprinkle over apples. Top with remaining crumbs.

Bake in moderate oven (350°) 45 minutes or until apples are tender. If you wish, serve topped with ice cream or custard sauce. Makes about 10 servings.

FRESH APPLE ROLLS

Welcome the apple season with this easy-to-prepare dessert

2 c. sifted flour	¼ c. chopped walnuts
2 tblsp. sugar	¼ c. raisins
4 tsp. baking powder	Ground cinnamon
½ tsp. salt	1½ c. sugar
3 tblsp. shortening	1 tblsp. flour
⅔ c. milk	½ tsp. salt
Melted butter or regular margarine	1 c. water
2 c. sliced, pared apples	1 tblsp. butter or regular margarine

Sift together 2 c. flour, 2 tblsp. sugar, baking powder and ½ tsp. salt into bowl. Cut in shortening until mixture is crumbly. Add milk and stir with fork to moisten. Turn on lightly floured surface and knead gently 10 times.

Roll dough into a 15 × 9″ rectangle. Brush with melted butter. Spread apples, walnuts and raisins evenly over surface of dough. Sprinkle with cinnamon. Roll up like jelly roll, starting on wide end. Cut into 12 slices and arrange in greased 13 × 9 × 2″ baking pan.

Bake in hot oven (400°) for 20 minutes.

Meanwhile, combine 1½ c. sugar, 1 tblsp. flour, and ½ tsp. salt in small saucepan. Gradually stir in water and 1 tblsp. butter. Stirring constantly, bring mixture to a boil and boil for 1 minute.

Pour over rolls and bake another 10 minutes or until golden brown. Makes 12 servings.

CHUNKY CIDER APPLESAUCE

Add a pour-over of heavy cream and a shake of cinnamon—yummy!

9 c. pared, sliced apples	½ c. sugar
½ c. apple cider	⅛ tsp. salt
1 tblsp. lemon juice	½ tsp. ground nutmeg

Combine apples, cider and lemon juice in 3-qt. saucepan. Bring to boil over medium heat. Simmer until apples are tender, for about 20 minutes.

Add sugar, salt and nutmeg; cook for 1 minute longer. Break up apples into chunks. Makes about 1 quart.

APPLE PINWHEELS IN SYRUP

A rich spicy sauce bubbles all through this hearty fall dessert

Pastry for 2-crust pie	¼ tsp. salt
4 c. grated apples	¼ c. butter or regular
1 tsp. ground cinnamon	margarine
¾ c. sugar	½ tsp. vanilla
½ c. dark brown sugar, firmly	2 c. hot water
packed	Whipped cream

Roll pastry into 14 × 12″ rectangle. Combine apples and cinnamon, spread over pastry evenly; then roll up as for jelly roll. Slice into 1½″ pieces, sealing edges with toothpicks, and place in 11 × 7 × 1½″ baking dish sealed side down.

Bake in moderate oven (400°) 15 minutes.

Combine sugar, brown sugar, salt, butter, vanilla and water in 2-qt. saucepan and bring to a full boil. Pour over rings. Return to oven and bake 15 to 20 minutes more, basting twice, until apples are tender. Serve warm with whipped cream. Makes 8 servings.

SNOWY GLAZED APPLE SQUARES

Top each serving with a large scoop of creamy vanilla ice cream

2½ c. sifted flour
½ tsp. salt
1 c. shortening
2 eggs, separated
Milk
1½ c. crushed corn flakes

8 medium tart apples, pared and sliced (about 5 cups)
1 c. sugar
1½ tsp. ground cinnamon
Glaze (directions follow)

Combine flour and salt in bowl. Cut in shortening until mixture is crumbly. In a measuring cup, beat egg yolks with enough milk to make ⅔ c. Add to mixture; toss lightly.

Divide dough almost in half. Roll larger portion to fit 15½ × 10½ × 1″ jelly roll pan. Sprinkle with corn flakes. Spread apples over corn flakes. Combine sugar and cinnamon; sprinkle over apples. Roll out remaining dough. Place on top; seal edges.

Beat egg whites until foamy; spread on crust.

Bake in moderate oven (350°) 1 hour. Cool slightly; spread with Glaze. Cut into squares. Makes 15 servings.

Glaze: Combine 1¼ c. sifted confectioners sugar, 3 tblsp. water and ½ tsp. vanilla. Mix until smooth.

DELICIOUS CHERRY DESSERT

This easy-to-make dessert can double as a breakfast or snack treat

1 c. butter or regular margarine
1½ c. sugar
4 eggs
1 tsp. vanilla
2¾ c. sifted cake flour

1½ tsp. baking powder
½ tsp. salt
1 (1 lb. 5 oz.) can prepared cherry pie filling
Confectioners sugar

Cream together butter and sugar until light and fluffy. Add eggs, one at a time, beating well after each addition. Add vanilla.

Sift together flour, baking powder and salt. Gradually stir dry ingredients into creamed mixture. Reserve 1 c. batter; set aside. Spread remaining batter in greased 15½ × 10½ × 1″ jelly roll pan. Spread cherry pie filling over batter. Top with spoonfuls of reserved batter.

Bake in moderate oven (350°) 40 minutes or until golden. Cool and sprinkle with confectioners sugar. Cut into 3 × 2″ slices. Makes about 2 dozen.

VARIATIONS

Blueberry: Substitute 1 (1 lb. 5 oz.) can prepared blueberry pie filling and ½ tsp. lemon extract for prepared cherry pie filling.

Mincemeat: Substitute 2 c. prepared mincemeat and 1 tsp. cornstarch for prepared cherry pie filling.

APPLE PIZZA PIE

Looks dramatic and tastes divine . . . so easy to fix for a fall dinner

1 ¼ c. unsifted flour
1 tsp. salt
½ c. shortening
1 c. shredded Cheddar cheese
¼ c. ice water
½ c. powdered non-dairy "cream"
½ c. brown sugar, firmly packed
½ c. sugar

⅓ c. sifted flour
¼ tsp. salt
1 tsp. ground cinnamon
½ tsp. ground nutmeg
¼ c. butter or regular margarine
6 c. sliced, pared apples, ½″ thick
2 tblsp. lemon juice

Mix 1¼ c. flour and 1 tsp. salt; cut in shortening until crumbly. Add cheese. Sprinkle water over mixture gradually; shape into ball. Roll pastry into 15″ circle on floured surface; place on baking sheet and turn up edge.

Combine powdered non-dairy "cream," brown sugar, sugar, ⅓ c. flour, ¼ tsp. salt, cinnamon and nutmeg. Sprinkle half of this mixture over pastry. Cut butter into remaining half until crumbly. Arrange apple slices, overlapping them in circles on crust. Sprinkle with lemon juice and remaining crumbs.

Bake in very hot oven (450°) 30 minutes or until apples are tender. Serve warm. Makes 12 servings.

BAKED FRUIT DESSERT

This is also a delicious accompaniment for ham, roast pork or poultry

1 (1 lb. 14 oz.) can pineapple chunks
1 (1 lb.) can sliced peaches
½ c. sugar
2 tblsp. cornstarch
2 tblsp. lemon juice

2 tblsp. raisins, plumped
1 c. shredded Cheddar cheese
1 c. soft bread crumbs
3 tblsp. melted butter or regular margarine

Drain pineapple and peaches, reserving juice. Combine sugar and cornstarch in small saucepan. Gradually stir in reserved fruit juice and lemon juice. Cook over medium heat, stirring constantly, until mixture boils. Boil for 1 minute; remove from heat.

Combine peaches, pineapple, raisins and cheese in 8″ square baking dish. Pour on sauce. Combine bread crumbs and butter; sprinkle on top.

Bake in moderate oven (350°) 30 minutes or until lightly browned. Serve warm. Makes 6 to 8 servings.

LEMON PUDDING CAKE

Top with a puff of whipped cream and a stemmed maraschino cherry

4 eggs, separated
⅓ c. lemon juice
1 tsp. grated lemon rind
1 tblsp. melted butter or regular margarine

1½ c. sugar
½ c. sifted flour
½ tsp. salt
1½ c. milk

Beat together egg yolks, lemon juice, lemon rind and butter until thick and lemon-colored. Combine sugar, flour and salt. Add dry ingredients alternately with milk, beating well after each addition. Beat egg whites until stiff. Blend into egg yolk mixture on low speed of electric mixer. Pour mixture into 8″ square baking dish. Set in a pan of hot water.

Bake in moderate oven (350°) 45 minutes or until golden. Cut into squares. Makes 6 to 9 servings.

CHOCOLATE PUDDING CAKE

"A favorite, because we all like chocolate," a Nebraska woman says

1½ c. sifted flour
1 c. sugar
3 tblsp. cocoa
3 tsp. baking powder
¾ tsp. salt
¾ c. milk
1½ tblsp. melted butter or
   regular margarine

2 tsp. vanilla
¾ c. chopped walnuts
½ c. brown sugar, firmly
   packed
¼ c. sugar
3 tblsp. cocoa
1¾ c. boiling water
Whipped cream or ice cream

Sift together flour, 1 c. sugar, 3 tblsp. cocoa, baking powder and salt into a bowl. Add milk, butter and vanilla; beat well. Stir in walnuts. Spread batter in greased 13 × 9 × 2" pan.

Combine brown sugar, ¼ c. sugar and 3 tblsp. cocoa. Sprinkle over batter. Pour boiling water over all.

Bake in moderate oven (350°) 40 minutes.

Cut in 12 squares. Serve warm topped with whipped cream or ice cream. Makes 12 servings.

MAKE-AHEAD-AND-CHILL DESSERTS

These desserts are perfect for the busy homemaker. Whether for family, friends or company all these finales can be made the day before. While coffee is perking, reach into the refrigerator where dessert is ready and waiting.

LEMONY CHEESE CAKE

A Pennsylvania farm woman says her friends always rave about this

1⅓ c. graham cracker crumbs
⅓ c. sugar
3 tblsp. melted butter or regular
   margarine
½ tsp. ground cinnamon
2 lbs. cream-style cottage cheese,
   sieved

1⅓ c. sugar
4 eggs, separated
1 c. dairy sour cream
3 tblsp. flour
1½ tsp. vanilla
2 tsp. grated lemon rind

Combine graham crumbs, ⅓ c. sugar, butter and cinnamon; mix well. Press mixture into greased 9″ spring form pan.

Combine cottage cheese, 1⅓ c. sugar, egg yolks, sour cream and flour; beat well. Add vanilla and lemon rind. Beat egg whites until stiff. Fold into cottage cheese mixture. Pour into crust.

Bake in moderate oven (350°) 1 hour 10 minutes. Turn off heat. Let stand in oven for 15 minutes. Remove from oven and cool well. Makes 12 servings.

ST. LOUIS CHEESE CAKE

Graham cracker crumbs can be substituted for the zwiebach crumbs

1 c. zwiebach crumbs	1 c. sugar
¼ c. melted butter or regular margarine	1 tsp. vanilla
	¼ tsp. salt
3 (8 oz.) pkg. cream cheese, softened	1 c. dairy sour cream
	3 tblsp. sugar
⅓ c. milk	½ tsp. vanilla
4 eggs	

Combine zwiebach crumbs and butter; mix well. Press mixture in 9″ spring form pan.

Beat together cream cheese and milk. Beat in eggs, one at a time, beating well after each addition. Gradually beat in 1 c. sugar. Add 1 tsp. vanilla and salt; beat well. Pour mixture into crust.

Bake in moderate oven (350°) 35 minutes or until lightly browned. Remove from oven and cool for 10 minutes.

Combine sour cream, 3 tblsp. sugar and ½ tsp. vanilla. Spread over top of cake and bake in very hot oven (475°) 5 minutes. Remove from oven and let cool. Refrigerate overnight. Makes 12 servings.

CHERRY-TOPPED CHEESE CAKE

An easy-to-prepare dessert that needs no baking . . . just chill

18 graham crackers, crushed	½ c. sifted confectioners sugar
3 tblsp. sugar	1 tsp. vanilla
½ c. melted butter or regular margarine	1 envelope whipped topping mix
1 (8 oz.) pkg. cream cheese	1 (1 lb. 8 oz.) jar prepared cherry pie filling

Combine graham crumbs, sugar and butter; mix until crumbly. Press into 8″ spring form pan.

Beat together cream cheese, confectioners sugar and vanilla. Prepare whipped topping mix according to package directions. Fold into creamed cheese mixture. Pour into crust. Spread pie filling on top. Chill several hours. Makes 10 servings.

CREAMY CHEESE CAKE

A real old-fashioned cheese cake with a bright red strawberry sauce

3 c. cream-style cottage cheese, drained

5 eggs, slightly beaten

¼ tsp. salt

1 tsp. vanilla

¼ tsp. almond extract

1 c. sugar

¾ c. sifted flour

1½ c. milk

Tangy Jam Sauce (recipe follows)

Whipped cream

Press cottage cheese through sieve. Add eggs, salt, vanilla and almond extract to cheese; blend thoroughly.

Combine sugar and flour; slowly blend into cheese mixture. Add milk; blend well. Pour into buttered 9″ square baking dish. Set dish in pan of water.

Bake in moderate oven (350°) 1 hour or until knife inserted halfway between side and center comes out clean. (Surface may be pale.) Cool on rack. Cut in squares and serve with Tangy Jam Sauce and whipped cream. Makes 6 to 8 servings.

Tangy Jam Sauce: Combine ½ c. strawberry jam, ½ tsp. lemon juice, ¼ tsp. vanilla; blend thoroughly.

FOR THE HOLIDAYS

A medley of recipes that fit right into the Thanksgiving and Christmas seasons! Tiny jeweled Surprise Macaroon Tarts make perfect Christmas gifts. Tart Cranapple Squares are bright and festive, as is the Crisp Cranberry Crumble—especially good topped with a puff of cream and grated orange rind. All these dishes will make merry eating for the holidays.

SURPRISE MACAROON TARTS

A perfect choice for a Christmas dessert buffet or afternoon tea

2 c. sifted flour
½ c. sugar
¼ tsp. salt
1 c. butter or regular margarine
1 c. quick-cooking rolled oats
¼ c. water
2 eggs, separated
½ c. sugar

3 tblsp. orange juice
1 tblsp. melted butter or regular margarine
1 c. coconut macaroon crumbs
¼ tsp. almond extract
Peach, pineapple or strawberry preserves or red currant jelly

Sift together flour, ½ c. sugar and salt. Cut in butter until mixture resembles coarse crumbs. Stir in oats. Add water gradually until mixture holds together. Form into 48 balls.

Press balls evenly into small muffin cups about 1¾" diameter, forming small tart shells.

Combine egg yolks and ½ c. sugar; beat until light and fluffy. Beat in orange juice and melted butter. Stir in macaroon crumbs and almond extract.

Beat egg whites until stiff and fold into mixture.

Spoon about ¼ tsp. of preserves into each tart shell. Top with macaroon mixture.

Bake in moderate oven (350°) 25 minutes or until golden brown. Makes 4 dozen.

TART CRANAPPLE SQUARES

Simply luscious dessert when topped with softened vanilla ice cream

3 c. sifted flour
1 tblsp. sugar
1 tsp. salt
1 c. shortening
1 egg, separated
Milk
1 c. crushed corn flakes
4 c. sliced, pared apples

2 c. fresh or frozen cranberries
2 c. sugar
½ c. unsifted flour
1½ tsp. ground cinnamon
2 tblsp. butter or regular margarine
1½ c. sifted confectioners sugar
3 tblsp. lemon juice

Sift together 3 c. flour, 1 tblsp. sugar and salt into a mixing bowl. Cut in shortening until mixture resembles coarse crumbs.

Beat egg yolk in 1-cup measuring cup. Add enough milk to make ¾ c. Add milk mixture gradually, using a fork, until dough forms a ball.

Roll two-thirds of dough on a floured surface to 15 × 12″ rectangle. Place in 13 × 9 × 2″ pan. Dough should extend halfway up the sides of the pan.

Sprinkle corn flakes over crust. Top with half of apples and cranberries. Combine 2 c. sugar, ½ c. flour and cinnamon. Sprinkle half of dry mixture over fruit. Top with remaining apples and cranberries. Sprinkle with remaining dry mixture. Dot with butter.

Roll out remaining dough to fit top of pan. Place top crust over filling. Make vents in crust.

Beat egg whites until stiff. Spread over top crust.

Bake in hot oven (400°) 40 to 45 minutes or until golden. While still hot, pour over a glaze made by combining sifted confectioners sugar and lemon juice. Makes 12 servings.

CRISP CRANBERRY CRUMBLE

Holiday season guests will ask for seconds when you serve this

1 c. brown sugar, firmly packed	4 c. whole cranberries
1 c. sifted flour	1 c. sugar
¾ c. quick-cooking rolled oats	2 tblsp. cornstarch
1 tsp. ground cinnamon	1 c. water
½ c. melted butter or regular margarine	½ c. chopped walnuts
	Whipped cream or ice cream

Combine brown sugar, flour, oats, cinnamon and butter; mix until crumbly. Press half of mixture in 9″ square baking dish. Place cranberries in a layer over crust.

Combine sugar and cornstarch in small saucepan. Slowly stir in water. Cook over medium heat, stirring constantly, until thick and clear. Pour sauce over cranberries.

Add walnuts to remaining crumb mixture. Sprinkle over top.

Bake in moderate oven (350°) 1 hour or until golden brown. Cut into squares and top with whipped cream or ice cream. Makes 6 to 9 servings.

CRANBERRY TRENTON DESSERT

This cranberry dessert is so good served either warm or cold

3 c. chopped cranberries
3 c. chopped tart apples
1 tblsp. cornstarch
⅓ c. light brown sugar, firmly
  packed
¾ c. sugar
½ tsp. salt
1 tsp. vanilla
1 c. quick-cooking oats

½ c. light brown sugar, firmly
  packed
⅓ c. sifted flour
2 tblsp. crushed corn flakes
½ tsp. salt
¼ c. butter or regular
  margarine
½ c. chopped nuts

Combine cranberries, apples, cornstarch, ⅓ c. brown sugar, sugar, ½ tsp. salt and vanilla. Pour into buttered 11 × 7 × 1½" baking dish.

Mix together oats, ½ c. brown sugar, flour, corn flakes and ½ tsp. salt. Cut in butter until mixture is crumbly; stir in nuts. Sprinkle evenly over top of cranberry mixture.

Bake in moderate oven (350°) 35 to 40 minutes. Top with whipped cream, if you wish. Makes 10 servings.

CHEWY CRANBERRY SQUARES

A new way to serve cranberries . . . delicious snack or dessert

1½ c. sifted flour
1½ tsp. baking powder
½ tsp. salt
¾ c. sugar
6 tblsp. butter or regular
  margarine

2 eggs
1½ tblsp. lemon juice
1 c. chopped walnuts
¾ c. jellied cranberry sauce, cut
  in ¼" cubes

Sift together flour, baking powder and salt.

Cream together sugar and butter until light and fluffy. Add eggs and lemon juice; beat until smooth and creamy.

Stir dry ingredients into creamed mixture. Gently fold in nuts and cranberry cubes. Pour batter into greased 13 × 9 × 2" pan.

Bake in moderate oven (350°) 25 to 30 minutes. Cut into squares while still warm. Makes 24 bars.

SUET PUDDING

Rum or lemon extract can be substituted for vanilla in the sauce

1 c. ground suet	1 tsp. ground cinnamon
1 c. molasses	½ tsp. ground cloves
1 c. milk	½ tsp. ground nutmeg
3 c. unsifted flour	½ tsp. ground ginger
1½ tsp. salt	1 c. raisins
1 tsp. baking soda	Foamy Sauce (recipe follows)

Combine suet, molasses and milk.

Sift together flour, salt, baking soda, cinnamon, cloves, nutmeg and ginger. Combine dry ingredients with suet mixture. Stir in raisins. Turn into buttered 8-cup ring mold. Place in a large saucepan with 1″ boiling water.

Cover and steam for 2 hours 30 minutes, adding more boiling water, if necessary. Serve warm with Foamy Sauce. Makes 10 to 12 servings.

Foamy Sauce: Cream together ½ c. butter or regular margarine and 1 c. sifted confectioners sugar. Beat in 1 egg and 2 tblsp. vanilla. Place over hot water and stir until well heated. Makes 1½ cups.

Chapter 11

JAMS, JELLIES, RELISHES—
Homemade, of Course

It's often the small touches that add excitement to a meal. Perhaps it's a dish of spiced relish to pass with a baked bean supper . . . or a glass of sparkling-jewel jelly to brighten a breakfast or brunch.

We have a good assortment of jams, jellies and relishes that farm women simply wouldn't be without. Many of them have won ribbons at fairs, are regulars at church suppers and all of them would be the perfect homemade gift at holiday season—or any time of the year when a warm thought is particularly meaningful.

Pickled Pineapple, from a Washington homemaker, is easy to make—so easy in fact that she says she doesn't mind that it disappears so quickly. Made from ingredients that are usually on hand on the kitchen shelf—canned pineapple chunks, vinegar, salt, sugar and spices—this is a quickie to have on hand for emergencies.

Whenever Apple Relish is served to guests in a certain Wisconsin home, the recipe is always requested. It is a bit different—an interesting blend of red and green peppers, apples, pimientos and spices. Two relishes that are good accompaniments to meats are the Turnip and Onion Relish and Beet and Horseradish Relish.

The next time you make a batch of hot muffins or biscuits, do serve a pretty dish of homemade jelly. We have some sparkling beauties that are unusual. There's a bright green Refreshing Lime Jelly, a shimmering Tangy Lemon Jelly, pale Pink Grapefruit Jelly and a deep Sparkling Cherry Jelly. As a Christmas gift, an assortment in small jars would be a "conversation" gift. Save small jars such as mustard and maraschino cherry jars during the year and when the holiday season approaches you will have matching mini-jars for gifts.

For those who like jam we offer a deep purple Luscious Blueberry Jam and a Three-Fruit Jam that is a mouth-watering combination of apples, peaches and pears.

JELLIES AND JAMS IN JEWEL COLORS

These shimmering jellies and jams make a spectacular collection in emerald, ruby and topaz colors. Turn them into your prettiest cut-crystal dish; you'll be proud to say "I made them myself."

REFRESHING LIME JELLY

This adds a refreshing contrast to a curried chicken and rice dinner

1 c. lime juice (about 6 limes)
2½ c. water
1 pkg. powdered fruit pectin

5 c. sugar
5 to 6 drops green food color

Combine lime juice and water in large saucepan. Add powdered fruit pectin; mix well. Bring to a hard boil over high heat, stirring constantly. Stir in sugar all at once. Bring to a full rolling boil and boil for 1 minute, stirring constantly. Remove from heat. Stir in food color. Skim off foam with metal spoon.

Ladle into hot, sterilized glasses. Cover immediately with ⅛" hot paraffin. Makes about 5¼ cups.

TANGY LEMON JELLY

Use this tart jelly as a different filling for a two-layer white cake

½ c. lemon juice
1 tblsp. grated lemon rind
1½ c. water

4¼ c. sugar
1 bottle liquid fruit pectin
3 to 4 drops yellow food color

Combine lemon juice, lemon rind and water in bowl. Let stand for 10 minutes. Strain and pour into a large saucepan.

Add sugar to juice mixture; mix well. Bring to a hard boil over high heat, stirring constantly. At once stir in liquid fruit pectin. Bring to a full rolling boil and boil for 1 minute, stirring constantly. Remove from heat. Stir in food color. Skim off foam with metal spoon.

Ladle into hot, sterilized glasses. Cover immediately with ⅛" hot paraffin. Makes 5 cups.

SPARKLING CHERRY JELLY

After-school snack: peanut butter and cherry jelly sandwiches

2 c. bottled cherry drink
3½ c. sugar
2 tblsp. lemon juice

½ bottle liquid fruit pectin
¼ tsp. almond extract
4 drops red food color

Combine cherry drink, sugar and lemon juice in large saucepan; mix well. Bring to a hard boil over high heat, stirring constantly. At once stir in liquid fruit pectin. Bring to a full rolling boil and boil for 1 minute, stirring constantly. Remove from heat. Stir in almond extract and food color. Skim off foam with metal spoon.

Ladle into hot, sterilized glasses. Cover immediately with ⅛" hot paraffin. Makes 5 cups.

PINK GRAPEFRUIT JELLY

Surprise your friends with a jar of this very different jelly

3 c. canned or bottled grapefruit
   juice
1 pkg. powdered fruit pectin

4 c. sugar
7 drops red food color

Combine grapefruit juice and powdered fruit pectin in large saucepan; mix well. Bring to a hard boil over high heat, stirring constantly. Stir in sugar all at once. Bring to a full rolling boil and boil for 1 minute, stirring constantly. Remove from heat. Stir in food color. Skim off foam with metal spoon.

Ladle into hot, sterilized glasses. Cover immediately with ⅛" hot paraffin. Makes 5 cups.

LUSCIOUS BLUEBERRY JAM

For a quick and luscious dessert, spoon this over lemon sherbet

1½ qts. blueberries
2 tblsp. lemon juice

7 c. sugar
1 bottle liquid fruit pectin

Thoroughly crush blueberries, one layer at a time, making 4½ c. (Add extra blueberries, if necessary.)

Combine blueberries and lemon juice in a large saucepan. Add sugar; mix well. Place over high heat, bring to a full rolling boil and boil hard for 1 minute, stirring constantly. Remove from heat. Stir in liquid fruit pectin. Stir and skim with metal spoon for 5 minutes to cool slightly and prevent floating fruit.

Ladle into hot, sterilized glasses. Cover immediately with ⅛″ hot paraffin. Makes 9 cups.

THREE-FRUIT JAM

Tastes simply scrumptious on hot buttered cornmeal muffins

2 c. cut-up, pared apples	1 pkg. powdered fruit pectin
2 c. cut-up, peeled peaches	1 tsp. butter or regular
2 c. cut-up, pared pears	margarine
2 tblsp. lemon juice	5 drops yellow food color
6 c. sugar	

Combine apples, peaches, pears and lemon juice in a large saucepan. Cook over medium heat, stirring constantly, until fruit is almost tender. Stir in sugar, powdered fruit pectin, butter and food color. Place over high heat, bring to a full rolling boil and boil for 1 minute, stirring constantly. Remove from heat. Stir and skim with metal spoon for 5 minutes to cool slightly and prevent floating fruit.

Ladle into hot, sterilized glasses. Cover immediately with ⅛″ hot paraffin. Makes 6 cups.

CANTALOUPE HONEY

An original from a Maryland farm wife . . . good on biscuits

2 large very ripe cantaloupe	½ c. lemon juice
(5 lb.)	¼ tsp. salt
5 c. sugar	½ tsp. ground nutmeg

Peel cantaloupe and cut into wedges. Put through coarse blade of food chopper. Measure ground pulp and liquid. Add water, if necessary, to bring measure to 5 cups. Combine pulp, sugar, lemon juice and salt in a large saucepan. Bring to a boil, stirring constantly, until sugar is dissolved. Reduce heat. Simmer, stirring frequently, for 1 hour 15 minutes or until mixture is thick as honey. Remove from heat.

Stir in nutmeg. Stir and skim for 5 minutes. Ladle mixture into hot, sterilized jars; seal. Makes 5 cups.

CRANBERRY-BANANA CONSERVE

An unusual and tasty combination of flavors from a Kansas cook

1 (1 lb.) pkg. fresh cranberries	7 c. sugar
1½ c. water	½ bottle liquid fruit pectin
5 large ripe bananas	1 tblsp. lemon juice

Combine cranberries and water in saucepan. Simmer for 5 minutes. Mash bananas to a smooth pulp (should measure 3 cups). Add to cranberries along with the sugar. Bring quickly to a full rolling boil. Boil for 1 minute longer, stirring constantly. Remove from heat. Stir in liquid fruit pectin. Skim and stir conserve for 3 minutes.

Pour into hot, sterilized jars; cover immediately with ⅛" paraffin. Makes 5 pints.

HORSERADISH JELLY

This sparkling jelly is perfect accompaniment with ham and beef

½ c. horseradish	3½ c. sugar
1½ c. water	½ bottle liquid fruit pectin
3 tblsp. lemon juice	1 drop yellow food color
⅛ tsp. salt	

Combine horseradish, water, lemon juice and salt in a large saucepan.

Add sugar to horseradish mixture; mix well. Bring to a hard boil over high heat, stirring constantly. Boil hard for 3 minutes. Remove from heat. At once stir in liquid fruit pectin. Stir in food color. Skim off foam with metal spoon.

Ladle into hot, sterilized glasses. Cover immediately with ⅛" hot paraffin. Makes 4 cups.

REAL EASY REFRIGERATED RELISHES

This is a unique and delicious collection of relishes that capture the full flavor of garden fruits and vegetables. They do not have to be processed or preserved. You simply make and put them in a large bowl or container, then cover and refrigerate. Grand to prepare when you are pushed for time and yet want to have a homemade relish on hand.

PICKLED CARROTS

Even those who don't like carrots will enjoy this crisp spicy relish

2 lbs. carrots, pared and sliced
½ c. chopped green pepper
1 (3½ oz.) jar cocktail onions, drained
1 (10½ oz.) can condensed tomato soup
1 c. sugar
¾ c. wine vinegar
½ c. salad oil
1 tsp. salt
1 tsp. prepared mustard
1 tsp. Worcestershire sauce
¼ tsp. pepper
Lettuce

Cook carrots until tender. Drain and cool. Combine carrots, green pepper and onions in bowl. Mix together soup, sugar, vinegar, salad oil, salt, prepared mustard, Worcestershire sauce and pepper. Pour over vegetables. Cover and refrigerate at least 2 days. Drain and serve in lettuce cups. Makes 6 to 8 servings.

BEET AND CABBAGE RELISH

Stays super crisp. Take it to the bazaar . . . it will be a best seller

2 (1 lb.) cans beets, drained and chopped
4 c. finely chopped cabbage
½ c. horseradish
1 c. sugar
¾ c. light corn syrup
1½ tsp. salt
⅛ tsp. pepper
1 c. vinegar
1 c. water

Combine beets, cabbage, horseradish, sugar, corn syrup, salt and pepper in large bowl. Combine vinegar and water in saucepan. Bring to a boil.

Pour hot vinegar mixture over vegetables. Stir thoroughly. Cover and refrigerate. Or pour into jars; seal and refrigerate. Makes 2 quarts.

UNCOOKED POTPOURRI RELISH

This contains just about every vegetable in the garden

¾ c. red wine vinegar
½ c. olive oil
¼ c. water
2 tblsp. sugar
1½ tsp. salt
1 tsp. orégano leaves
¼ tsp. pepper
½ medium cauliflower, cut in flowerets
2 carrots, cut in 2" strips

2 stalks celery, cut in 1" slices
1 green pepper, cut in 2" strips
1 (4 oz.) jar pimientos, drained and cut in strips
½ c. sliced pimiento-stuffed olives
2 medium onions, sliced
1 clove garlic
1 bay leaf

Combine vinegar, oil, water, sugar, salt, orégano and pepper in a large skillet or Dutch oven. Add cauliflower, carrots, celery and green pepper. Bring to a boil, stirring occasionally. Reduce heat; simmer, covered, for 5 minutes. Cool. Combine cooked vegetables with pimientos, olives and onions.

Place garlic clove and bay leaf in mixture and refrigerate at least 24 hours so vegetables can marinate. Remove bay leaf and garlic clove. Makes about 6 cups.

CRANBERRY RELISH

For a new garnish, fill scooped-out lemon halves with this zingy relish

4 c. fresh cranberries
3½ c. unsweetened pineapple juice
2 envelopes unflavored gelatin
½ c. cold water

2 c. sugar
1 c. chopped pecans
½ c. diced green grapes
1 (8½ oz.) can pineapple tidbits, drained

Cook cranberries in pineapple juice until cranberries pop (about 8 to 10 minutes). Soften gelatin in water. Stir into hot cranberries. Stir in sugar. Chill until syrupy.

Fold in pecans, green grapes and pineapple. Chill until set. Makes 7 cups.

BAKED ORANGE SLICES

This makes a most unusual conversation-piece garnish for ham

2 medium oranges
1 c. sugar
½ c. water

$\frac{1}{16}$ tsp. cream of tartar
1 stick cinnamon

Cut unpeeled oranges into ¼" slices. Arrange orange slices in 11 × 7 × 1½" baking dish. Combine sugar, water, cream of tartar and cinnamon stick in a saucepan. Simmer for 5 minutes. Remove cinnamon stick. Pour hot syrup over orange slices.

Bake in slow oven (300°) 1 hour. Turn slices once during baking. Cool.

Store in covered jar. Refrigerate overnight or at least 8 hours. Serve as a garnish/relish with meats or poultry. Makes 8 servings.

SPICED FRUIT

Wreathe a crispy brown roast of pork with this spicy array of fruits

1 (1 lb. 13 oz.) can cling
  peach halves
½ c. cider vinegar
½ c. sugar
1½ sticks cinnamon
8 whole cloves
12 prunes

2 oranges, peeled and cut in ½"
  thick slices
1 (1 lb. 13 oz.) can pear halves,
  drained
1 (1 lb. 4 oz.) can pineapple
  chunks, drained

Drain peaches and reserve 1¼ c. juice. Combine peach juice, vinegar, sugar, cinnamon and cloves in 3-qt. saucepan. Bring to a boil; reduce heat. Simmer for 5 minutes.

Arrange peaches, prunes, oranges, pears and pineapple in a large bowl. Pour hot syrup over fruit. Let cool. Cover. Refrigerate overnight. Remove cinnamon sticks and cloves before serving. Makes 8 cups.

PICKLED PINEAPPLE

Economical and elegant gift for Christmas . . . make a triple batch

1 (1 lb. 14 oz.) can pineapple
chunks

1¼ c. sugar

¾ c. vinegar

$\frac{1}{16}$ tsp. salt

12 whole cloves

1 stick cinnamon

Drain pineapple, reserving 1¼ c. juice. Combine juice, sugar, vinegar, salt, cloves and cinnamon in saucepan. Simmer, uncovered, for 10 minutes. Add pineapple chunks. Bring to a boil. Remove from heat. Cool. Refrigerate several days. Remove cinnamon stick and cloves before serving. Makes 6 to 8 servings.

TREASURED COUNTRY RELISHES

When the flower garden is in full bloom and vegetables are ready for harvest and heavy on the vine, farm wives get out their canning kettle and chopping boards to preserve the bounty of summer.

Many of these recipes have been made and savored for several generations . . . we present these relishes with our Test Kitchens' "seal of approval."

APPLE CHUTNEY

Swirl this spicy chutney through a casserole of baked beans

3 qts. coarsely chopped, pared
apples

2 medium green peppers,
chopped

1¼ c. chopped onion

1 lb. raisins

10 maraschino cherries,
chopped

1 lb. brown sugar

2 c. dark corn syrup

3¼ c. vinegar

2 tblsp. mustard seeds

2 tblsp. ground ginger

2 tblsp. lemon juice

1 tblsp. salt

1 tsp. grated lemon rind

1 clove garlic, minced

Combine all ingredients in a large saucepan. Bring to a boil, stirring constantly. Reduce heat. Simmer for 35 minutes or until mixture thickens.

Ladle into hot, sterilized jars, filling to within ½″ from top. Adjust lids. Process in boiling water bath (212°) 5 minutes. Remove jars from canner. Complete seals unless closures are self-sealing type. Makes 13 half-pints.

CRANBERRY CHUTNEY

Serve with poultry or cold meat—extra jars make nice gifts

1 (1 lb. 14 oz.) can fruit cocktail
½ c. orange juice
½ c. sugar
¼ c. light brown sugar, firmly packed
¼ c. cider vinegar
½ tsp. ground cloves
¼ tsp. red pepper
½ tsp. salt
2 c. cranberries
1 c. chopped, unpared apples
1 tblsp. finely chopped candied ginger
1 small clove garlic, minced
¾ c. raisins

Drain fruit cocktail. Reserve 1¼ c. syrup. Combine reserved 1¼ c. syrup, orange juice, sugar, brown sugar, vinegar, cloves, pepper and salt in 3-qt. saucepan. Bring to a full boil, stirring often. Add cranberries, apples, ginger, garlic and raisins. Cook until berries pop, for about 5 minutes. Stir in fruit cocktail. Simmer, stirring often, until mixture thickens slightly, for about 15 minutes.

Pour into hot, sterilized jars. Seal immediately or store in refrigerator. Chutney will thicken as it cools. Makes about 5 cups.

SPICED CRANBERRIES

Lightly stir spiced berries through vanilla pudding for a parfait

2 (1 lb.) pkgs. fresh cranberries
6 c. sugar
1⅓ c. vinegar
⅔ c. water
1 tblsp. ground cinnamon
1 tsp. ground cloves
1 tsp. ground allspice

Combine cranberries, sugar, vinegar, water, cinnamon, cloves and allspice in a saucepan. Boil gently, stirring occasionally, for 40 minutes or until mixture thickens.

Ladle into hot, sterilized jars, filling to within ½″ from top. Adjust lids. Process in boiling water bath (212°) 5 minutes. Remove jars from canner. Complete seals unless closures are self-sealing type. Makes 2 pints.

APPLE RELISH

A Wisconsin woman is invariably asked for this popular recipe

15 apples, pared (about 4 lbs.)	2 c. vinegar
6 medium green peppers	4 tsp. salt
4 medium onions	1 tsp. celery seeds
2 (4 oz.) jars pimientos, diced	1 tsp. turmeric
4 c. sugar	

Chop apples, green peppers and onions using coarse blade of food chopper. Combine apple mixture with pimientos, sugar, vinegar, salt, celery seeds and turmeric in large saucepan. Bring to a boil; reduce heat. Simmer for 10 minutes.

Ladle into hot, sterilized jars, filling to within ½″ from top. Adjust lids. Process in boiling water bath (212°) 10 minutes. Remove jars from canner. Complete seals unless closures are self-sealing type. Makes 8 pints.

PEAR RELISH

Chock-full of vegetables that complement the flavor of the pears

6 lbs. ripe pears (18 medium)	2 c. diced onion
3 c. sugar	1 c. diced green pepper
2 c. white vinegar	1 (4 oz.) jar pimientos, drained
½ c. yellow mustard	and diced
2 tblsp. salt	¼ c. raisins

Pare pears and cut lengthwise into eighths.

Combine sugar, vinegar, mustard and salt in 6-qt. kettle. Bring to a boil and add pears, onion, green pepper, pimientos and raisins. Bring to a boil; reduce heat and simmer for 10 minutes or until pears are tender.

Ladle into hot, sterilized jars, filling to within ½″ from top. Adjust lids. Process in boiling water bath (212°) 20 minutes. Remove jars from canner. Complete seals unless closures are self-sealing type. Makes 6 pints.

BEET AND HORSERADISH RELISH

Brightly colored and brightly flavored . . . always popular at picnics

4 c. ground cooked beets	¾ c. sugar
1 c. prepared hot horseradish	1½ tsp. salt
1 c. vinegar	½ tsp. paprika

Combine all ingredients in saucepan. Heat to the boiling point.

Ladle into hot, sterilized jars, filling to within ½″ from top. Adjust lids. Process in boiling water bath (212°) 5 minutes. Remove jars from canner. Complete seals unless closures are self-sealing type. Makes 6 half-pints.

TURNIP AND ONION RELISH

Two robust vegetables team to produce a most intriguing relish

5 c. shredded white turnips	3 c. white vinegar
2 c. chopped onion	¾ tsp. paprika
4 tsp. salt	1 tsp. yellow food color
4 c. sugar	

Combine turnips, onion and salt and let stand for 1 hour. Drain.

Combine sugar, vinegar, paprika and food color in saucepan. Bring mixture to a boil. Add drained turnip mixture and simmer for 1 minute.

Ladle into hot, sterilized jars, filling to within ½″ from top. Adjust lids. Process in boiling water bath (212°) 5 minutes. Remove jars from canner. Complete seals unless closures are self-sealing type. Makes 3 pints.

MIXED VEGETABLE RELISH

Spunky in flavor, this colorful relish is delicious with meats

3 c. finely chopped carrots	1 c. light corn syrup
1½ c. finely chopped onion	1½ tblsp. salt
1 c. finely chopped green pepper	1½ tsp. mustard seeds
1 c. finely chopped cabbage	1½ tsp. celery seeds
2 c. cider vinegar	¼ c. diced pimientos

Combine carrots, onion, green pepper and cabbage in a large bowl. Cover vegetables with boiling water. Let stand for 5 minutes. Drain well.

Combine vegetables, vinegar, corn syrup, salt, mustard and celery seeds in 6-qt. saucepan. Bring to a boil, stirring constantly. Reduce heat and simmer, stirring occasionally, for 25 minutes or until mixture thickens. Add pimientos during the last 5 minutes of cooking time.

Ladle into hot, sterilized jars, filling to within ½" from top. Adjust lids. Process in boiling water bath (212°) 10 minutes. Remove jars from canner. Complete seals unless closures are self-sealing type. Makes 5 to 6 half-pints.

GARDEN WALK PICKLES

The bounty of the garden in a jar . . . a Blue Ribbon winner

6 large cucumbers, sliced	1 lb. carrots, cut in slices
1 qt. chopped tomatoes	1 pt. cut-up celery (1" pieces)
6 medium onions, sliced	1 medium cauliflower, cut in
4 green peppers, cut in strips	flowerets
1 c. salt	8 c. white vinegar
1 gal. water	7 c. sugar
1 pt. cut-up small green beans, (1" lengths)	¼ c. mixed pickling spices
	4 tblsp. mustard seeds
1 pt. lima beans	2 tblsp. celery seeds

Soak cucumbers, tomatoes, onions and green peppers overnight in a brine made of 1 c. salt to 1 gal. water.

Next day, drain and cover with boiling water. Drain and set aside. Cook green beans, lima beans, carrots, celery and cauliflower in salted water for 20 minutes. Drain and set aside. Boil together vinegar, sugar, pickling spices, mustard and celery seeds. Add all vegetables. Simmer for 15 minutes.

Ladle into hot, sterilized jars, filling to within ½" from top. Adjust lids. Process in boiling water bath (212°) 5 minutes. Remove jars from canner. Complete seals unless closures are self-sealing type. Makes 6 quarts.

Chapter 12

DO STAY FOR A BITE TO EAT
(Snacks, Sandwiches and Soups)

Hospitable country cooks are famous for their reputation of always being able to serve something good to eat on the spur of the moment. Whether a car full of relatives drops by to say hello, or a husband invites a cattle buyer to stay for lunch, a farm woman welcomes her unexpected guests and turns out an outstanding meal in no time at all.

In this chapter you will find some of their favorite snacks, soups, and sandwiches that fill the bill for all situations. We have recipes that are perfect to stir up and serve on a cold winter day after a snowmobiling party. There are specials that youngsters will love, such as Pizza Burgers or Miniature Pizzas. Both recipes can be made ahead and popped in the freezer and then you will be prepared when your children race in and ask "Mom, may Kathy and Barby stay for lunch?"

Teen-agers love a big batch of bubbling cheese fondue after the football game. We have several varieties they will be eager to try: Golden Pizza Fondue, Double Cheese Fondue or Bacon Cheddar Fondue. The grown-ups will like these too.

Tuna Party Ball and Salmon/Pecan Ball team beautifully with frosty cold glasses of tomato juice as a first course appetizer. Pass a plate of our homemade Health Crackers, plain or with a thin slice of cheese.

We have he-man hearties too, such as Barbecued Beef Buns, Meatball and Lentil Soup, and Runzas. (Runzas are sturdy homemade giant-size rolls filled with sausage, cabbage, onion, carrots and seasonings—they make a big hit with the hungry field crew.)

Many of these recipes can be frozen so that all the work is done ahead—that's how country women produce hearty snacks in a few minutes. Others are quick and easy recipes that can be put together while the coffee perks. Every one has been family tested and then tested in our Countryside Test Kitchens.

HEARTY SOUPS FOR SUPPER

A great big pot of homemade soup simmering on the stove can provide a nourishing meal for a hungry family or unexpected guests. Just ladle the soup into large bowls and pass a basket of crackers. Or if there is time, stir together a batch of corn muffins to add special eating pleasure.

Every one of these soups is thick with vegetables . . . the stick-to-the-rib variety that the men in the family will like.

MEATBALL AND LENTIL SOUP

A nutritious and complete meal that is ideal for lunch or supper

1 lb. lentils, rinsed and drained	1 (1 lb.) can stewed tomatoes
2 tsp. salt	½ tsp. marjoram leaves
1 bay leaf	½ tsp. salt
2½ qts. water	⅛ tsp. pepper
Meatballs (recipe follows)	1 c. sliced carrots, ½" thick
1 c. chopped onion	1 c. sliced celery, ½" thick
⅓ c. bacon drippings	

Combine lentils, salt, bay leaf and water in 6-qt. kettle. Bring to a boil; reduce heat and simmer, covered, for 45 minutes. Do not drain. Meanwhile, prepare Meatballs.

Sauté onion in bacon drippings. Stir in tomatoes, marjoram, salt and pepper; bring to a boil. Add tomato mixture, Meatballs, carrots and celery to cooked lentils. Bring to a boil; reduce heat and simmer, covered, for 30 minutes. Makes 3½ quarts.

Meatballs: Combine 1 lb. ground beef, ½ c. dry bread crumbs, 2 beaten eggs, ¼ c. milk, 2 tblsp. finely chopped onion, 2 tblsp. finely chopped parsley, 1 minced garlic clove, ¾ tsp. salt, ½ tsp. marjoram and ⅛ tsp. pepper. Mix lightly and shape into 15 meatballs. Brown meatballs in ¼ c. hot oil in 8" skillet. Drain and set aside.

GREEN BEAN SOUP

A traditional, hearty Amish soup that will please your whole family

1 meaty ham bone, about 2 lbs.	¼ c. chopped fresh parsley
2 qts. water	4 sprigs summer savory,
4 c. cut-up green beans (1″ pieces)	chopped or 1 tsp. dried savory
3 c. cubed potatoes	1 tsp. salt
2 medium onions, sliced	¼ tsp. pepper
	1 c. light cream

Cook ham bone in water in 6-qt. saucepan until tender, for about 1½ hours. Remove meat from bone and cut in chunks. Put back in soup base.

Add green beans, potatoes, onion, parsley, savory, salt and pepper. Bring to a boil; reduce heat and simmer, covered, for 20 minutes or until vegetables are tender. Skim off excess fat.

Just before serving, stir in light cream. Makes about 3½ quarts.

CREAM OF POTATO SOUP

An excellent choice for Christmas Eve supper, with cornmeal muffins

6 c. sliced potatoes (5 large)	¼ tsp. pepper
½ c. sliced carrots	2 c. milk
6 slices bacon	2 c. light cream
1 c. chopped onion	Finely shredded Cheddar cheese
1 c. sliced celery	Parsley sprigs
1½ tsp. salt	

Cook potatoes and carrots in boiling water until tender. Drain.

Sauté bacon until crisp in skillet. Drain on paper towels. Crumble. Sauté onion and celery in 2 tblsp. of the bacon fat until tender (do not brown).

Combine potatoes, carrots, onion mixture, bacon, salt, pepper, milk and cream. Simmer for 30 minutes. (Do not boil.) Garnish with shredded Cheddar cheese and parsley. Makes about 2 quarts.

CLAM / VEGETABLE CHOWDER

Hearty soup that is especially good during the cold winter months

4 slices bacon
1 c. chopped onion
1 qt. clam broth
1 c. water
2 c. diced, pared potatoes
1 c. diced celery
1 c. sliced, pared carrots
½ c. chopped green pepper

1 (9 oz.) pkg. frozen cut green
   beans, thawed
1½ tsp. salt
½ tsp. thyme leaves
⅛ tsp. pepper
4 c. canned tomatoes
1 tblsp. chopped fresh parsley
2 (7 oz.) cans minced clams

Fry bacon in Dutch oven until crisp. Drain and crumble.

Sauté onion in bacon fat until tender. Stir in clam broth, water, potatoes, celery, carrots, green pepper, green beans, salt, thyme and pepper. Bring to a boil; reduce heat and simmer for 20 minutes or until vegetables are tender.

Add bacon, tomatoes, parsley and undrained clams. Heat well. Makes about 2½ quarts.

PASTA AND BEAN SOUP

Truly a meal-in-a-dish . . . a crowd-pleaser after a football game

1 lb. dry great northern beans
2 qts. water
2½ tsp. salt
1 large whole carrot
6 strips bacon
½ c. chopped onion
½ c. chopped celery
1 small clove garlic, minced

1 (1 lb.) can stewed tomatoes
½ bay leaf
½ tsp. orégano leaves
½ tsp. salt
¼ tsp. pepper
¼ c. water
1 c. ditalini or small elbow
   macaroni

Soak beans 8 hours or overnight. Rinse and drain. Combine beans, 2 qts. water, 2½ tsp. salt and carrot; simmer in 6-qt. pot for 2 hours or until beans are tender.

Fry bacon in skillet until crisp. Remove and drain on paper towels. Reserve ¼ c. bacon drippings. Add onion, celery and garlic. Sauté until tender (do not brown). Stir in tomatoes, bay leaf, orégano,

½ tsp. salt, pepper and ¼ c. water. Bring to a boil; reduce heat. Simmer 30 minutes.

Cook macaroni according to package directions. Drain.

Purée half of the beans. Cube carrot. Crumble bacon. Combine all ingredients. Makes 3½ quarts.

FISH AND CLAM CHOWDER

Choose any of your favorite fish fillets for this superb chowder

1 c. chopped onion	2½ tsp. salt
½ c. butter or regular margarine	¼ tsp. pepper
	2 c. water
6 medium potatoes, pared and cubed	1½ lbs. frozen fish fillets, thawed
1½ c. sliced, pared carrots	2 (7½ oz.) cans minced clams
1 c. sliced celery	2 qts. milk

Sauté onion in melted butter in Dutch oven until tender (do not brown).

Add potatoes, carrots, celery, salt, pepper and water. Arrange fish fillets on top of vegetables. Bring to a boil; reduce heat. Cover. Simmer for 15 to 20 minutes or until vegetables are tender.

Add undrained clams and milk. Heat mixture over low heat. Do not boil. Makes about 3 quarts.

HEARTY TOMATO RICE SOUP

So quick and easy to prepare . . . soup is ready in just 20 minutes

1 lb. ground beef	2 beef bouillon cubes
1 c. chopped onion	⅓ c. regular rice
½ c. chopped celery	1 tsp. salt
1 tblsp. butter or regular margarine	½ tsp. chili powder
	1 bay leaf
1 (1 lb. 12 oz.) can tomatoes	2½ c. water

Sauté ground beef, onion and celery in melted butter in Dutch oven until meat is well browned.

Stir in tomatoes, beef bouillon cubes, rice, salt, chili powder, bay leaf and water. Bring to a boil; reduce heat. Cover. Simmer for 20 minutes. Makes 2 quarts.

YOU'RE INVITED FOR CHEESE FONDUE

Last-minute entertaining can be carefree when you serve cheese fondue. Be sure to keep several types of cheese in your refrigerator and you'll be ready to turn out a bubbling dish of golden fondue almost at a moment's notice. These fondues made a big hit when we tested them in our Countryside Kitchens at FARM JOURNAL. In fact, if there is any left over, refrigerate and then the next day simply spread the chilled mixture on thick slices of bread and broil until hot and bubbly—a marvelous lunch in minutes!

BACON CHEDDAR FONDUE

Crusty French bread cubes or raw vegetables make good dippers

5 slices bacon	1½ lbs. sharp Cheddar cheese, shredded
1 c. chopped onion	1 tsp. Worcestershire sauce
1 clove garlic, finely minced	1 tsp. dry mustard
1 (10½ oz.) can condensed cream of mushroom soup	3 dashes Tabasco sauce
1 c. milk	Fresh parsley

Fry bacon until crisp and brown in 3-qt. heavy saucepan. Drain and crumble; set aside. Add onion and garlic to ¼ c. bacon drippings; sauté until tender (do not brown). Add soup. Slowly stir in milk, over medium heat; blend until smooth.

Add cheese, a little at a time, stirring until melted. Add bacon, reserving some for garnish. Add Worcestershire sauce, dry mustard and Tabasco sauce.

Pour into fondue pot and keep warm. Garnish with bacon and parsley. If mixture becomes too thick, stir in a little hot milk. Makes 5 cups.

CLAM CHEESE FONDUE

A mild-flavored fondue that's delicious with crisp raw vegetables

2 (7 oz.) cans minced clams
Milk
2 tblsp. minced onion
2 tblsp. minced celery
3 tblsp. butter or regular
  margarine

¼ c. flour
½ lb. Colby cheese, shredded
½ lb. Brick cheese, shredded
2 tsp. Worcestershire sauce

Drain clams, reserving broth. Add enough milk to reserved broth to make 2 cups.

Sauté onion and celery in melted butter in 3-qt. heavy saucepan until tender (do not brown). Stir in flour. Gradually stir in reserved broth mixture. Cook, over medium heat, stirring constantly until thickened.

Add cheeses, a little at a time, stirring until melted. Add clams and Worcestershire sauce.

Pour into fondue pot and keep warm. If mixture becomes too thick, stir in a little hot milk. Makes about 4 cups.

DOUBLE CHEESE FONDUE

Dunk chunks of caraway-studded rye in this bubbling fondue

2 tblsp. minced celery
¼ c. butter or regular
  margarine
¼ c. flour
1 c. milk
1 c. light cream

¾ lb. Swiss cheese, shredded
¼ lb. Brick cheese, shredded
1 tsp. Worcestershire sauce
¼ tsp. dry mustard
¼ tsp. onion salt
$\frac{1}{16}$ tsp. cayenne pepper

Sauté celery in melted butter in 3-qt. heavy saucepan until tender. Stir in flour. Gradually stir in milk and cream. Cook, stirring, until thick.

Slowly add cheeses; stir until melted. Add Worcestershire sauce, dry mustard, onion salt and cayenne pepper.

Pour into fondue pot and keep warm. If mixture gets too thick, stir in some hot milk. Makes 4 cups.

GOLDEN PIZZA FONDUE

Spread any left-over fondue on English muffins and broil until bubbly

1 tblsp. minced onion
1 clove garlic, finely minced
2 tblsp. butter or regular
    margarine
3 tblsp. flour
1 (1 lb.) can stewed tomatoes
½ tsp. basil leaves

½ tsp. orégano leaves
⅛ tsp. cayenne pepper
⅛ tsp. pepper
½ c. milk
1 lb. mild Cheddar cheese,
    shredded
1 tblsp. grated Parmesan cheese

Sauté onion and garlic in melted butter in 3-qt. heavy saucepan until tender (do not brown). Add flour. Stir in tomatoes, breaking them up with spoon. Add basil, orégano, cayenne pepper and pepper. Cook over medium heat, stirring, for 5 minutes. Slowly stir in milk.

Add Cheddar cheese, a little at a time, stirring until melted. Add Parmesan cheese.

Pour into fondue pot and keep warm. If mixture becomes too thick, stir in a little hot milk. Makes about 4 cups.

SPECIALS FOR THE YOUNGER SET

Teen-agers and youngsters love hot dogs and hamburgers. These snacks make use of both of their favorites and are instant successes when served at a party or picnic. Adults like them too—one farm woman makes the Miniature Pizzas four batches at a time and freezes them for holiday entertaining.

MINIATURE PIZZAS

A must for teen-age get-togethers with icy cold soft drinks or punch

½ lb. bulk pork sausage
½ c. chopped onion
⅓ c. chopped green pepper
1 clove garlic, minced
1 (15 oz.) can tomato sauce
1 (4 oz.) can mushrooms,
    undrained

1 tsp. chili powder
1 tsp. orégano leaves
½ tsp. basil leaves
8 English muffins, split
1 (10 oz.) pkg. Cheddar cheese,
    shredded

Brown pork sausage in 10″ skillet until meat begins to turn color. Add onion and green pepper. Sauté until tender (do not brown). Add garlic and cook for 1 minute. Stir in tomato sauce, mushrooms, chili powder, orégano and basil. Bring to a boil; reduce heat and simmer for 20 minutes. Stir mixture occasionally. If mixture is too thick, add water. Cool well.

Place English muffin halves on a baking sheet. Spoon on mixture. Sprinkle with cheese. Freeze. When frozen, wrap in aluminum foil and freeze.

To Serve: Place frozen pizzas on a baking sheet. Bake in very hot oven (450°) 12 minutes. Makes 16 miniature pizzas.

RUNZAS

These hearty sandwiches can be eaten hot or cold

2 (13¾ oz.) pkgs. hot roll mix
1 lb. ground beef
1 lb. bulk pork sausage
3 c. chopped cabbage
2 c. finely chopped onion
1 c. shredded carrot
2 tblsp. water

1 tblsp. Worcestershire sauce
1½ tsp. salt
½ tsp. orégano leaves
½ tsp. ground nutmeg
¼ tsp. pepper
1 egg, beaten
1 tblsp. water

Prepare hot roll mix according to package directions. Let rise.

Meanwhile, brown ground beef and pork sausage in large skillet. Combine cabbage, onion, carrot and water in 10″ skillet. Steam for 10 minutes. Add to browned meat. Add Worcestershire sauce, salt, orégano, nutmeg and pepper. Drain and cool completely.

Turn dough onto floured surface. Divide dough into 12 parts. Roll each in a 6″ circle. Place ½ c. meat mixture in center. Bring edges of circle to center and pinch together. Brush with combined egg and water. Let rise for 30 minutes.

Bake in hot oven (400°) 15 minutes or until golden brown. Makes 12 sandwiches.

BARBECUED BEEF BUNS

Pass bowls of potato chips, crisp dill pickles and carrot sticks

1½ lbs. ground beef	2 tblsp. lemon juice
1 c. chopped onion	4 tsp. prepared mustard
1½ c. ketchup	2 tsp. salt
1 c. water	¼ tsp. pepper
¼ c. sugar	⅛ tsp. cayenne pepper
¼ c. Worcestershire sauce	12 hamburger buns or rolls
2 tblsp. cider vinegar	

Brown ground beef in large skillet until meat turns color. Add onion and cook until meat is well browned.

Add ketchup, water, sugar, Worcestershire sauce, vinegar, lemon juice, mustard, salt, pepper and cayenne pepper. Bring mixture to a boil; reduce heat and simmer for 30 minutes, stirring occasionally. Skim off excess fat.

Serve spooned over hamburger buns. Makes about 4 cups or 12 servings.

PIZZA BURGERS

Pizza fans will ask for more when you serve these great sandwiches

½ lb. ground beef	¼ tsp. salt
½ lb. pork sausage	¼ c. dry bread crumbs
½ c. ketchup	6 hamburger buns
⅓ c. water	3 slices American cheese
1 tsp. orégano leaves	

Brown ground beef and sausage in 10″ skillet. Remove excess fat. Stir in ketchup, water, orégano, salt and bread crumbs. Heat mixture well.

Lay opened hamburger buns on broiler rack. Spoon mixture on bottoms of hamburger buns. Cut each slice of cheese into four strips. Lay 2 strips of cheese crisscross fashion on each.

Place under broiler until cheese melts. Makes 6 servings.

HOT DOG CURLS

Your children will especially like this new way to serve hot dogs

½ c. chopped onion
½ c. chopped green pepper
½ c. chopped celery
1 tblsp. butter or regular
   margarine
1 lb. frankfurters, sliced
   lengthwise

1 tblsp. flour
1 (8 oz.) can tomato sauce
½ c. water
6 frankfurter buns or rolls,
   toasted

Sauté onion, green pepper and celery in butter in skillet until tender (do not brown).

Add frankfurters and fry until they curl up and are deep red in color. Stir in flour and cook until slightly brown. Add tomato sauce and water. Cover and simmer for 10 minutes.

Serve spooned over frankfurter buns. Makes 6 servings.

CRUNCHY NUGGETS

A breakfast cereal that tastes equally well as an evening snack

3 c. unsifted graham flour
2½ c. unsifted flour
1 c. sugar
1½ tsp. salt

1½ tsp. baking soda
1¼ c. molasses
1½ c. sour milk

Combine graham flour, flour, sugar, salt and baking soda in a large bowl. Add molasses and sour milk; stir well. Spread mixture in greased 13 × 9 × 2″ cake pan. Bake in very slow oven (250°) 1 hour 45 minutes. Turn out on rack. Let stand, uncovered, overnight.

Cut into squares and grate on a medium grater. Spread half of mixture in a shallow roasting pan. Bake in moderate oven (350°) 45 minutes, stirring every 15 minutes. Cool and store in tightly covered container. Makes 12 cups.

GOLDEN CRISPIES

Youngsters will like this for an afternoon snack . . . nourishing too

4 c. rolled oats	½ c. flaked coconut
2 c. raw wheat germ	¾ c. brown sugar, firmly packed
1 c. hulled sunflower or sesame seeds	¾ c. cooking oil
	⅓ c. water
1 c. chopped walnuts	2 tblsp. vanilla

Combine all ingredients and mix well. Spread in 15½ × 10½ × 1" jelly roll pan. Bake in moderate oven (350°) 1 hour, stirring frequently. Cool and store in tightly covered container. Makes about 10 cups.

PARTY SNACKING

When you are planning a big feast, it's a good idea to give your guests a few nibbles. Pass a tray filled with glasses of well-chilled tomato juice and one of our handsome cheese balls. Or for a lighter snack, make a batch of homemade Health Crackers and serve with cups of steaming chicken broth.

HEALTH CRACKERS

These crisp crackers are perfect complements to soups or cheeses

3 c. quick-cooking rolled oats	¾ c. salad oil
2 c. unsifted flour	1 c. water
1 c. raw wheat germ	1 egg white, slightly beaten
3 tblsp. sugar	Sesame or poppy seeds
1 tsp. salt	Garlic or onion salt

Combine oats, flour, wheat germ, sugar and salt. Add oil and water, stirring until mixture leaves the sides of the bowl. Divide dough into quarters.

Roll out each quarter on a slightly floured surface to make 12 × 10" rectangle. Roll dough up loosely around rolling pin and place on lightly greased baking sheet. Cut into squares, triangles, rectangles or diamonds. Brush with egg white. Sprinkle with sesame seeds or poppy seeds and garlic salt or onion salt.

Bake in moderate oven (350°) 15 to 20 minutes or until golden brown. Makes about 8 dozen.

SALMON / PECAN BALL

An unusual hostess gift . . . wrap in plastic film and tie with ribbon

1 (1 lb.) can salmon, drained
    and flaked
1 (8 oz.) pkg. cream cheese,
    softened
1 tblsp. lemon juice
1 tblsp. grated onion

1 tsp. horseradish
¼ tsp. salt
½ c. chopped pecans
⅓ c. chopped fresh parsley
Assorted crackers

Combine salmon, cream cheese, lemon juice, onion, horseradish and salt; mix well. Chill mixture for 2 hours.

Shape chilled salmon mixture into a ball. Roll in combined pecans and parsley. Chill until serving time. Serve with assorted crackers. Makes 1 salmon ball.

TUNA PARTY BALL

Prepare the day before the party and refrigerate until needed

2 (7 oz.) cans tuna, drained and
    flaked
1 (8 oz.) pkg. cream cheese,
    softened
2 tblsp. minced celery
1 tblsp. minced onion
1 tblsp. lemon juice

2 tsp. prepared mustard
¼ tsp. salt
⅛ tsp. cayenne pepper
1 hard-cooked egg
Sliced pimiento-stuffed olives
Assorted crackers

Combine tuna, cream cheese, celery, onion, lemon juice, mustard, salt and pepper. Remove white from egg and chop finely. Add to tuna mixture and mix well. Chill mixture for 2 hours.

Shape chilled tuna mixture into a ball. Sieve egg yolk. Garnish tuna ball with sliced olives around the sides and egg yolk on top. Chill until serving time. Serve with assorted crackers. Makes 1 tuna ball.

FESTIVE CHEESE BALL

A zesty cheese spread that is great on thin slices of rye bread

1 lb. sharp Cheddar cheese,
   shredded
2 oz. blue cheese, crumbled
2 tblsp. Worcestershire sauce
1 tblsp. finely chopped onion
½ c. mayonnaise

5 drops Tabasco sauce
1 c. finely chopped walnuts
¼ c. chopped fresh parsley
½ tsp. paprika
Assorted crackers

Combine Cheddar cheese, blue cheese, Worcestershire sauce, onion, mayonnaise and Tabasco sauce. Mix well. Chill mixture for 2 hours.

Shape chilled cheese mixture into a ball. Combine walnuts, parsley and paprika. Roll cheese ball in walnut mixture. Chill until serving time. Serve with assorted crackers. Makes 1 cheese ball.

MINIATURE MEATBALL SNACKS

A tasty, hot hors d'oeuvre that's sure to please all your guests

12 slices white bread
Softened butter or regular
   margarine
1 lb. ground beef
2 tblsp. grated onion
1 tblsp. Worcestershire sauce
1 tsp. prepared mustard

½ tsp. salt
½ tsp. celery salt
½ tsp. garlic salt
½ tsp. ground nutmeg
4 drops Tabasco sauce
¼ c. chili sauce
8 slices process American cheese

Remove crusts from bread slices. Toast bread on one side under broiler. Spread untoasted side with butter and cut into four squares. Arrange squares on broiler pan, toasted side down.

Combine ground beef, onion, Worcestershire sauce, mustard, salt, celery salt, garlic salt, nutmeg and Tabasco sauce. Mix together well. Shape into 48 small meatballs. Place meatballs on bread squares. Make a small dent on top of each meatball with thumb. Broil 4″ from source of heat for 5 to 6 minutes or until meat is well browned and edges of bread are toasted.

Fill small dent of each meatball with chili sauce. Cut each slice of cheese in half and each half into 6 strips. Place 2 strips crisscross fashion on each meatball. Place under broiler until cheese melts. Serve hot. Makes 48.

CUCUMBER DIP

Good choice for snack while playing cards or watching television

1 (8 oz.) pkg. cream cheese, softened
¾ c. grated cucumber
2 tsp. finely chopped green pepper
1½ tsp. grated onion
2 tblsp. lemon juice
¼ tsp. salt
⅛ tsp. pepper
Raw vegetables, chips or crackers

Combine all ingredients. Chill. Serve with raw vegetables, chips or crackers. Makes about 1½ cups.

INDEX